A HIERARCHICAL VISION OF ORDER

Understanding Chinese Foreign Policy in Asia

Antoine Roth

First published in Great Britain in 2024 by

Bristol University Press
University of Bristol
1-9 Old Park Hill
Bristol
BS2 8BB
UK
t: +44 (0)117 374 6645
e: bup-info@bristol.ac.uk

Details of international sales and distribution partners are available at bristoluniversitypress.co.uk

© Bristol University Press 2024

British Library Cataloguing in Publication Data
A catalogue record for this book is available from the British Library

ISBN 978-1-5292-2750-5 hardcover
ISBN 978-1-5292-2793-2 paperback
ISBN 978-1-5292-2751-2 ePub
ISBN 978-1-5292-2752-9 ePdf

The right of Antoine Roth to be identified as author of this work has been asserted by him in accordance with the Copyright, Designs and Patents Act 1988.

All rights reserved: no part of this publication may be reproduced, stored in a retrieval system, or transmitted in any form or by any means, electronic, mechanical, photocopying, recording, or otherwise without the prior permission of Bristol University Press.

Every reasonable effort has been made to obtain permission to reproduce copyrighted material. If, however, anyone knows of an oversight, please contact the publisher.

The statements and opinions contained within this publication are solely those of the author and not of the University of Bristol or Bristol University Press. The University of Bristol and Bristol University Press disclaim responsibility for any injury to persons or property resulting from any material published in this publication.

Bristol University Press works to counter discrimination on grounds of gender, race, disability, age and sexuality.

Cover design: blu inc
Front cover image: Shutterstock / grebeshkovmaxim

Bristol Studies in East Asian International Relations

Series Editors: **Yongjin Zhang**, University of Bristol, UK,
Shogo Suzuki, University of Manchester, UK and
Peter Kristensen, University of Copenhagen, Denmark

This series publishes cutting-edge research on the changing international politics of East Asia. It covers the security dynamics, the causes of conflict and cooperation, and the ongoing transformation of the region, as well as the impact of East Asia on the wider global order.

The series contributes to theoretical debates within the field of International Relations. Topics studied in East Asia can shed fresh light on disciplinary debates while the theoretical insights can challenge and enrich the propositions of mainstream IR theories which have been derived mostly from the European experience. In welcoming theoretically informed and theoretically innovative works, this series plays an important role in developing and establishing new Asian schools of thought in International Relations theory.

Also available

Middle Powers in Asia Pacific Multilateralism
A Differential Framework
By **Sarah Teo**

China's Rise and Rethinking International Relations Theory
Edited by **Chengxin Pan** and **Emilian Kavalski**

China Risen?
Studying Chinese Global Power
By **Shaun Breslin**

The Responsibility to Provide in Southeast Asia
Towards an Ethical Explanation
By **See Seng Tan**

Find out more at

bristoluniversitypress.co.uk/
bristol-studies-in-east-asian-international-relations

International advisory board

Amitav Acharya, American University, Washington D.C., US
Mark Beeson, University of Technology Sydney, Australia
Barry Buzan, London School of Economics and Political Science, UK
Zhimin Chen, Fudan University, Shanghai, China
Ja Ian Chong, National University of Singapore, Singapore
Paul Evans, University of British Columbia, Canada
Rosemary Foot, University of Oxford, UK
Evelyn Goh, Australian National University, Australia
Linus Hagström, Swedish Defense University, Sweden
Miwa Hirono, Ritsumeikan University, Japan
Yuichi Hosoya, Keio University, Japan
Weixing Hu, University of Hong Kong, China
Xiaoming Huang, Victoria University of Wellington, New Zealand
Christopher R. Hughes, London School of Economics and Political Science, UK
Yang Jiang, Danish Institute for International Studies, Denmark
Hun Joon Kim, Korea University, South Korea
Jing Men, College of Europe, Belgium
Nele Noesselt, University of Duisburg-Essen, Germany
John Ravenhill, University of Waterloo, Canada
Masayuki Tadokoro, Keio University, Japan
Yu-Shan Wu, National University of Taiwan, Taiwan

Find out more at

bristoluniversitypress.co.uk/
bristol-studies-in-east-asian-international-relations

Contents

Acknowledgements		vi
Introduction		1
1	Aspects of Asia as an International System	20
2	The Ideal of Hierarchical Order	42
3	Statecraft in the Long Imperial Era	59
4	China's Forced Entry into International Society and the Transformation of the Ideal of Hierarchical Order	80
5	The Pursuit of a Hierarchical Order in the People's Republic of China	101
6	Moral Discourse and Ritual in Contemporary Chinese Diplomacy	120
7	Traditional Tools of Rulership in the Modern World	144
Conclusion		167
References		179
Index		213

Acknowledgements

Many people have contributed to the completion of this book. It is issued from a PhD dissertation completed under the supervision of Takahara Akio at the University of Tokyo. My most special thanks go to him for his kind and steady support as I grappled with the challenge of constructing my argument and finding something meaningful to say about China's relations with its neighbours. I must also thank Kawashima Shin for his guidance, as well as Matsuda Yasuhiro and Kohara Masahiro for their judicious criticism and comments. My thanks as well to fellow members of our study group at the University, and in particular to Lim Jaewhan and Li Hao, who always gave constructive feedback and raised stimulating questions, and to Zheng Huangyan, who offered me friendship and precious moral support during all my years in Tokyo. Financially, my research was supported by a scholarship from the Japanese Ministry of Education, Culture, Sports, Science, and Technology, and by a grant from the Japanese Society for the Promotion of Science. I am grateful for this too. Outside the University of Tokyo, very special thanks must go to Felix Kuhn, with whom I shared many an evening discussing various topics related to this book, and who shaped my thinking in more ways than he knows. My loving gratitude, finally, to my family and to Marica in particular. This book could not have come together without her unconditional affection and support during my years of research and writing.

Introduction

Sixty years is a particularly meaningful number in the traditional Chinese calendar, the completion of a cycle and the beginning of a new one. On the 60th anniversary of the People's Republic of China (PRC) in 2009, marked by a grand military parade in the centre of Beijing and many festivities, the Chinese Communist Party (CCP) had indeed a lot to celebrate. It had successfully hosted the Olympic Games and used it as a sort of coming-out party, displaying to the world the fruits of China's economic miracle. While the West was mired in the deepest recession since the 1930s, China had avoided a complete crash thanks to a massive fiscal stimulus. The G20, where China could play a prominent role, replaced the G8 as the main forum to discuss global economic issues. China was also about to surpass Japan to become the second-largest economy on the planet, an ascent symbolizing the success of its growth strategy and the enormous economic (and military) capabilities that it had acquired. In short, things were mostly going China's way and a sense that the world's centre of gravity was shifting eastwards was spreading in the PRC and around the world.

Against this background, an increasingly confident CCP declared that a 'new situation' (*xin xingshi*) had arisen. At the fourth plenum of the 17th CCP Central Committee in mid-2009, this new situation was described thusly:

> The world is currently in a period of major developments, major changes and major adjustments. The multi-polarisation of the world; the deep development of economic globalisation; the constant progress of science and technology; the far-reaching influence of the international financial crisis; the new change occurring in the structure of the world economy; the new situation appearing in the international balance of power; the new characteristics emerging in the global thought and culture exchanges, mixing and confrontation; the continued dominance of developed nations in terms of economy, science and technology, etc.; the trend toward intense comprehensive national power competition and intense battle for all kinds of strengths; the growing number of unstable and uncertain factors; [all

these trends] present new opportunities and new challenges for our country's development.¹

This assessment referred to the uncertainties of the modern world – transnational threats like terrorism, global warming, the erosion of state authority due to economic globalization – but also acknowledged that China's power had risen compared with that of the West. It emphasized the need for China to strengthen its position in an international arena seen as fundamentally competitive. The 'new situation' thus opened the door to a more assertive foreign policy posture to guard against new threats and seize new opportunities to advance China's interests. The expression became increasingly prevalent in high-level speeches in the following years, especially after the start of the presidency of Xi Jinping in 2012 (Bradley, 2014). This all culminated with Xi's proclamation of a 'new era' (*xin shidai*) at the 19th Party Congress in October 2017, signalling that the change in China's understanding of its international environment in the previous decade or so, and the ensuing shift in its foreign policy, had become the new normal.

How China's foreign policy posture would adapt to meet the demands of the 'new situation' became clear in the years after 2009. This period saw a growing shift away from Deng Xiaoping's admonishment to 'bide our time and keep a low profile' (*taoguang yanghui*, literally 'hide one's brilliance and nourish obscurity') on the international stage. Under this policy, China had become increasingly engaged in international affairs, but had largely done so by embedding itself ever more deeply in existing international structures. It emphasized its respect for prevailing norms and practices in order to reassure other countries that its rise would be peaceful and create a stable international environment while it focused on building its strength at home.

More recently, however, China has become less shy about taking the initiative and using its growing resources to increase its international footprint, especially in its neighbourhood. It has launched major economic and diplomatic initiatives like the Asian Infrastructure Investment Bank (AIIB) or the Belt and Road Initiative (BRI, or 'One Belt One Road', *yidai yilu* in Chinese), asserted its territorial claims in the East and South China Sea, and expanded its maritime activities more generally. Rhetorically as well, Chinese leaders have displayed greater confidence and affirmed their intentions to take centre stage in international society. In 2009, President Hu Jintao was merely encouraging

---

¹ '中共中央关于加强和改进新形势下党的建设若干重大问题的决定' [Decisions of the CCP Central Committee on several important questions regarding the strengthening and improvement of party construction under the new situation], *People's Daily Online*, 28 September 2009. On the development, since 2000, of similar concepts leading up to the 'new situation', see Heath, 2014: 116-8.

Chinese diplomats to be more 'active' in pursuing cooperation with other states and in promoting multilateralism.[2] By 2017, however, his successor Xi Jinping was ready to announce that China could take the lead (*yindao*) in creating a more just international order and preserving international security and stability.[3]

Studying China's vision of order

Such talk of reforming international order to make it 'more just' is omnipresent in speeches by Chinese leaders, but they remain rather vague on what that concretely entails. It is clear, however, that the new order they seek to create should see the influence of Western powers, the United States (US) chief among them, and the liberal values they promote diminish significantly. When studying China's vision of international order, then, many observers have focused on the Chinese challenge to US leadership of international order or to liberal norms (Ikenberry, Wang, and Zhu, 2015; Jones, 2018; Johnston, 2019; Tobin, 2020; Doshi, 2021). These studies share a focus on the Chinese attitude towards existing international structures and norms, although they differ in their conclusion as to how deep and comprehensive the PRC's challenge towards them actually is. They devote comparatively less attention to China's own order-building efforts. Furthermore, they tend to reduce international order to America's domination of it, or alternatively to disaggregate order into a series of distinct regimes covering different issue areas like security, trade, and the environment. By doing so, they can lose sight of the fact that order can also be understood as something more fundamental, a sort of 'political constitution of world politics' that sets the basic parameters within which states interact with each other (Hurrell, 2007: 3).

This understanding of order, adopted in this book, has been developed most of all by the English School of international relations theory. It is aptly described by Evelyn Goh as 'sustained, rule-governed interaction amongst a society of states that share common understandings about their primary goals and means of conducting international affairs' (Goh, 2013a: 169).[4] Scholars in the English School tradition have written illuminating works on China's search for great power status in a global international society dominated until now

---

[2] '第十一次驻外使节会议在京召开' [11th ambassadorial conference convenes in Beijing], 20 July 2009, www.fmprc.gov.cn/chn/pds/gjhdq/gjhdqzz/mzblwelm/xgxw/t574427.htm.

[3] '习近平首提 "两个引导" 有深意' [The 'Two Leaderships' put forward by President Xi Jinping have deep meaning], *Studying China*, 21 February 2017.

[4] In Hedley Bull's famous definition, international society is formed by a group of states who, 'conscious of certain common interests and common values ... conceive themselves to be bound by a common set of rules in their relations with one another, and share in the working of common institutions' (2002: 13).

by Western powers, as well as on the issue of leadership in that society in an age of power transition between the US and the Middle Kingdom (Suzuki, 2008; Buzan, 2010; Clark, 2011a; 2014; Zhang Xiaoming, 2011; Zhang Yongjin, 2015; 2016; Foot, 2020; Zhang and Buzan, 2020). As such essays make clear, if the question is whether China is seeking to alter international order beyond removing its most liberal elements and challenging the US' dominant position, at first glance the answer seems to be no. China embraces a strong vision of state sovereignty (the most basic building block of modern international relations), advocates 'peaceful coexistence', conducts diplomacy and concludes treaties with other states, and actively engages in multilateralism in the United Nations (UN) and in other global organizations.

Yet if China does not question the basic features of international order, it does seek to alter them to recover the central position it believes is its right, and to fit its own values and purposes. This book examines this Chinese vision for a Sinocentric international order. It follows in the footsteps of scholars like Nadèje Rolland (2020), who have written expertly on the topic, but takes a different approach in three ways. Firstly, it focuses on Asia, China's immediate neighbourhood where its growing weight is the most deeply felt and where it has been most keen to invoke its cultural traditions as guides to its foreign policy. Secondly, it embraces a broad historical perspective to highlight the ways China's contemporary vision of order is shaped by the country's traditional political culture and imperial heritage. Finally, it takes as its central theme the hierarchical nature of this vision, which is grounded in the belief that, to be stable, this order must reflect the difference in status between the PRC and smaller states. The objective of this book is thus to show how the ancient tradition of viewing order hierarchically still informs Chinese designs for Asia today. Before presenting the outline of this argument, I will first explain this choice to focus on Asia, the historical roots of contemporary Chinese foreign policy, and the concept of hierarchy.

China and its 'periphery'

It is in Asia that the PRC has been most proactive in trying to reshape international structures as its power has grown. Its leaders tend to refer to the region as the 'periphery' (*zhoubian*), implying that China itself is its natural centre. As Xi Jinping puts it, this 'periphery' deserves special care due to its 'extremely important strategic significance'.[5] From a realist perspective, it is inevitable that, like other great powers before it, a stronger

---

[5] '习近平在周边外交工作座谈会上发表重要讲话' [Xi Jinping gives an important speech at the Peripheral Diplomacy Work Conference], *Xinhua Online*, 25 October 2013. See also Heath, 2014: 120.

China will seek to dominate its immediate surroundings to ensure that no neighbour or outside power can threaten its security and challenge its superior position (Mearsheimer, 2010; Lind, 2018). China indeed seems to consider its 'periphery' a natural sphere of influence – a sort of 'extended Sinosphere', as Japanese Sinologist Amako Satoshi puts it (Aoyama and Amako, 2015: 202–3).

The exact contours of this sphere, just like the geographical extent of Asia, can be hard to narrow down and are open to interpretation. As Aoyama Rumi points out, though, a conception that includes all the regions bordering China – North-East Asia, South-East Asia, South Asia, and Central Asia – is what accords best with official Chinese writings on 'peripheral diplomacy' (2013: 14–5). China's relations with each of these regions of course have their own particularities, institutional frameworks, and set of salient issues, but the very existence of the concept of peripheral diplomacy does suggest that China has a comprehensive vision for order in its neighbourhood. Asia thus seems the most relevant place to analyse in depth Chinese preferences for international rules and norms. This is where examining the contemporary relevance of historical and cultural legacies becomes crucial. David Kang (2007; 2010) has been a trailblazer in this respect, emphasizing the importance of studying Asia's past for hints about what Chinese leadership will look like in the future.[6] There are, however, many reasons to quibble with his understanding of the 'Sinocentric order' (Callahan, 2012: 9–11). This book takes Kang's injunction to study China's past seriously but seeks to improve on his diagnosis and offer a more accurate and nuanced analysis of traditional Chinese modes of rulership and their modern fate.

Linking imperial past and present

Knowledgeable experts like Mark Mancall (1963), John Fairbank (1969), or Lucian Pye (1968; 1988; 1990) have, decades ago, already noted the weight that long-standing traditions still exerted on the politics and policies of the 'new China' founded in 1949. This is unsurprising, since an intense consciousness of the past has always been, and continues to be, a distinctive feature of Chinese political culture. Some have even described the study of history as the true religion of the Middle Kingdom (Han Yu-shan, 1955: 1; Huang Chun-chieh, 2004; Yu Shicun 2012; Wang

---

[6] Kang also looks at other East Asian states' stances towards China during the imperial era and reactions to its rise today. This is also an important topic of study, but one beyond the remit of this book which focuses on the Chinese side of these relationships.

Fei-ling, 2015 : 47). If that is the case, the CCP is an ardent believer. The readings of history it offers are partial and far from innocent. They are used to legitimize its domestic rule and foreign policy not only through hagiographic depictions of its own history, but also through invocations of an idealized vision of China's imperial past and of the country's 'traditional culture' the Party claims to be the custodian of (Ai, 2015; Ford, 2015; Mayer, 2018).[7]

Yet it would be a mistake to conclude from this that Chinese traditions are simply a tool of propaganda for a regime always in search of the best ways to consolidate its hold on power and gain international acceptance. No matter how biased their understanding of it is, there is every indication that Chinese leaders take the study of history very seriously and look to the past, both near and far, for lessons and guidance. One sign of that is the regularity with which they pepper their speeches with allusions to Chinese classics and famous historical episodes. Another is the CCP's declared objective to achieve the 'great rejuvenation of the Chinese nation' (*Zhonghua minzu weida fuxing*), which most modern Chinese leaders have alluded to in one form or another – Xi Jinping more than any other before him – and which explicitly harkens back to lost imperial splendour, an idealized vision of the past where China was admired by all and surrounded by deferential neighbours. China's past, and the inspiration the country's pre-modern traditions offer its leaders today as they seek to reshape international order, is therefore a natural focus of enquiry for outside observers as well.

Although some scholars and writers seem to have accepted more or less wholesale the official CCP narrative that imperial China was supremely peaceful and benevolent, and that the PRC will be equally so once it returns to a position of international primacy (Jacques, 2009; Hsiung, 2012), others have been less naïve and offered a more critical analysis (for example, Ford, 2010; French, 2017; Wang Fei-ling, 2017; Schuman, 2020). Their work usefully highlights various aspects of China's imperial model with relevance today, such as its authoritarian nature and totalitarian potential, a close association of political legitimacy with moral virtue, a constant push and pull between civilizational rhetoric and geopolitical calculations, and China's enduring sense of superiority and centrality.

---

[7] The fascination with Chinese traditions is not limited to government spheres either, as more and more Chinese scholars now look to their own history and culture to analyse and guide their country's foreign policy. Among the most well known are Zhao Tinyang (2006), Yan Xuetong (2008; 2011a), and Qin Yaqing (2016), but the list goes on and on (for example, Wang Shengcai, 2006; Ye Zicheng, 2007; Xiao and Niu, 2010; Shi Yinhong, 2015).

Some other observers, however, stress the need for caution in following this kind of long historical approach, which risks exaggerating China's maladaptation to the Western norms of modern international society and downplaying the impact of the radical changes in the country's international environment over the centuries. They have noted the diversity and heterogeneity of Chinese intellectual traditions, the complexity of its actual historical experience, and the crucial role played by the new currents of thought embraced during the 20th century (most notably nationalism and Marxism-Leninism) in informing the Chinese world view today (Schwartz, 1968; Kim, 1979: 90–3; Hunt, 1984; Kawashima, 2007: 29–34; Miller, 2009; Callahan, 2015). In this debate, then, one side emphasizes the lines of continuity in the history of China's engagement with the world, while the other focuses on the points of rupture. This book seeks to take a middle path between the two sides, establishing the link between China's imperial past and its present while still taking due precautions to account for the country's fluctuating fortunes and the radical changes that accompanied its forced entrance into the modern society of nation states.

Hierarchy and its varieties

The pivotal concept on which this book's argument about historical continuity in China's vision of order relies is that of hierarchy. The Oxford dictionary defines hierarchy as 'a system in which members of an organization or society are ranked according to relative status or authority' (Stevenson, 2010: 825). In such a system, 'actors are organized into vertical relations of super- and subordination' (Mattern and Zarakol, 2016: 624). Stratification is in fact a basic feature of all international societies, including our contemporary global society of nominally equal sovereign states (Luard, 1976: Ch. 9). This reality is routinely, if often only tacitly, acknowledged in all writings about international relations through the common use of terms such as superpower, great powers, middle powers, and small powers, or core, semi-periphery, and periphery, which all imply gradation and inequality (Clark, 1989: 2; Dunne, 2003: 304). A burgeoning academic literature has also focused more specifically on questions of hierarchy and status in international relations (for example, Simpson, 2004; Hobson and Sharman, 2005; Donnelly, 2009; Lake, 2009; Volgy et al, 2011; Paul, Larson, and Wohlforth, 2014; Pouliot, 2016; Renshon, 2017; Zarakol, 2017; Mcconaughey, Musgrave, and Nexon, 2018).

In writings about the modern international society and its European origins, the forms of hierarchical relations most commonly identified are management of international affairs by great powers, whose special rights and duties are recognized by other states, and hegemony exercised by one dominant state with some degree of social consent (Bull, 2002: 196 ff.;

Watson, 2007: 104–7; Clark, 2009; 2011b). Many have described post-Cold War East Asia as a prominent instance of an international society at the regional level where a hegemon, namely the US, has assumed managerial functions with the support of a constituency of allies and with the tacit consent of other states (Beeson and Berger, 2003; Mastanduno, 2003; Beeson, 2004; Ikenberry, 2004; Inoguchi and Bacon, 2005; Clark, 2011b: Ch. 8; Goh, 2013b).

The modern institutions of great power management and hegemony are, however, not the best lens through which to study China's understanding of its contemporary place in Asia. The country undoubtedly sees itself as a great power, and is recognized as such by the whole of international society. Notably, it seats on the United Nations Security Council as one of the five permanent, veto-wielding members – the clearest and most prominent marker of great power status. However, China has strongly emphasized its determination to forge its own path as it steps up on the international stage, conducting a 'major country diplomacy with Chinese characteristics' (*Zhongguo tese daguo waijiao*) free from the standards set by Western great powers of the past.[8] In Xi Jinping's words, China's diplomatic work needs to have 'a distinct Chinese feature, Chinese character and Chinese style'.[9]

Therefore, even if the country has come to embrace Western concepts like that of a 'responsible great power' (*fuzeren daguo*) – a great power that fulfils its managerial functions and refrains from actions that cause disorder or injustice – as a way to counter the impression that a rising China might pose a threat (Wang Yizhou, 1999: 26, Scott, 2010: 83–4), it has also made clear that it would take more responsibility on its own terms, based on its own sense of the proper conduct of a great power, and not as part of a process of 'Westernization' (Liu Feitao, 2004: 32; Li Jie, 2007: 157–8; Deng Yong, 2014: 124–5). Some Chinese scholars have stressed that to truly take responsibility, a great power needs not only the necessary national strength, but also the freedom to choose how to manage international affairs according to its own agenda and its own values (Liu Feitao, 2004: 28, Jin Canrong, 2014: 33–5). China has embraced the language of great power management, then, recognizing its usefulness as an internationally acceptable frame to talk about its increasingly prominent role on the international stage, but this does not tell us much about how exactly it aims to assume its 'responsibilities',

---

[8] To drive this point home even more, the CCP insists on translating the word for 'big country' (*daguo*) as 'major country' instead of 'great power' in official pronouncements.
[9] '习近平出席中央外事工作会议并发表重要讲话' [Xi Jinping chairs the Central Diplomatic Work Conference and gives an important speech], *Xinhua Online*, 29 November 2014.

especially at the regional level where it is most eager to emphasize its own values and to stake out its leadership claim.

One direction it is adamant it will not take is to attempt to establish a Chinese hegemony in Asia to replace the American one, of which it is very critical. It may have been true during the era of 'keeping a low profile' that China had learned to begrudgingly accept the US' central role in the region and to 'live with the hegemon', in the words of Jia Qingguo (2005; see also Goh, 2005; Foot, 2009). This argument is, however, harder to maintain since 2009, in this new period of increased activism and self-confidence. Xi Jinping now openly states that 'it is for the people of Asia to run the affairs of Asia, solve the problems of Asia and uphold the security of Asia'[10] and promotes international institutions that are of China's own making, do not necessarily include the US, and are certainly not led by it. China further emphasizes its determination to behave differently as a regional overseer to an America routinely accused of 'hegemonism' or 'hegemonic behaviour'.[11]

Such criticism hints at the strongly negative connotation that 'hegemony' (*baquan*) holds in the Chinese language and psyche. The Xinhua Dictionary defines a hegemon as 'a state that commits aggression, pressures other states, and increases its influence through military or economic power' (Institute of Linguistics, CASS, 2012: 10) This reflects the traditional understanding of the concept, whereby the 'way of the hegemon' (*badao*) is rule through the use of raw power, which compares negatively with the 'way of the king' (*wangdao*), or rule through moral virtue to which any dominant state should aspire. Following the 'way of the hegemon' may sometimes become necessary to preserve order, but should not be something to aspire to. As will be discussed later in this book, this understanding of hegemony was reaffirmed in the early 20th century by seminal political leaders like Sun Yat-sen and Li Dazhao, and remains the one used by the CCP today when it condemns the hegemonism and power politics attributed to Western great powers and promises to offer a better way.

Considering this, centring our whole discussion of China's designs for its relations with smaller neighbours on the idea of hegemony would put us on shaky ground. It still has its uses in a more limited way. Even Chinese scholars admit that the use of the 'way of the hegemon' may be necessary to ensure the country's interests when faced with hostile conditions.[12] The question

---

[10] Xi Jinping, 'New Asian Security Concept for new progress in security cooperation', 21 May 2014, www.fmprc.gov.cn/mfa_eng/wjdt_665385/zyjh_665391/201405/t20140527 _678163.html.

[11] See, among countless examples, this commentary criticizing US freedom of navigation operations in the South China Sea: 'Opinion: U.S.-called freedom of navigation is hegemonism in disguise', *Xinhua*, 19 November 2015.

[12] Interview with a prominent scholar at Fudan University, Shanghai, 9 March 2018. See also 陈向阳 [Chen Xiangyang], '哈中国特色大国外交是对'务实王道'的返本开新'

to be examined is, therefore, what the conditions are where China deems a turn towards hegemonic practices – that is, the use of force for coercive purposes – justified. As a description of the way China seeks to organize its relations with smaller states overall, though, hierarchy itself, rather than any specific form, is a better fit. As a general principle, any discussion of the world view of active participants in international life should take care to be framed in terms that would be recognizable to those participants (the technical expression for this is 'subjective adequacy'),[13] or risk attributing them intentions and ideas that they in fact do not possess (Navari, 2009: 43). If this book takes as its guiding concept that of hierarchy, it is because, out of the many lenses through which to approach the universal question of how to organize relations between states of unequal size and power, this is the one that most accords with the Chinese world view.

In discussions of China's imperial past, hierarchy is omnipresent. Its domestic governance model was premised on a clear vertical organization of society, just as its foreign relations were premised on the superiority of the Son of Heaven over any ruler he would interact with. The relations of 'superior and inferior' (*shangxia*) are a prominent theme in classical political writings and imperial histories, and hierarchy has been identified time and again as a pillar of the Chinese system of thought, and of Confucianism in particular (Nakamura, 1964: Ch. 23; Fei Xiaotong, 1992: Ch. 4; Hwang Kwang-Kuo, 2011: 109–11). Today's Chinese leaders refrain from using similar language to avoid hurting the sensibilities of their foreign counterparts, but are still comfortable pointing out the different expectations facing big and small states regarding their behaviour in the international arena and are obsessed by their country's international status (*guoji diwei*) (Deng Yong, 2008).

Several scholars have argued that a hierarchical understanding of the world still underpins China's foreign policy and its vision of international order today (Callahan, 2008; Harris, 2014: 6; Buzan, 2018: 15–18). It is an important theme in the works mentioned previously that highlight the elements of continuity between China's imperial past and the PRC. In fact, in some of those works, China's hierarchical world view may even be overemphasized to reinforce the impression of a radical opposition between it and the Western conception of international society, ignoring both how much today's China has adapted itself to prevailing international norms and how common elements of hierarchy are in Western traditions and practices as well. Ironically, by putting so much emphasis on the opposition of a

---

[Great power diplomacy with Chinese characteristics is a return to and renewal of the 'pragmatic Way of the King'], *China Online*, 17 May 2017.
[13] See Weber, 1968: 11, 20.

'hierarchical China' and an 'egalitarian West', such arguments avoid the need to describe the specifically Chinese understanding of hierarchy as it relates to international order, limiting themselves to an insistence on China's sentiment of superiority towards 'barbarians', to by now cliché discussions of the so-called 'tribute system' – largely based on early Ming practices but too often made to represent the whole of 2,000 years of imperial foreign policy – and of China's dissatisfaction with the way the contemporary international order works. What is needed, then, is a more rigorous examination of the Chinese conception of hierarchy, how it relates to the actual foreign relations of various dynasties, and how it evolved and changed with China's entrance into the modern society of nation states. In the rest of this introduction, I will outline how this book seeks to go about offering such an examination.

Systemic constraints

The core of my argument deals with the traditional Chinese vision of hierarchical order and its influence on Chinese foreign policy throughout the ages, but it starts with a bit of context setting. I have mentioned earlier the importance, in any discussion of continuities in Chinese history, of properly taking into account the complexities and lines of rupture that have marked it. This is the objective of Chapter 1, which uses the distinction between system and society operated by the English School to discuss certain external constraints on China's ability to achieve its vision of order in its surroundings and some of the radical changes that have reshaped its external environment in the 19th and 20th centuries. In the understanding of scholars like Hedley Bull and Adam Watson, the social aspect of international relations relates to the common rules, norms, and institutions agreed upon by states to regulate their relations. In contrast, according to Bull's classical definition, a system implies only that 'two or more states have sufficient contact between them, and have sufficient impact on one another's decisions, to cause them to behave – at least in some measure – as parts of a whole' (2002: 9). This definition, associated with the realist tradition of international relations theory (Wight, 1991), therefore has a mechanistic connotation.

In practice, states brought together by systemic pressures have always developed at least a thin layer of social rules, if only to facilitate trade and communications as a matter of expediency (Watson, 1987: 151; James, 1993: 272–4). In other words, the social and systemic aspects of international relations coexist and are always intertwined. The system–society distinction can therefore best be thought of as a useful methodological device that reminds us of the necessity to consider the 'complex and multidimensional reality' of international politics from different angles, including both a physical or systemic perspective and a social one that takes into account states' intentions, perceptions, and values (Dunne and Little, 2014: 94).

The first angle, systemic analysis, focuses on structural factors influencing state behaviour from the outside. Those include geography, available technologies relating to transport and communication, and the military power of a given state relative to that of its neighbours. They can also include social facts themselves, that is, institutionalized understandings that have become so commonly accepted and universally shared that they come to have 'effects separate from the particular attitudes or orientations immediately in the heads of the participants' and therefore acquire system-like features (Navari, 2009: 51). When considered under this angle, the changes in structural conditions occurring over the course of Asia's history, and especially after the intrusion of Western imperial powers, become clear. The strength of the Chinese empire fluctuated widely, from unity and military might sufficient to expand by subjugating surrounding polities, to weakness and vulnerability to invasion, to complete disintegration and long periods of fragmentation; the 'Western impact' brought about one such period of weakness and vulnerability, but also new systemic norms of inter-state interactions that China had to adapt to. Economic and social structures, techniques of warfare, and means of travel and communication also evolved greatly over the centuries, and especially rapidly over the last 150 years. Chapter 1 is devoted to discussing those changes. It argues that China is today in a position of strength that approaches the one it occupied at the apogee of the greatest dynasties, but that the increase in the volume and intensity of interactions between states in the modern world and the existence of new norms of legitimacy that form the universal ground rules for contemporary international relations present new challenges as it seeks to shape international order in its neighbourhood.

Hierarchical order as a Weberian ideal type

The book then shifts perspectives to try to see Asia through Chinese eyes by examining the values it holds and the rules and norms it believes should govern its relations with neighbours. This is, in other words, the social part of my analysis, which takes most of the following pages and examines China's vision of an Asian society of states with itself at the centre. My central argument is that a hierarchical vision of international order, with differentiated roles assigned to China and to the smaller states that surround it, has been a constant guide for political elites over the course of the country's long history, and continues to shape various aspects of its foreign policy today, from its moralizing discourse about international relations to its use of diplomacy as a means to demonstrate its superior status and its employment of various tools to guide, coerce, and induce other states into accepting their assigned position in a Sinocentric regional architecture.

To make this argument, I begin by drawing a picture of the concept of hierarchy as it relates to order in traditional Chinese political thought. Said picture takes the form of a Weberian ideal type. Max Weber's objective in conducting sociological investigations was 'the knowledge of the cultural significance of concrete historical events and patterns' (Weber, 1949: 111). One of the most important tools Weber developed for his purpose was the 'ideal type', which is 'formed by the one-sided *accentuation* of one or more points of view and by the synthesis of a great many diffuse, discrete, more or less present and occasionally absent *concrete individual* phenomena which are arranged according to those one-sidedly emphasized viewpoints into a unified *analytical* construct' (emphasis in original) (Weber, 1949: 90). An ideal type thus aims to illuminate one particular aspect of an infinitely complex reality that the analyst believes to be significant and meaningful for social actors. It is an abstraction, a 'mental construct (Gedankenbild) [that] cannot be found empirically anywhere in reality', but can then be used as a reference and point of comparison during the examination of said reality to better understand important aspects of it (Weber, 1949: 90, 93).

Crucially, ideal types are formed by '[relating] events to values' (Keene, 2009: 106), and thus are grounded in the premise that saying anything meaningful about the behaviour of a given social actor means first understanding his motivations based on his particular, culturally inspired value orientation. An ideal type is thus, 'in effect, an interpretation of the social world in terms of a particular set of cultural values' (Keene, 2009: 107). We should be careful, though, not to confuse ideal types, as 'pure' analytical concepts, with the complex set of ideas actually present in the minds of people at any given historical period (Weber, 1949: 94–6). The two are, of course, closely related: ideal typification seeks to distil the essence of the widely held beliefs of a group of people – in our case the conception among the Chinese political elite of what a harmonious world order ought to look like – which does serve as a guide for their action in concrete situations. Yet those beliefs will necessarily vary from individual to individual within that group. They are not necessarily always consistent, often ambiguous, and sometimes contradictory. An ideal type, on the contrary, should be clearly and logically stated, and remain a fixed point used for analysis. It is, thus, nothing more than a heuristic tool with which we can compare the behaviour of actual social actors to better understand their significance.

Considering the concept of hierarchical order in Chinese political thought in such terms can facilitate the task of determining, through comparison of ideal type and actual foreign relations, the impact a hierarchical world view had on Chinese behaviour in different ages by accentuating aspects that are relevant to it. My ambition is, however, emphatically not to attempt to explain the whole of China's foreign relations. Reasoning in terms of ideal types means acknowledging the possibility of several overlapping interpretations of the same complex reality, which can all claim validity as long as they have identified and revealed certain of its essential features (Weber, 1949: 91; Keene, 2009: 108). For instance, the historical patterns of China's foreign relations can be analysed in terms of its visions for orderly political relations, as I do here, but equally so in terms of security and Chinese decision making regarding the use military force,[14] or in terms of commerce and China's participation in Asian trade networks.[15] Those approaches focus on different facets and meanings of the same set of practices, like the paying of tribute, which will be discussed here. All reveal something meaningful about the nature of China's interactions with its neighbours that remain significant for us today. This book is, thus, written in the hope of providing one such viewpoint that may be of interest to contemporary observers of Asian international politics and Chinese foreign policy, but has no pretension to eclipse other such attempts. My approach is rather complementary to the ones mentioned earlier, seeking to illuminate a different side of the vast and complex topic that is China's relations with the outside world, a side that has been left in the shadows by other works with a different focus.

To follow the Weberian method, then, means first to construct an ideal-typical image of a hierarchical order as it can be abstracted from the basic system of values and principles that is typically thought of as China's traditional political culture, and then to use this ideal type as a fixed point against which to evaluate the designs and policies of past Chinese statesmen and of those who lead the country today. It is a process that first seeks to draw a picture of 'the order in the minds of actors' – namely, in our case, Chinese leaders – and then to examine how their actions have sought to reproduce said order in the real world (Hollis and Smith, 1990: 87). Chapter 2 deals with the first part of this process, the ideal type construction, while the chapters that follow analyse the Chinese historical record from the imperial era to the present day.

Building an ideal type requires a solid foundation, which means choosing the right set of values. Chinese culture is, of course, far from a monolithic entity. The formative age of intellectual effervescence that preceded the

---

[14] There is in fact a healthy and long-standing debate about the nature of China's historical 'strategic culture' and propensity to use military force in its search for security (Johnston, 1995, 1996; Zhang Shu Guang, 1999; Swaine and Tellis, 2000; Scobell, 2002; Zhang Tiejun, 2002; Scobell, 2003; Feng Huiyun, 2007; Ni Lexiong, 2008; Wang Yuan-kang, 2011; Liu Tiewa, 2014).

[15] Japanese scholars have been at the forefront of efforts to identify the economic forces driving diplomatic relations behind the façade of a China-imposed hierarchy (for example, Hamashita, 1990; 1997; Ueda, 2005; Iwai, 2006; 2009; Nakajima, 2018).

unification of the empire by the Qin was later dubbed that of the 'hundred schools' and laid the foundations for a variety of philosophical currents (some more successful and enduring than others). In later centuries, Buddhism came to occupy an important space in China's intellectual and religious life, while extended periods of rule by 'conquest dynasties' established by Inner Asian nomadic polities also left their mark (Waley-Cohen, 2006). Less directly and more generally, Chinese culture was from very early times until at least the Song dynasty (which, faced with more powerful 'barbarian' neighbours to which it had to submit, strove to more consciously define the 'Chineseness' of Chinese culture to shore up its self-esteem) influenced by constant interactions and mixing with, or absorption of, other polities of the Eurasian landmass (Ge Zhaoguang, 2014: 83–93). This is all before the fundamental questioning of long-held traditions and widespread exploration of European philosophical writings that the 'Western shock' of the 19th century provoked.

It is clear, however, where the Chinese cultural mainstream lies, namely in the synthesis of Confucian and Legalist thought – sometimes dubbed 'Imperial Confucianism' – which during the Han dynasty became the backbone of the imperial moral and legal system and remained so for most of the following two millennia (Hsiao Kung-chuan, 1979: 467–8; Fairbank and Goldman, 2006: 62–3; Zhao Dingxin, 2015: 274 ff.).[16] Imperial Confucianism did not remain static, of course, and underwent a particularly deep rethink from the late Tang to the early Ming (Bol, 1992; Farmer, 1995: 24–9). Yet, its centrality to the Chinese imperial model remained mostly unchallenged. The official orthodoxy was strongly rooted enough to give distinct colours to the elements of foreign culture that made their way into the Middle Kingdom.[17] This was the case for Buddhism, which adapted to Chinese social and political institutions as it spread and saw some of its core concepts brought in line with classical Chinese texts (Taoist as

---

[16] Briefly stated, Confucianism is a doctrine that emphasizes personal ethics, moral government, and the maintenance of social harmony through respect for ancient traditions, chief among them the practice of rituals and music. Legalism advocates instead strengthening the authority of the state through the strict enforcement of standards of behaviour and the judicious use of various techniques of statecraft. It should be noted that the terms 'Confucianism' and 'Legalism' are inaccurate and unsatisfactory translations of their Chinese equivalents – literally, the school of the scholars (*rujia*) and the school of *fa* (*fajia*), a term with a much broader meaning than simply law – which were themselves settled upon a posteriori to designate an ensemble of important texts sharing a similar outlook on politics and society (see Goldin, 2011). They are used in this book for lack of a better and commonly agreed upon alternative.

[17] China's most famous 20th century writer, Lu Xun, colourfully calls Chinese culture a 'soy sauce vat' (*jianggang*) that soaks whatever enters it (quoted in Barmé, 2008: 187).

well as Confucian) through translation (Nakamura, 1964: 209–12, 266–8, 291–4; Ch'en, 1973; Fairbank and Goldman, 2006: 79–81).

The same can in fact be said of the Chinese form of communism that inspired the founding of the PRC in 1949. Its early adherents avowedly rejected Chinese traditions, but were still brought up steeped in them and their doctrine drew in various ways on deeply rooted strains of thought. One could mention, for instance, the reverence for the new 'classics' that were the writings of the first generations of Marxists and revolutionaries, an affinity for authoritarian principles of government, an inclination towards moral idealism and ideological conformism, or an emphasis on practical learning as a basis of policy making (de Bary, 1988: 99–104; Pye, 1988: 31–2; Mizoguchi, Ikeda, and Kojima, 2007: 240–1). This is a reminder that, although China's modern transition brought about a fundamental rupture with its past, bringing about a 'post-Confucian era' (de Bary, 1988: 105 ff.), elements of continuity do exist and are worth exploring.

To identify these elements of continuity when it comes to China's vision of international order, then, Chapter 2 starts by building an ideal type of hierarchical order based on the foundational texts of Confucianism and Legalism that formed the bedrock of the imperial orthodoxy. It identifies the following five assertions that underpin it. First, the maintenance of order is the primary purpose of political power. Secondly, inequalities in resources and capabilities between members of society are an inescapable fact of life. A stable order needs to reflect and rationalize those inequalities and therefore requires the enforcement of a strict vertical differentiation of the roles of various social actors. Third, the hierarchical structure of society and the high position occupied by some of its members can only be justified in moral terms, since other forms of domination are unsustainable. Fourth, the glue that holds order together is an equal dedication of all members of society to following the rules of ritual, simply understood here as proper behaviour that accords with reason and civilization, so as to periodically reaffirm their acceptance of their prescribed position. Fifth, the three main tools at the disposal of the state to ensure that all behave according to ritual norms are its control over names (or language more broadly), the prestige derived from its military strength and from the consistent imposition of punishments on transgressors, and its ability to offer material benefits to incentivize good conduct.

I should stress here that these five assertions are deeply inter-related and form a logical chain. It is to guarantee order that a stable social hierarchy must be established; it is to make hierarchy acceptable that those in a superior position must exhibit exceptional moral qualities; it is through behaviour according to the rules of propriety that moral virtues are concretely expressed and that the hierarchy is maintained on a day-to-day basis; the ruler at the top of the pyramid has a duty to use the tools at its disposal to ensure that the rules of propriety are respected. They are discussed separately in the following chapters only for the sake of convenience and clarity of analysis.

From the imperial era to the Xi Jinping era

The largest portion of this book is devoted to the analysis of China's historical experience in imperial times, during the period of transition to the modern era, and under the PRC, seen through the lens of the ideal type of hierarchical order described previously. Chapter 3 on the long imperial era examines how the aspiration to establish a stable hierarchical order was reflected in actual Chinese statecraft at a time where the Confucian–Legalist synthesis truly was the ruling orthodoxy. It highlights the unshakeable assumption of Chinese superiority over all its neighbours even in the face of a very different reality, the variety and purpose of Chinese techniques of 'rule through ritual', the enduring obsession with assigning the appropriate rank and status to all the rulers sending envoys to China as a precondition to the establishment of stable ties with them, and the consistency in the use of the empire's wealth and power to enforce 'proper relations' between polities. This chapter therefore identifies the concrete shape that key aspects of the Chinese vision of order took when applied to the real world, so as to later trace how they survived contact with the modern society of states.

Chapter 4 turns its attention to the late 19th and early 20th centuries, the pivotal decades during which China's modern understanding of international order took shape. It aims to account both for the radical transformation in China's fate this period represents and the lines of continuity between imperial past and modern Chinese statecraft. To do so, it examines the profound changes in the Chinese world view and conduct of foreign relations that accompanied the country's traumatic entrance into the modern society of sovereign states, while highlighting the ways in which traditional modes of thinking about the outside world did endure. It analyses the shift towards an understanding of order as an objective to be achieved once China has recovered its strength, the country's continuing aspiration to be recognized as first among Asian states, its renewed sense of moral superiority both over its neighbours and over Western great powers seen as predatory and corrupt, and its obsession with questions of status on the international stage within the new framework of Western-style diplomacy. These all later became important features of the PRC's foreign policy.

Both chapters rely on the work of the many scholars who have written detailed and illuminating accounts of the history of Chinese foreign relations, and introduce in particular a range of Japanese scholarship on the topic that remains little known in the English-speaking world. This is unfortunate because the insights of Japanese historians have proven particularly valuable during the writing of this book, steeped as they are in the shared intellectual traditions and writing system of what Nishijima Sadao (1983) calls the 'East Asian cultural sphere' while still maintaining a helpful degree of distance and detachment from their topic of study. Including their work in the analysis conducted in these pages allows me, I hope, to present a more well-rounded and nuanced take on the legacies of China's past.

Having identified the most enduring aspects of Chinese designs for a hierarchical order and the form in which they survived China's entrance into the modern society of states, the final three chapters examine their role in driving Chinese foreign policy since the founding of the People's Republic, and especially in the contemporary period under Xi Jinping. Here, the argument relies as much as possible on authoritative primary sources – Chinese leaders' speeches and official documents – supplemented where necessary by references to Chinese scholars' comments and analyses of government policies, as well as to English and Japanese language scholarship. Chapter 5 focuses on the link between order and hierarchy themselves. It discusses PRC statesmen's efforts to present themselves as leaders of the developing world, and of Asian states in particular, in the establishment of a more just international order than the one dominated by Western states. It also describes how, even as it denounced the existing international order, China made steady efforts to raise its status within said order by pursuing economic development, raising its 'comprehensive national power', and obtaining the support of its neighbours in that endeavour. The chapter finally shows that, under Xi Jinping, a stronger China has become much more proactive about 'taking leadership' and clearer about its expectation that neighbouring states will accept its role as overseer of Asia and behave with the necessary deference.

Chapter 6 turns to the modern role of morality in China's diplomatic discourse and ritual in its diplomatic practice. It shows how PRC leaders justify their international leadership ambitions by claiming for their country unique virtues based on the 'righteous' norms of international affairs it promotes. It also analyses the PRC's attempts to impose standards of 'correct' behaviour on neighbouring states that involve diplomatic shows of deference and self-restraint in avoiding China's 'red lines'. Those features of Chinese foreign policy were already evident before Xi Jinping came to power, but he has doubled down on them, presenting the CCP as the inheritor of ancient Chinese virtues and seeking to create a pattern of diplomacy that regularly reaffirms the PRC's place at the centre of Asia.

Chapter 7 discusses finally the modern use of traditional tools of statecraft. It highlights notably the enduring focus on mastery of language, as seen in the CCP's efforts to establish a sophisticated international propaganda apparatus, and its recreation of a modern 'ranks and titles' system through its partnerships network. It also discusses the use of military might both to boost the PRC's reputation for power and resolve and to 'punish' those who offend it, as well as the reliance on growing economic resources to incentivize deference from neighbours both through promises of investments and assistance and through threats of economic retaliations against any 'provocation'. In those ways, Chinese power is used to obtain compliance with a vision of hierarchical order meant to be sustained through the cultivation of moral virtues by participating states, and more concretely through frequent ritualized diplomatic interactions. Though its shape may be very different, this vision of order still embodies principles and values inherited from China's imperial past.

1

Aspects of Asia as an International System

The purpose of this chapter is to highlight several important structural factors of Asia seen as an international system which constrain and influence China's ability to shape its relations with neighbours. This is meant to serve as a prelude to our main argument. The aim of this book is to study the attraction that one idea, namely hierarchy as it relates to order, has exerted on Chinese statesmen in their dealings with the outside world, serving as a figurative pole star towards which they have oriented themselves time and again. This means we will emphasize continuity in the intellectual realm. It is therefore important to bring nuance to that argument with a reminder that, whatever continuity there has been in China's understanding of what a stable and harmonious order should look like, its international environment itself has been anything but stable or unchanging over the course of its long imperial history, to say nothing of the transition to the modern society of states.

The features we will highlight here all relate to Asia understood as a system, that is, as a group of polities brought into sustained contact by economic and geopolitical forces. Discussion in those terms will thus focus on power, technology, and other factors conditioning to an extent states' behaviour independently of their aspirations or values. As discussed in the introduction, this can include normative elements as well if they become so widely and unquestionably accepted as to form another conditioning factor, weighting on states or pushing them in a certain direction regardless of immediate intent. In the following pages, then, we highlight some important systemic forces and their fluctuations that have set the conditions for China's foreign relations over the centuries. We will put particular emphasis on how much structural change the modern transition brought to Asia and how this change has altered the nature of China's relations with its neighbours, redefining the boundaries within which it can pursue the ideal of hierarchical order. Specifically, the three forces discussed are the distribution of power in the system, its interaction capacity as determined by available technologies, and hegemonic beliefs about basic principles of legitimacy.

Types of asymmetry

Asia is an asymmetrical system, in the sense that a unified China is, generally speaking, more powerful than its neighbours and occupies a central position both geographically and figuratively. Power is understood here in the classical sense, namely, as the combination of elements that give a state the capacity to shape the behaviour of others. As Martin Wight writes of the power of modern states, 'its basic components are size of population, strategic position and geographical extent, and economic resources and industrial production. To these must be added less tangible elements like administrative and financial efficiency, education and technological skill, and above all moral cohesion' (1978: 26). All these elements make a powerful state able to mould its environment, notably by building a large and effective military force. If we generalize this definition with a few adjustments to make it more broadly applicable, a state's power thus includes physical attributes (size, population, geographical features), the economic resources at its disposal, and the effectiveness of its internal organization, all of which determine the military force it can put to bear on others. Therefore, when we describe Asia as an asymmetrical system, we mean that China is bigger and more populous, wealthier, more effective as a centralized administrative state, and more militarily mighty than its neighbours. This statement may be true generally speaking, but requires a lot of qualifications and elaboration to accurately reflect a much more complex reality, as we will see shortly.

Before that, though, we should say a few words about the general impact of asymmetry on the shape of Asian international relations. Brantly Womack has done the most to popularize discussions of asymmetry in international relations, particularly as it applies to China's place in Asia. The centrepiece of his work is a study of Sino–Vietnamese relations throughout the centuries (2006), but the 'asymmetry theory' that he has sought to elaborate is perhaps most clearly spelled out in a 2009 essay (see also Wills, 2009, expanding on the same theme). One can question several aspects of his arguments – notably his charitable view of China's restraint in the use of force and his eagerness to use the word 'theory' even if it is unclear how universally applicable his findings are – but they helpfully remind us that the differences in size and power between China and its neighbours have important consequences for the nature of their relationship.

Most obviously, developments in China will have a disproportionate impact on the whole region, as its ability to project power abroad is dependent on its degree of internal cohesion. Chinese actions are also a more important factor in any of its neighbours' strategic calculations than their own behaviour is in China's, at least individually if not collectively. That is, the general asymmetry of the system leads to an asymmetry in attention between neighbours for whom China looms extremely large and China itself, for whom the actions of individual neighbours are generally a peripheral concern. The result can be a certain insularity and a certain difficulty to accurately assess China's international environment, especially since, due to its sheer size, the likelihood is low that senior officials in the capital will have had significant experience of interactions with foreigners. China's disproportionate size and sense of its centrality in Asia can also lead to an assumption that interactions with the outside world will conform to the same principles as those that prevail in domestic politics, and that the same policy tools will remain effective. Furthermore, internal considerations will likely prevail over foreign policy ones, and foreign relations will be expected to contribute to domestic priorities. Namely, the purpose of foreign policy will be to reinforce domestic stability by avoiding any disruption to the internal order and by reinforcing the prestige of Chinese leaders in the eyes of their population.

The asymmetry of Asia, which one would expect to facilitate Chinese efforts to realize its vision of order, thus also creates impediments to such efforts by opening a potential gap between its expectations of how the outer world will behave and the reality. This is doubly true because, as was mentioned earlier, a more complex picture hides beneath the general asymmetry of China's relations with its neighbours. Indeed, despite its disproportionate size and population, rare have been the cases where this has translated into superior power without caveats. To demonstrate this, we will offer a brief overview of the dynamics of China's foreign relations across the imperial period and the modern one. In the former case, China's neighbours can be divided into four geographical categories, namely, Inner Asia, the South and Korea, the maritime world, and Central and South Asia.

Inner Asia

China's most defining foreign relation throughout the imperial era was with its mostly nomadic western and northern neighbours in Inner Asia. Here is how Frederick Mote describes this region and its inhabitants:

> 'Inner Asia' in distinction to 'Central Asia', is used here to designate the vast region east of the Pamirs and extending all the way to the Pacific Ocean. It includes Tibet and Xinjiang in the west, north of China Proper from the latitude of China's Great Wall all the way to but not including the Siberian forests and tundra, and east to the Pacific coast. Inner Asia is thus defined as the 'interior' of East Asia, whether seen from Russian Siberia or from China. ... Owen Lattimore has used

the expressive geographical metaphor of the 'Inner Asian Sea' for the steppes and deserts stretching from Manchuria to the Pamirs, seeing its oasis as islands and the edges of the sedentary societies encircling as its shores. This well describes the historical relationship of the sown (that is, of sedentary agriculture) to the steppe, the sedentary 'shore and islands dwellers' to the 'sea-roaming' nomads. ... The Inner Asian core area offered conditions that permitted the highest development of the potential in nomadism, sustained by its wandering herds of cattle and sheep and the use of camels and horses for transport or for war. Only under conditions which to them represented failure would those nomads settle down in one place long enough to scratch out and harvest a summer's crop. They looked with scorn on farmers, and though dependent on neighboring farming peoples for grain, iron, textiles, and other essentials, they much preferred to acquire those by raiding or coercive exploitation. Agriculturalists and nomads thus coexisted in an unbalanced symbiosis, nomads needing items that only stable agricultural communities could provide, while their sedentary neighbors needed nothing from the nomads, yet could not evade their demands. (Mote, 1999: 23, 25, 27–8; see also Barfield, 1992: 16–24)

China's relation with Inner Asia was still an asymmetrical one, but not in the traditional sense. The imbalance of population between the sown and the steppe was clear. Accurate counts are hard to establish, but it is, for instance, estimated that the Han dynasty ruled over 54 million people around 150 BC while facing a Xiongnu nomadic federation perhaps 1.5 million strong (Loewe, 1974: 80–1). In the tenth century AD, those numbers were around 80 million for China and 5 million for the whole of Inner Asia (Mote, 1999: 26). The economic imbalance was equally in evidence. The nomads depended on the resources they extracted from the Chinese empire, which for itself was interested only in the exotic goods from other parts of Eurasia that reached it through Inner Asia and in the sturdy horses and other livestock bred there (Yü Ying-shi, 1967: 198–200).

In other dimensions of power, the balance was not to China's advantage. Chinese practices of state administration may have been particularly refined and effective for managing a sedentary population but the loose tribal federation model developed by the inhabitants of the steppes was equally well adapted to their way of life, and capable of assembling an impressive war machine. Indeed, the military balance of power was clearly in the steppe's favour for much of the imperial era, leading to a situation of reverse asymmetry whereby the nomads were much more likely to prevail over the Chinese than to be dominated by them. The limits of the Chinese world were defined early on under the Qin and Han by their confrontation with the powerful Xiongnu empire which dominated the steppe, a pattern of opposition between equally powerful steppe and sown that frequently repeated later on, including during other great Chinese dynasties like the Tang and the Ming (Barfield, 1992: 8–16). Outside of those periods, Chinese history is characterized by the almost constant dominance of nomadic or semi-nomadic tribes, many of them coming out of Manchuria, who established 'conquest dynasties' over part or all of the Middle Kingdom. All these inevitably had to adopt the Chinese administrative model to rule over Chinese populations but mostly strove to retain their separate identity.

Their rulers also generally had greater success than purely Chinese counterparts in effectively dealing with other Inner Asian polities, culminating with the Mongol domination of large parts of the Eurasian landmass and the Qing's conquest of virtually all of Inner Asia. Traditional Chinese ways of wielding power had proven much less effective in taming the people of the region, and the necessity to adopt the ways of the steppe to rule over the steppe was further demonstrated by the few Chinese rulers successful in that endeavour, such as Han Wudi, Tang Taizong, or the early Ming emperors (Waldron, 1990: 73–6; Chang Chun-shu, 2007: 161 ff.; Lewis, 2009b: 146, 149–50).

Outside of these examples, the steppe was where China's sense of superiority met with the harsh reality of its vulnerability against the techniques of warfare of polities that, with the exception of the adaptable Tang, only Inner Asian conquerors themselves were able to durably subjugate. This pattern of reverse asymmetry forced Chinese rulers to adapt their aspirations for foreign relations that conformed to the ideal of hierarchical order to their often precarious circumstances, although the nomadic conquerors' own embrace of this ideal provided some solace. As we will see in a later chapter, situations where Chinese dynasties coexisted on Chinese territory with equally or more powerful 'barbarian' ones, in particular, revealed their attachment to this ideal even when they were themselves not necessarily at the top of the pyramid.

Korea and the South

In contrast to Inner Asia, China's relations with the polities to its South and on the Korean peninsula were straightforwardly asymmetrical. None of them could indeed compare with the Middle Kingdom in all dimensions of power listed previously, be it size and population, economic wealth, administrative sophistication, or military strength. This did not mean, though, that China could necessarily shape its relations with them fully in accordance with its ideals.

After a tumultuous early history that included the formation of various native kingdoms in political and military competition among themselves and with the inhabitants of Manchuria as well as several full-scale Chinese invasions, a Sinicized but independent unified kingdom emerged on the Korean peninsula in 676. Despite its superior power, China was unable to assert its dominance militarily thereafter and had to settle for only symbolic demonstrations of submission from Korean rulers. In later periods, Korea shared with China an acute vulnerability to military threats from Inner Asian conquerors while continuing to look to the Middle Kingdom for trade and cultural inspiration.

The military element was also prevalent in China's relations with polities it encountered as the empire expanded southwards from its cradle in the northern Central Plains (*zhongyuan*). This included today's Northern Vietnam, which was conquered early and remained a part of the Chinese world, even if only nominally so, whenever the imperial centre of power was too weak to control this remote region, until the disintegration of the Tang allowed a local ruler to definitively assert independence in 938 (Fitzgerald, 1972: 19–25; Holcombe, 2001: 143–62). Thereafter, Vietnam exemplified a typical pattern of asymmetrical relation with China – hence Womack's choice of it as his main case study – whereby it took great inspiration from its civilization, modelled its state institutions on Chinese ones, traded heavily, and offered regular demonstrations of deference. It also found itself in military confrontation with every dynasty from the Song onwards. Each of these conflicts was of a different nature, but all shared two attributes, namely, that they ended in defeat or retreat for the Chinese side but did not cause long-term disruptions to the regular course of Sino–Vietnamese relations.

The military factor also remained consistently important in China's relations with the polities and kingdoms that used to occupy today's Yunnan and Guizhou provinces. Like other mountainous or hilly areas in the South, Chinese control over local ethnic groups remained nominal at best until very late in the imperial era, and the region is a multi-ethnic patchwork still today (Herman, 2006; Herman, 2007). Those areas were the target of several military expeditions during the early dynasties – including one famous episode involving legendary statesman Zhuge Liang, immortalized in the *Romance of the Three Kingdoms* – but whatever control was established as a result proved fleeting and local rulers remained firmly in charge despite whatever declarations of allegiance they had to provide (Fitzgerald, 1972: 39–49; Yang Bing, 2009: 72 ff.).

It was one of those local rulers who managed to take over the domains of his neighbours to create the Nanzhao kingdom around the same time as the foundation of the Tang dynasty. Nanzhao proved a geopolitically active and expansionist actor on the Chinese empire's border, alternating between alliance and military confrontation with the Tang and posing a frequent threat to their outlying provinces. The successor Dali kingdom was more pacific and sought regular tributary and trading relations with the Song, without ever entering into armed conflict with them. The conquest of Dali by the

Mongols marked the beginning of the end of Yunnan as an independent entity, as the Ming who took over the province and the Qing after them made increasingly determined efforts to Sinicize the region and integrate it fully into the empire. The full takeover of Yunnan brought China into closer contact with the inhabitants of today's Burma (which had already been the target of several Mongol expeditions) and northern Laos, with whom it fought several conflicts for control of the borderlands (Suzuki, 1981; Mote, 1999: 711–3).

Altogether, then, China's relations with Korea and with polities on its southern border come closest to archetypical asymmetry, with some caveats. A clear asymmetry in material power ensured that these neighbours never posed an existential threat to the Chinese empire and that they usually considered it wiser to willingly offer demonstrations of deference rather than open themselves to invasion. China's superior might did not, however, prevent it from losing control of regions that were once part of its territory – or from gaining control of them only late in the case of Yunnan and other parts of today's South China. In fact, smaller neighbours most often held the advantage in armed confrontations that took place far from the Chinese centre of power, in environments inhospitable to Chinese troops. With military means repeatedly proving ineffective, China had no choice but to settle for the symbolic demonstrations of submission that were offered.

The maritime world

When it comes to China's relations with lands only reachable by sea, such military considerations played only a minor and intermittent role. Indeed, few were the rulers of the Middle Kingdom who mounted maritime expeditions to remote shores. The most famous ones are the voyages through the South China Sea and beyond undertaken by admiral Zheng He for the Ming Yongle emperor between 1405 and 1433, with large contingents of soldiers in toe to awe local rulers into submission (for example, Levanthes, 1994; Miyazaki, 1997; Wade, 2005; Dreyer, 2007; Terada, 2017). Earlier expeditions include raids ordered by a Sui ruler against the kingdom of Linyi in Central Vietnam and against islands in the East China Sea – which ones exactly remains a point of debate (Wang Gungwu, 1958: 64–5; Lo Jun-pang, 2012: 45–7) – and attempts at an invasion of Japan, of the kingdom of Champa (a successor of Linyi), and of the island of Java by the Mongols after their conquest of China (Lo Jun-pang, 2012: 247–83, 287–91, 303–8).

Outside of these isolated events, though, relations between China and overseas kingdoms – including most of continental South-East Asia as well, separated on land from the Middle Kingdom by Yunnan, Burma, and Vietnam, as highlighted previously – were mostly limited to trade. Cultural exchanges also played an important role in the case of Japan and later of the

Ryukyu Islands. China was mostly known as a vast and wealthy empire where countless commercial opportunities awaited and thus attracted a growing stream of foreign merchants, scholars, and monks to its shore, starting as early as the Han dynasty (Wang Gungwu, 1958: 20–1).

The asymmetry of power between China and polities of the maritime world thus did not play an important role in their relationship. When the rulers of the Middle Kingdom so desired, they could indeed bring superior military strength to bear on whoever their targets were, but this was a hazardous and expensive endeavour and they seldom chose to do so. The pull of the Chinese economy and civilization was nevertheless enough to ensure a steady flow of visitors that could be counted as tribute bearers coming to bow before the Son of Heaven, whether they were in fact envoys of faraway rulers or rather simple merchants, religious men, or scholars. Interactions with the maritime world thus served to comfort Chinese rulers in their confidence in their own superiority and ability to make at least parts of the world bow before them.

Central and South Asia

The Chinese empire's military-political interactions with Central Asia – understood here as the lands west of the Pamir Mountains and east of the Caspian Sea – were equally rare, limited as they were to the three most expansionary dynasties of the Han, Tang, and Qing (Yü Ying-shi, 1986: 410; Sen, 2003: 27–34; Newby, 2005; Lewis, 2009b: 158–9). Even in those cases, the empire's presence and influence in this remote region did not prove very stable or durable. As for other dynasties like the Song or the Ming, the 'Inner Asian sea' remained as big an obstacle as the ocean itself, and relations with Central Asia could only concern matters of trade and diplomacy, where China was not really in a position to assert its superiority.

The rarity of military-political interactions was even more evident when it came to the Indian subcontinent, as only the Tang truly had sustained exchanges there (Sen, 2003: 16–25). Even then, aside from one small military campaign in retaliation for an attack on a Tang envoy, Chinese power was not part of the equation, as the desire for cultural and commercial exchanges and friendly diplomatic relations drove contacts (Sen, 2003: 22–4). The only other recorded instance of military conflict in that region over the course of China's imperial history is an intervention by the Qing to help their Tibetan vassal repel a Nepalese invasion and subdue that assertive neighbour. This intervention remained an exception, though, and Tibet generally managed its relations with the Indian subcontinent on its own (Mote, 1999: 938–9).

Overall, then, Central Asia and South Asia remained distant lands separated from China proper by vast deserts and high mountains that formed a formidable barrier to sustained military-political interactions. It was, with the few exceptions highlighted previously, impossible for Chinese rulers to project their power so far away, but no threat to their sense of centrality and superiority came from those regions either. The exception to this was the cultural realm, where the spread to East Asia of Indian-born Buddhism in the early centuries of the Common Era pushed China to confront the notion that there were sources of civilization outside of itself (Sen, 2003: 8–12; Ge Zhaoguang, 2014: 53–7).

Modern transition

That early challenge was nothing, though, compared with the 'Western shock' or 'Western impact', the expression often used to designate the forced opening of China and Japan by Western imperial powers. In fact, this 'shock' was but the culmination of a long process of Western advances on China's periphery on all sides. Direct contact with an expanding Russian empire began very early, in the mid-17th century, although in that case the Qing were able to find a mutually acceptable modus vivendi with their adversaries after a few initial skirmishes (Mancall, 1971). China's rulers remained relatively unconcerned about Western encroachment from the South until the Opium Wars, as the European empire builders did not reach its borders until the mid-19th century, while seafaring merchants and envoys initially followed traditional customs in their dealings with Chinese authorities. This masked for a while the dramatic shift in the balance of power in China's disfavour.

The late 19th and early 20th centuries indeed saw the most complete reversal to date of asymmetry in China's foreign relations, seeing it confronted by Western powers (and eventually by a Westernized Japan) who not only dominated it militarily and exploited it economically but also forced it to look to another civilization for inspiration in profoundly reforming its state model and its belief system. This was not the first time that China had come under foreign cultural influence, as noted previously, but never had the shock been so direct and intertwined with considerations of material power. Needless to say, in that period China was in no position to realize its preferred vision of order.

The 'new China' – to use the CCP's expression – that emerged at the other end of this ordeal was still initially weak for a country of its size, and was facing a periphery radically transformed in many respects. One important new development was, furthermore, the unprecedented level of interactions between it and the rest of the world beyond Asia, even after Western powers largely left the region (with the exception of the Soviet Union and the US, of course). China was now an actor in the great game of power not only at the regional level, but also at the global one, and this broader context became a significant factor in its strategic calculations. In this book, though, our focus will remain on Asia itself and on China's immediate surroundings. The division of this periphery into the four categories used earlier does not make sense anymore in this post-1949 world. A more apt categorization would be to distinguish between East Asia, Russia and Central Asia (formerly the Soviet Union), and South Asia.

East Asia

The PRC initially was economically weak and had limited capacities to project power far from its eastern and south-eastern borders. It was preoccupied by the threat posed to it by US activities on the South-East Asian mainland and on the Korean peninsula, and focused most of its available material resources on assisting the Lao, Vietnamese, and Korean communist movements in their conflict with the global superpower.[1] This immediate preoccupation with territorial security and the dominant presence of the US throughout the region made it quite challenging to achieve any design for regional order that it might have had in those early days, although it was far from inactive, as we will see in later chapters.

China's situation steadily improved after the start of reform and opening up in the late 1970s thanks to an entente forged with the US during the 1980s, which lessened the pressure on its eastern and south-eastern flank. It also made successful efforts to mitigate potential threats by engaging the region after the end of the Cold War even as its power steadily rose. With this rise, which gathered pace after 2000, East Asia is now becoming an asymmetrical system perhaps more comprehensively than at any time in its history. China's economic resources and military capabilities now outstrip even Japan, its most powerful neighbour, and the maritime sphere has, with the exponential growth in Chinese naval capabilities, become just another area for it to spread its wings.

A few factors make this picture more complicated, though. The first is the role of the US, still the world's foremost superpower. Its numerous military assets in the region go some way towards mitigating the general asymmetry in China's favour, but beyond the overall balance of power and the US–China competition,[2] the relevance of America's presence for individual countries in their relations with China varies greatly. Japan is probably the only country that can avail itself of a solid and wide-ranging alliance with the superpower

---

[1] Chen Jian (2001) offers an excellent account of this early Cold War period seen through Chinese eyes.

[2] The trend in the last few years in fact seems to be towards military superiority for the Chinese side in Asian waters (see Hiroyuki Akita, 'Future balance of power haunts US as China bulks up', *Nikkei Asia Review*, 16 March 2021).

that supplements its already sophisticated defence capabilities and provides some reassurance in dealing with the challenge of China's growing maritime advances. The alliance with South Korea, on the other hand, is squarely aimed at countering the threat from North Korea, and any role for it in relations with China remains a matter of much contention (Chung, 2001; Yoo, 2012). In South-East Asia, the Philippines is the US' most prominent treaty ally. The relationship has had many ups and downs due to the two countries' former status as colonizer and colonized, including notably the closure of the US base on the archipelago in 1992. As concerns over China's rise – fuelled in particular by its seizure of Mischief Reef in 1994 – have grown, the Philippines has renewed its commitment to the alliance, although the wild shifts in policy that its presidential, personality-driven political system produce continue to be a factor of instability (San Pablo-Baviera, 2003: 345; Avila and Goldman, 2015: 12–14). In any case, the alliance has until now been of little help in confronting China's maritime advance in the South China Sea.

Other South-East Asian states face a diverse set of circumstances in terms of the extent of their defence links with America and of the degree of their exposure to Chinese military power. Among direct neighbours, Vietnam is particularly exposed due to a shared border and acute territorial disputes in the South China Sea and particularly keen to develop security cooperation with America (their enmity of the 1960s and 1970s is mostly forgotten). Laos and Myanmar, with settled land borders, are both less exposed and much less close to the global superpower. Further south, Malaysia and Indonesia are also less exposed due to distance and to a lower degree of acuteness in their territorial (or rather jurisdictional in Indonesia's case) disputes with China in the South China Sea, and have cordial but not very deep defence ties with the US. Singapore, without a direct stake in the South China Sea disputes but strategically located at the mouth of the Malacca Strait, is also only moderately exposed but has become one of the pillars of support for the maintenance of America's military power in East Asia. Least exposed are Cambodia and Thailand, without common borders with China or maritime disputes. Both have seen a decline in defence ties with the US in recent years, although from a different basis. Cambodia's were not extremely developed to start with, but Thailand has been a treaty ally of the US since 1954. A Joint Vision Statement was agreed on in 2012 to reinvigorate this alliance,[3] but this could not mask the growing strains in the relationship as the Thai elite reassessed its strategic value and sought more evenly balanced ties between the US and China – a trend that only accelerated after a military coup in 2014 (Prasirtsuk, 2013: 34–6; Storey, 2015; Busbarat, 2016: 238–40).

---

[3] Text of the statement at https://archive.defense.gov/releases/release.aspx?releaseid=15685.

The dilemma faced by Thailand to balance relations with the US and with China in the security realm and to avoid upsetting the latter by being too closely aligned with the former is one that it shares with virtually all states in East Asia, including other US allies like South Korea and the Philippines (but not Japan, the only state that remains largely immune to this dynamic and fully committed to its alliance). The very existence of this dilemma highlights the systemic impact of the rise of Chinese power. It also shows that America's regional military presence is no silver bullet allowing other states to fully mitigate the asymmetry of their position vis-à-vis China.

In the economic realm, the picture is even more uniformly one of decreasing US importance and ever-growing Chinese power. America was the foremost economic partner for many East Asian countries until the turn of the millennium, but its position has more recently steadily declined as that of China has risen (Rajah, 2019: 3–5). This is most notable in the area of trade, where the US consumer market absorbs an ever-lower proportion of Asian exports, but also visible in the realm of foreign direct investments, where intra-regional flows increasingly dominate (Murakami, 2016).[4] A more important factor counteracting China's weight from now on may thus be efforts at regional integration and diversification that exclude it. The Trans-Pacific Partnership, in which Japan has taken a leading role after the withdrawal of the US, and which offers its Asian members other links with wealthy states in the Americas (Canada, Mexico, Chile), may, if enlarged to include other states in the region and other economies outside it, become an important contravening force to the trend towards China becoming the core of the regional economy. With a mind to prevent such an occurrence, China itself has now applied for membership of the partnership, although its prospects for accession remain far from clear at the time of writing.[5]

Overall, then, there are a few caveats to the general statement that East Asia today is more than ever an asymmetrical system, but neither the presence of the US nor inter-Asian economic linkages excluding China do more than mitigate to some extent the fact that Chinese power is ever more disproportionate to that of its neighbours. Even in the case of Japan, the shift in the balance of power to China's advantage is clear.

---

[4] See also Kawate Iori, 'China sidelining US in Asia with growing economic clout', *Nikkei Asian Review*, 6 January 2018; John Reed and Valentina Romei, 'Who dominates the economies of South-East Asia?', *Financial Times*, 1 May 2018.

[5] Another emerging factor of uncertainty is the battle between the US and China for the dominance of new technologies. This could put East Asian countries in the uncomfortable position of having to choose which side's technological standards to adopt at the risk of cutting itself from the other.

Russia and Central Asia

When it started its existence, communist China was in a reversed asymmetrical relation with the Soviet Union to its north and west. Not only was the latter more powerful materially speaking, but it was also a crucial teacher in guiding Chinese efforts to rebuild its economic and political structure along socialist lines. The relations between the two sides quickly turned sour, with the Soviet Union eventually becoming the biggest threat to China's security. Here too, the situation started to change after the beginning of reform and opening up and became radically different with the collapse of the Soviet Union. For the first time in their common history, China started to develop an asymmetrical relation with a greatly weakened Russia, which gave it the confidence to promote the construction of an ever-closer partnership to be held as a model for relations with other great powers. All the while, it could steadily increase its presence in Mongolia and in the newly independent states of Central Asia, where Russia maintains strong security ties but where the pull of China's own economic might has proven more and more irresistible. Those states have become dependent on China for investments and trade opportunities and their security ties are growing at a clip that makes the precarious position of a less powerful Russia increasingly apparent (Swanström, 2005: 579–82; Wislon, 2021).

South Asia

There is no clear historical precedent for the high level of interactions between China and South Asia in the post-1949 era, made possible by the PRC's full takeover of Tibet and Xinjiang after 1949 and by new transport technologies that make the Himalaya, the world's greatest natural barrier, a less imposing obstacle. The exponential growth of the PRC's maritime capabilities has more recently also helped it increase its military presence in the Indian Ocean. Here again, it started with a relatively weak hand but has developed an increasingly asymmetrical relation with states in the region. The shift is particularly striking when it comes to India, Asia's other giant, which started from a position of rough parity in the 1950s – which did not prevent it from badly losing the Sino–Indian war of 1962 – but has fallen far behind due to China's unprecedented economic boom. Now the PRC's capacity to put pressure on India on their disputed border and to roam the seas surrounding the subcontinent greatly worries Indian strategists, while its attractiveness as an economic partner is as irresistible for South Asian states as it is for other neighbours.

Looking back at the evolution of the balance of power in various regions of Asia, then, we can draw a few general lessons. First, and unsurprisingly, China's ability to make neighbours act in conformity with its vision of order has historically been correlated with how deeply and comprehensively asymmetric its relation with them was, with countries exposed to the full brunt of Chinese power like Vietnam at one end of the spectrum and militarily superior nomads at the other. This augurs well for China's ability to shape the regional order in the current era as its power relative to that of all its neighbours keeps growing. Secondly, though, the number of truly asymmetrical relations in China's favour was relatively low, with only the few countries in the second historical category highlighted previously (the South and Korea) qualifying. Despite this, the example of the pre-modern maritime world, where military power was rarely a factor, shows that economic wealth and cultural achievements were sometimes enough to attract tribute bearers, or at least individuals who could be received as such. Here again, China's current conditions seem favourable as both its power projection capabilities and its economic (if not cultural) appeal keep growing along with the number of neighbours directly subject to its influence.

This is because the most radical change that occurred with the transition to the modern era – besides the reshaping of China's neighbourhood by Western powers, of course – was to give China an unprecedented ability to overcome the natural barriers to its expansion and to put an end to Inner Asian nomadic power that had been such a challenge in the past. New technologies played a crucial role in that transition, which brings us to the second systemic feature of Asia worth highlighting, namely the exponential growth in its interaction capacity.

Interaction capacity

The usefulness of power is in large part determined by the ease with which it can be deployed throughout a system. The world's greatest army may be of little use if dispatching it away from its home base is too much of a logistical challenge. This is why the means of transport, communication, and organization available at any point in time is one of the defining features of a system. Yet their importance is not limited to military considerations. Every other aspect of human interaction, be it political, economic, or cultural, equally relies on our ability to meet each other and conduct exchanges in the first place. This ability has grown considerably over time and especially in the past two centuries or so. Richard Little and Barry Buzan have proposed a useful way to understand the factors that enable or limit the scope of exchanges between polities within a system with their concept of 'interaction capacity'. Here is how they describe it:

> Interaction capacity ... refers to the amount of transportation, communication, and organizational capability within the unit or system. ... It refers to the carrying capacity of a social system, its physical

potential for enabling the units within it to exchange information, goods, or blows. ...

Three factors mediate interaction capacity:

- whether geographical factors make movement easy or difficult;
- what physical technologies are available for transportation and communication; and
- what social technologies are available for transportation and communication.

In a low-technology environment, interaction capacity is strongly shaped by geography. High mountains, vast swamps, and open oceans can simply block contact between communities on either side of them. Open steppelands make movement easy once horses or camels are available, as do navigable rivers once even quite primitive boats become available. With the development of larger and sturdier ships, and knowledge about navigation, seas can become highways rather than barriers. ... As physical technologies improve, geography becomes decreasingly important, and the large-scale movement of goods, information, people, and armies between any two points in the system becomes first possible, and then commonplace. ...

Social technologies of transportation and communication include language (esp. the development of lingua francas and writing), shared ideas (religion, diplomacy, economics), money and bills of exchange, and more concrete systems of rules and institutions. (Buzan and Little, 2000: 80–3)

The quantum leap that the transition to modernity induced in all aspects of interaction capacity is as striking in Asia as it is elsewhere. That is not to say that this capacity was static for the whole duration of the Chinese imperial era, of course. Seafaring transportation steadily improved over the centuries, with great contributions from China itself. It indeed developed increasingly sophisticated navigational science and technologies and its merchant vessels were for a long time the largest in the world (Mote, 1999: 719). As mentioned earlier, Chinese rulers seldom used these improving means of navigation to launch military expeditions, the voyages of Zheng He being a notable exception. Behind this attention-grabbing event, though, seafaring advances enabled the growth of a vigorous exchange of goods and ideas in the East Asian maritime world already during the Tang dynasty, but even more so during the Song and after (Haneda, 2013).

The interaction capacity of Asia, or at least of a part of it, was also significantly boosted by the emergence, in the early centuries of the Common Era, of what Nishijima Sadao calls the 'East Asian world', a 'cultural sphere' centred on China and also including the Korean peninsula, Japan, and Vietnam (later joined by the Ryukyu Islands), all of whom shared the use of Chinese characters, Confucianism, Chinese-style legal codes, and the Chinese version of Buddhism (Nishijima, 1983: 397–400; Lee, 2000). All those common elements, and especially the use of a common writing system, made exchanges that much easier. The special role of Buddhism should also be highlighted, not only within the 'East Asian cultural sphere' but throughout the whole of Asia. Buddhist monks, moved by their faith to make often perilous pilgrimages to the centre of knowledge that China had become in this realm as well, were indeed instrumental in the spread of the fruits of its civilization, and the formation of the said cultural sphere. Before and beyond that, the spread of Buddhism from India to South-East Asia and to China through Central Asia and across the Inner Asian steppe fuelled a region-wide desire for cultural exchanges and for trade in religious products, both by sea and on land (Wang Gungwu, 1958: 53–5; Liu Xinru, 1988: 81–3; Lewis, 2009a: 152, 158–62). The volume of exchange was particularly important at the height of the Buddhist age during Tang times, although it certainly did not stop with the fall of that dynasty (Sen, 2007: 37–54; Lewis, 2009b: 147, 155–6).

In many other respects, though, the interaction capacity of Asia did not change much over the course of China's imperial history. Physical means of transport and communication on land are a case in point. Movement across the vast expanses of Inner Asia remained determined by the limitations of human locomotion, augmented only by the use of horses (in which China's nomadic and semi-nomadic neighbours had most often a clear advantage).[6] In the South, China's difficulties in overcoming the ecological barrier to its expansion were evident. The tropical and subtropical hills of South China and northern South-East Asia, with their unfamiliar climate and deadly illnesses, constituted a mortal threat to the Chinese soldiers dispatched from the dryer and colder North. The perils of these regions, immortalized in the Chinese psyche by the dreaded 'miasma' (*zhang*, a character created to replace the homonymous one for 'barrier') that makes frequent appearances in historical records, were a major reason for the difficulties encountered by Chinese rulers in controlling today's southern provinces until the very end of the imperial era, and for the advantage held in military confrontations by better acclimatized non-Chinese natives (Bello, 2005; Yang Bing, 2010).

---

[6] The three dynasties that managed to durably establish control over most of Inner Asia – the Chinese Tang and the 'barbarian' Yuan and Qing – all did raise Asia's interaction capacity on land during their reign by building sophisticated transport and communication (and oversight) networks on their vast territory (Barfield, 1992: 205–6; Millward, 1998: 118–21; Arakawa, 2010).

The southern ecological barrier did not prevent the exchange of envoys and information, and neither did the basic nature of on-land means of communication, but they did slow interactions down. Whether by land or by sea, it usually took weeks or even months for rulers to exchange messages even in the best of conditions. This inherently limited the number of diplomatic interactions that were possible. Another limitation was institutional.[7] The default mode of communication among Asian polities was the travelling embassies that carried messages between capitals (Zhang Feng, 2014: 48). Regular diplomatic interactions themselves took place exclusively at the court of various rulers. Delegates did sometimes conduct negotiations outside of that context on the field of battle or close to political borders, but there was no institutionalized mechanism to do so. Such 'on the ground' contacts remained ad hoc, dictated by the need of the moment.

Both in terms of physical technologies and of these kinds of 'social technologies', as Buzan and Little call them, the transition to the modern era has radically increased Asia's interaction capacity. The role in this revolution of new means of transport and communication – railways, air travel, modern maritime propulsion technologies, the telephone, the Internet, and satellite communications – is well known and does not need elaborating (see Buzan and Little, 2000: 277–88 for a summary). On the social side, the adoption in Asia of the Western diplomatic customs of permanent embassies and regular mutual state visits, along with the multiplication of multilateral forums and conferences, which give state representatives frequent occasions to interact with each other, has been equally transformative.

The consequences of these tectonic changes are mixed when it comes to China's ability to realize its vision of order. On one hand, as already highlighted earlier, new technologies make the projection of Chinese power far from its shores and borders much easier while also increasing the capacity for economic exchanges and thus the attractiveness of China's growing wealth. Furthermore, as we will argue in later chapters, regular, Chinese-led diplomatic interactions play an important part in this vision both as a framework to deal with ever-changing international conditions and as a means to display China's majesty and ability to receive the deference of others. The modern world offers more occasions than ever to achieve those objectives with its constant stream of bilateral and multilateral meetings.

On the other hand, the multiplication of interactions with other states makes it more likely that one of them will eventually act in a way that goes against Chinese wishes, and thus makes order maintenance more difficult.

---

[7] Diplomatic institutions are understood here in a very mechanical sense as loci of exchange and negotiation, regardless of what political entities participate in said exchanges or what is discussed within them.

This is doubly problematic for PRC leaders since the exponential growth of means of communication and information diffusion has made control of how contacts between states are presented to the general public increasingly challenging. When diplomatic interactions were limited to the ruler's court in front of a select audience, it was relatively easy to stage them in a way that accorded with the Chinese world view. Compromises could be made when necessary in the knowledge that the only witnesses would be those present on the spot and that the only records of interactions made for posterity would be by Chinese chroniclers or emissaries to foreign lands, who could reconcile any 'improper' exchange with the Chinese world view. Differing accounts by those on the other side of these exchanges were irrelevant.

Such adaptation to contrarieties is harder in a world where inter-state meetings happen in front of rolling cameras and are chronicled by armies of journalists. The control of information about diplomatic interactions is in fact a bigger challenge today than it was even 70 years ago, as the simple telephone, photograph, and radio have been supplanted by television and then by the World Wide Web and omnipresent smartphones. Chinese leaders are determined to control what information the Chinese public has access to, but even a 'Great Firewall' around the national Internet and an army of censors cannot prevent all discussion of how the country appears on the world stage. This increases the pressure to ensure that China's interactions with other states conform with the 'proper order of things' in the first place.

Core principles of legitimacy

The third systemic factor shaping China's diplomatic behaviour is the set of hegemonic beliefs that characterize the contemporary international society and that China itself has fully embraced. By hegemonic beliefs, we mean here ideas about basic features of that society – who its members are, what rights and duties they hold – that are so widely shared and deeply accepted around the globe that they can be said to hold an undisputed position as foundational tenets of international relations, shaping and constraining the behaviour of state. In other words, they have acquired systemic features. Universal acceptance does not exclude differing interpretations of said beliefs, but the debate among these interpretations takes place within commonly accepted boundaries. One example is the belief in market capitalism. Virtually no state today, China included, rejects the idea that economies should be market-based, but opinions vary regarding the appropriate degree of state involvement in the market. Here, China, the most prominent advocate of state capitalism, stands in opposition to Western states adhering to the precepts of free markets.

More relevant to our discussion, however, are the hegemonic beliefs about the nature and conduct of a modern nation state. These are what Ian Clark calls a society's principles of legitimacy, which 'express rudimentary social agreement about who is entitled to participate in international relations, and also about appropriate forms in their conduct' (2005: 2). The sole legitimate members of international society today are nation states, and this status comes with a whole range of stipulations about appropriate conduct embodied in the core corpus of international law. Again, this does not imply full consensus regarding who counts as a nation state and what the boundaries of appropriate conduct are. Case in point, in East Asia, the international status of Taiwan is a deeply contentious issue while North Korea's nuclear programme and various exactions have led some to label it a 'rogue state', that is, a state whose membership of international society is put into question by its belligerent behaviour. Such controversies should not mask the fact that no Asian country disputes the basic tenets of today's principles of legitimacy and that they interact with each other as nation states in conformity with the most important norms of international law as expressed in the Charter of the United Nations, the Vienna Convention on the Law of Treaties, the Vienna Convention on Diplomatic Relations, and other fundamental treaties.

These fundamental norms include, notably, the right to equality of sovereign states – a topic of much interest in a study of hierarchy. We noted in the introduction how this judicial principle coexists in practice with clear inequalities both in terms of power and of status, rights, and responsibility within international society. We will also see in later chapters that China has its own interpretation of the exact meaning of equality. One point beyond dispute today, though, is every state's right to equality in matters of diplomatic protocol and ceremonial, official correspondence, and treaty making. This is another radical change that China has had to come to grips with as it has entered the modern international society. Indeed, it is precisely through such norms dictating how diplomatic interactions were to be conducted and how rulers should address each other in their correspondence that its vision of hierarchical order found its most concrete expression during imperial times. Those norms were inherently flexible and subject to negotiations to determine the nature of each individual relationship since the underlying foundations for them were themselves periodically negotiable.

We are referring here to the distinction between status foundations and status treatment proposed by Felix Kuhn (2019: 26–7). The latter refers to the way two states treat each other in practice in their concrete diplomatic encounters, while the former are the underlying principles that will form the more durable ground rules governing their diplomatic interactions. In Asia before the 19th century, status foundations were less enduring than they are today since relations between polities were in fact understood as the personal relations between their rulers. There were no systemic norms guiding those personal ties. Every ruler who could claim to have authority over a distinct group of people, be they roaming nomads or settled populations living on territories of various size, could also claim what we would today call 'international personality' and seek to build diplomatic ties with surrounding polities. The foundations for those ties were then negotiated based on the prevailing balance of power, each side's strategic needs and diplomatic acumen, and other factors. They also needed to be renewed (and occasionally renegotiated) after a leadership succession on either side. This left the space for the Chinese emperor to demonstrably assert his superiority wherever he could.

No such demonstration is possible today within the confines of codified diplomatic interactions, based as they are on principles of equality (Wood and Serres, 1970: 18). The foundations for those interactions have in the contemporary international society been systematized and bound to the principle of sovereign equality. Once a polity is recognized by international society as a sovereign nation state, the foundation for its relations with other members follows clear rules enounced in the fundamental treaties mentioned previously. Leaders and diplomats are only representatives of their state and are bound by those rules, which provide relatively strict guidelines governing status treatment and have become hegemonic beliefs.

These are the constraints within which China must operate as it seeks to shape the regional order according to the hierarchical inclinations that, as the next chapters will argue, are still very much a part of its world view today. As a result, the concrete manifestations of these inclinations are to be found not in the main diplomatic ceremonials, conducted as they are according to accepted rules of protocol meant to represent the equality of states, or in explicit form in treaties and diplomatic documents that will emphasize the same principles. They are to be found, rather, in the nuances of status treatment visible in the space surrounding its most formal parts, in the staging and framing of diplomatic interactions – especially when they take place on Chinese soil and involve multiple particpants – in the choice of standardized words and formulations used in a range of diplomatic documents, or in the informal and tacit rules of behaviour that become clear over the course of repeated exchanges or are hinted at in the public declarations of Chinese officials. Such manifestations of hierarchy are by necessity not front and centre as they may have been in imperial times, or as formally institutionalized, but that does not make them any less real or worth paying attention to.

The need to respect states' rights to equality is not the only modern principle of international legitimacy that has engendered new dynamics in China's relations with its neighbours. Another important aspect is the expectation that modern nation states will exert full control over a clearly demarcated territory. There is nothing new in China seeking exact demarcations of land borders with its neighbours and in laying claim to specific maritime areas. Those were regular occurrences in imperial times, giving rise to conflicts and negotiated solutions (Mancall, 1971: 286–304; Edwards, 1987: 35–7). Yet China's entrance into the modern international society brought a new urgency to the question of the delimitation of China's territory not only on land, but also at sea. Developments in international law in the 20th century have indeed led to the progressive territorialization of the maritime domain, granting exclusive rights of supervision and exploitation of natural resources to coastal states (Oxman, 2006). China has been particularly expansive in its claims to large parts of the East and South China Sea. The result has been a net increase in the potential points of friction between it and its neighbours. These have become test cases for Chinese efforts to shape a regional order where conflicts are resolved in a way that it finds acceptable.

Conclusion

To summarize the arguments of this chapter, focusing on some systemic features of Asia reveals how the dynamics of China's relations with its neighbours vary from case to case, and how far from static the history of the region was before the 'Western shock'. That event did lead to unprecedented transformations in all the areas discussed earlier, though, which needs to be fully taken into account in any study that emphasizes elements of continuity between China's imperial past and its present, such as this one. China has never been so able to project power throughout its neighbourhood, so intensely engaged in interactions with other Asian states, and has never shared with them such a well-established understanding of the basic rules governing their relations.

The impact of all those changes on China's ability to realize its vision of order is ambiguous, but it is undeniable that the modern international society comes with new constraints. We have shown how the general asymmetry of China's position relative to its neighbours used to mask a much more nuanced reality, where China was vulnerable to pressure from Inner Asia, limited in its expansion by natural barriers to its south and by the vastness of the ocean, and not necessarily capable of having its way even in the most clearly asymmetrical relations with Vietnam and Korea. The China that is rising after the 'century of humiliation' and the failure of the Maoist era to rebuild its national power is in that respect in a much stronger position, only partially undermined by the continuing presence of the US on its maritime periphery.

This stronger position, however, comes with the need to take into account the added complexities of the modern world, be it the much freer and faster flow of information, or the contemporary principles of legitimacy that are fundamental to international relations and to China's own identity as a modern nation state. In other words, both China's assets and the challenges and constraints it faces have grown. This ambiguity highlights the limits of thinking in terms of international system. One cannot simply conclude from the previous discussion that China is now on the verge of dominating its neighbourhood as never before due to its increasingly asymmetrical power, or on the contrary that it is so constrained in its foreign policy choice that it could only bring about marginal changes to the regional order. A systemic account cannot tell us much about China's preferences regarding said order either. For this, we must shift gear and enter the realm of ideas to examine China's own understanding of its environment and what it should look like on a normative level. This will be our task in the rest of this book. What this chapter has emphasized, though, is that China's international environment was never simple or straightforward, even before the transition to the modern world. This hints at a need for flexibility in adapting its vision of order to its concrete conditions. To be able to understand this process of adaptation, though, we must first spell out China's vision of order as it would exist in an ideal world. This will establish a basis on which to evaluate its historical experience in subsequent chapters.

2

The Ideal of Hierarchical Order

This chapter spells out the constitutive elements of the ideal type of hierarchical order grounded in China's traditional culture. These constitutive elements will then serve as a framework for the examination, in the chapters that follow, of China's concrete historical experience during the imperial era, during the period of transition to modern times, and under the People's Republic. Chinese foreign relations, like those of any major country, are complex, ever-evolving, and multifaceted. By accentuating some of their significant features, an ideal type can serve as a guide to wade through that complexity and identify one particularly meaningful and consistent Chinese foreign policy aim. Although we use core elements of ancient Chinese political philosophy to build this ideal type, we do not pretend that a hierarchical inclination sums up the whole of its rich and diverse cultural traditions, or that those traditions are the only force that drives its behaviour even today. This is not an attempt to comprehensively classify and study all aspects of Chinese foreign policy in light of different orientations either. Rather, by examining its relations with neighbouring states in light of a particular set of values that Chinese statesmen hold dear and that is incarnated in the ideal type of hierarchical order, we wish to emphasize one significant purpose they pursue when they engage in interactions with other polities and to show that this purpose has stayed important to them over the centuries and remains so today.

This ideal type has at its core the idea of a moral duty of the individual to accept his role in a ranked society and to follow the rules of proper behaviour specific to his rank, and of a moral duty of the ruler to enforce those rules and to lead by example so as to maintain social order. The underlying values that it most strongly reflects are, simply stated, the achievement of social order as a goal in itself, the cultivation of the virtues that sustain individuals in the fulfilment of their social role, and respect for social rules of proper behaviour. None of these is particularly unique to the Chinese. All societies seek to preserve order among their members, all belief systems contain a set of prescriptions for personal morality, and all societies set out some sort of rules for communal life and expect them to be respected. China is noteworthy, though, in elaborately combining the three to create a remarkably durable vision of an ideal harmonious society, which can only be maintained if its members are hierarchically ranked and organized. Equally noteworthy is the tendency to understand the power of the state as a tool meant to compensate for the failings of men that threaten the realization of this vision.

While the pursuit of a harmonious society is typically associated with Confucianism, the accumulation of power is the purview of Legalist thinkers, who have little patience for idealist thinking and for whom strengthening the state is a high purpose in itself. The genius of the Confucian scholars of the early Han dynasty was to recruit the Legalist precepts about building a strong and authoritarian state, which had been the basis of the Qin's success in unifying China, for the purpose of realizing the much more appealing vision of a harmonious society, thus creating the famous Confucian–Legalist synthesis that was to form the enduring backbone of the empire's ideological system (de Bary, 1988: 15–20; see also Graham, 1989: 370 ff.; Holcombe, 1997: 547–8; Lewis, 1999: 339 ff.).

Needless to say, successive generations of emperors had their own interpretation of that vision depending on their personal beliefs and the circumstances they faced. They varied greatly in their degree of dedication to it. It was, however, powerful enough to endure through thick and thin and even to survive, albeit much transformed, China's entrance into the modern society of states. Before examining that process, though, our first task is to spell out the structure of China's ideal orderly society not as it actually existed at any given time, nor necessarily as it existed in the minds of successive generations of statesmen, but rather in its purest form as early Chinese philosophers imagined it in reaction to the troubled conditions of their time. Since their writings became the foundation for the empire's whole system of thought, they are the perfect source from which to distil our ideal type of hierarchical order.

Order: the highest value

As noted earlier, how to achieve social order is a universal preoccupation, but it has always been particularly prevalent in the Chinese intellectual world. The Chinese cosmology, Mark Lewis points out, depicts organized human society as emerging from a 'primal chaos' that may have vanished, but '[survives] as a permanent background condition to human existence' and 'is the source of the specter of "chaos" [*luan*] that has haunted the Chinese imagination for millennia' (2005: 2). Richard Smith similarly points out that 'for some three thousand years, Chinese thinkers have been preoccupied with [the notion of order]' (2012: 3).

This preoccupation with order was at the centre of intellectual debates during the formative Spring and Autumn and Warring States periods, when different schools of thought sought solutions to the chaotic conditions of their time (Harle, 1998: 14–15). Although their propositions for re-establishing peace in the Chinese realm differed, they jointly contributed to the creation of a common discourse centred on concepts like governance (*zhi*), harmony (*he*), peace (*ping*), tranquillity (*an*), stability (*ding*), rectification (*zheng*), and an abhorrence of chaos (*luan*). They had a common purpose as well, namely, to recreate the order and unity of the realm that was commonly thought (regardless of reality) to have existed in a golden past before the disintegration of the central authority of the ruling Zhou dynasty (Sato, 2003: 120–5; Zhang Yongjin, 2014: 174).

Hence, thinkers as different as Mencius and Shang Yang, at two opposite ends of the spectrum between Confucian idealism and Legalist realism, expressed a similar yearning for order. Asked why he looks displeased, Mencius laments that heaven does not seem to want the realm to enjoy 'peace and order' (*pingzhi*) as it has not yet seen fit to make appear the true ruler that could bring this about.[1] Shang Yang, who in a way answered Mencius' call by setting the basis for the unification of China that put an end to the Warring States – even if the Confucian sage would have strongly disapproved of his methods – concurs that 'there is no greater benefit for the people in the empire than order'.[2] Those thinkers represent the two extremes of the Confucian–Legalist mainstream that eventually emerged, but in fact all the schools of thought of that period influenced each other through dialogue and mutual challenge. They shared much in terms of their conception of the problems they were trying to solve, if not in their prescriptions for solving them. It is therefore no exaggeration to state that the achievement of order is one of if not the primary purpose that animates Chinese political philosophy.

Social inequality: an inescapable reality

Core to all arguments about achieving order is the acceptance that humans differ in their capabilities, leading inevitably to the existence of different social classes. Social order, then, should be 'the rationalisation of existing human inequalities', giving each his proper role and place in a well-designed hierarchy so as to achieve a state of harmony reflecting the harmony of the

---

[1] In *Mencius* IV, 22. This text and all those quoted in this chapter and the next can, unless indicated otherwise, be found on the online platform of the invaluable Chinese Text Project (https://ctext.org/).
[2] *Book of Lord Shang*, 'Opening and debarring' 7 (translation by J.J.L. Duyvendak).

cosmos itself (Bodde, 1967: 46). Indeed, Xunzi, one of the most important thinkers of the late Warring States and the one perhaps closest to the middle ground between Confucianism and Legalism, explicitly links equality with disorder:

> Where the classes are equally ranked, there is no proper arrangement of society; where authority is evenly distributed, there is no unity; where everyone is of like status, none would be willing to serve the other. Just as there are Heaven and Earth, so too there exists the distinction between superior and inferior.[3]

Such distinctions must therefore be the basis on which 'human relationships' (*renlun*) are built. As Chinese sociologist Pan Guangdan notes, *renlun* 'express proper arrangements, classifications, and order' among the individuals that constitute a society (quoted in Fei Xiaotong, 1992: 65). To emphasize their importance, Mencius invokes the legendary emperors Yao and Shun of Chinese high antiquity, his favourite models of sage kings uniquely able to pacify the world: 'By the sages, the human relations are perfectly exhibited. He who as a sovereign would perfectly discharge the duties of a sovereign, and he who as a minister would perfectly discharge the duties of a minister, have only to imitate – the one Yao, and the other Shun'.[4] Only when human relationships are thus properly classified, and the respective rank that each should hold in the social hierarchy settled, can individuals accomplish the task expected of them and participate in the maintenance of social order.

Since the authority of the father over his son, of the master over his servant, or of the ruler over his subject is the natural order of things, then, the task of political thinkers is twofold. First is the need to create a system of thought that legitimizes those arrangements and makes them acceptable to all involved, offering both a guide to good governance for those in power and reasons to comply for the common folk. Second is the elaboration of ethical and practical principles to guide all individuals in the proper performance of their social role. Only thus can the stability of the social structure, and hence the peace and tranquillity of the realm, be guaranteed.

If all schools of thought of the Warring States shared this basic mission statement, they also agreed that a stable order should have only one centre and unify all the known world – or *tianxia*, 'all-under-heaven' – under one ruler. This dictum of 'stability in unity', most plainly expressed by Mencius,[5] was 'the common motto of the intellectual discourse of the

---

[3] In 'Regulations of a king' (Knoblock, 1990: 96).
[4] *Mencius* VII, 2 (translation by James Legge).
[5] *Mencius* I, 6: '[The king] asked: "How can all-under-heaven be stabilised?" I answered: "Stability is in unity"' (author's translation).

Warring States period', with different thinkers proposing different ways to achieve this desired state (Pines, 2012: 17). The ideal Chinese world order was thus a stable and all-encompassing hierarchy with the Son of Heaven at its centre – an ideal that endured throughout the imperial era, 'repeatedly reinforced through official rhetoric, imperial historiography, and other means of ideological production, turning into the pivotal principle of Chinese political culture' (Pines, 2012: 40).

Moral superiority: the legitimation of supremacy

If the man at the top of the hierarchy is supposed to rule over all-under-heaven, then, legitimizing his exalted position is an imposing task. The Legalists demand allegiance to any king able to understand the ways of the world and the needs of the moment, and on that basis to consolidate his power and establish a durable order. For the great Legalist master Han Fei, heavily influenced by Daoist philosophy, the function of the ruler is to design laws and regulations that are in accordance with the universal laws of nature and to serve as impartial overseer of that system. His absolute power results from his identification with the 'highly abstract cosmic force' of the Way, or with Heaven and Earth themselves (Pines, 2013: 70–1). Through such identification, he is able to always understand the needs of the moment and maintain order:

> When the sage rules, he takes into consideration the quantity of things and deliberates on scarcity and plenty. Though his punishments may be light, this is not due to his compassion; though his penalties may be severe, this is not because he is cruel; he simply follows the custom appropriate to the time. Circumstances change according to the age, and ways of dealing with them change with the circumstances.[6]

This rather abstract and detached vision of the ruler's role was not likely to attract much support, though. It is therefore unsurprising that the Confucian vision of the rightful ruler as the embodiment of morality and virtue eventually proved more appealing. The Master himself compares 'he who exercises government by means of his virtue ... to the north polar star, which keeps its place and all the stars turn towards it'.[7] The Chinese understanding of virtue, *de*, also contains the meaning of power or potency. This implies that the ruler possessing superior virtue will naturally attract the support of the common folk through his power of attraction: 'The relation between

---

[6] In 'Five Vermins' 2 (Han Feizi, 2003: 100).
[7] *The Analects* II, 1 (translation by James Legge).

superiors' and inferiors' virtue is like that between the wind and the grass. The grass must bend, when the wind blows across it'.[8]

As this quote suggests, virtue is not the unique remit of the ruler and should be practised by all members of society, but a rightful ruler is by definition more virtuous than anyone else. As Lucian Pye writes, 'in Chinese political culture there has always been the pretense if not the reality, that legitimacy is based on a claim to moral superiority' (1988: 103). The ruler must be the most virtuous person around or the order he presides over would crumble as 'the citizens would lose their sense of direction' (Shih Chi-yu, 1993: 31). The most important virtues in question are 'humaneness' or 'benevolence' (*ren*), and 'righteousness' or 'justice' (*yi*). *Ren* is at the centre of Confucius' entire discourse but its exact meaning is elusive. This is because, Fei Xiaotong suggests, 'the concept of *ren* is, in fact, only a logical synthesis, a compilation of all the ethical qualities of private, personal relationships' (1992: 75–6). Hence, being benevolent can simply mean being a good person, who cares for others and treats them always with 'earnestness, tolerance, trustworthiness, diligence, and generosity'.[9] The meaning of righteousness is equally open to interpretation, but it's association with trustworthiness[10] and courage (*yong*)[11] indicates the connotation of fulfilling one's duty and doing what is right no matter the circumstances (Tomiya, 2016: 33–5).

In both those qualities, Xunzi argues, the 'true king' (*wangzhe*) should excel in order to obtain the allegiance of all:

> His benevolence [*Ren*] fills the empire; his justice (*Yi*) permeates the land; his majesty pervades the country. His benevolence [*Ren*] fills the country, hence there is no one in the empire who does not cherish regard for him; his justice (*Yi*) permeates the land, hence no one in the empire fails to honor him; his majesty pervades the country, hence no one in the empire cares to oppose him.[12]

The one at the top of the social ladder should thus excel in benevolence and righteousness so as to guide all members of society to exhibit the same qualities in their respective role. What it means to behave virtuously will depend in practice on individuals' position in the social hierarchy since the

---

[8] *The Analects* XII, 19 (slight alteration of the translation by James Legge).
[9] *The Analects* XVII, 2 (author's translation).
[10] In *The Analects* I, 13: 'When agreements are made according to what is right, what is spoken can be made good' (translation by James Legge).
[11] In *The Analects* II, 24: 'To see what is right and not to do it is want of courage' (translation by James Legge).
[12] In 'Regulations of a king' (Dubs, 1928: 131). We will get to the third element, majesty (*wei*), in a moment.

principle of social distinctions also implies differentiation in the type of virtues that corresponds concretely to the all-encompassing *ren* and *yi*. If such personal ethics are meant to ensure social harmony and individuals' dedication to the fulfilment of their role, they are, however, not self-enforcing. There is need for a means to cultivate such dedication. That means, according to Confucian thought, is ritual (*li*).

Ritual: the means to maintain the social hierarchy

Li is a multifaceted and complex concept that has been the topic of countless studies.[13] A detailed discussion of the many ways it has permeated all aspects of Chinese life over the centuries is beyond the scope of this chapter. We will therefore limit ourselves to an overview of its role in building the hierarchical social order. *Li* is most often translated as 'ritual', a custom we will follow, but its general meaning is probably closer to the 'rules of proper conduct' proposed by Homer Dubs (1928).[14] *Li* should guide every individual in all his social interactions, encompassing 'the highest sense of morality, duty, and social order as well as the most minor rules of good manners, the minutia of polite forms' (Knoblock, 1994: 49). It could be approximated to civilized behaviour, or behaviour guided by reason.[15] It should thus not be understood simply as religious ritual – although *li* is an important means of communion between the earth's inhabitants and the heavenly realm and gives pride of place to practices such as ancestors' worship and imperial ceremonies – but rather as any behaviour that advances the greater purpose of social harmony and that has for this reason been standardized and codified by wise ancestors as a guide for future generations. *Li* thus incorporates 'any scripted performance meant to order the world' (Ing, 2012: 20).

The reason why *li* is so central to the Chinese vision of order through hierarchy is that 'it largely involves the behavior of persons related to each other in terms of role, status, rank, and position within a structured society' (Schwartz, 1985: 67). The *Guanzi*, an important Legalist text of the Warring States period close in orientation to that of Xunzi, explicitly links hierarchy and ritual: 'When the distinction between ruler and minister and between superior and inferior is fixed, the system of rituals is established'.[16] This

---

[13] For example, Hsü, 1932: 90–104; Nishi and Koito, 1941; Ch'ü T'ung-tsu, 1965: 226–41; Fehl, 1971; Schwartz, 1985: 67–75; Knoblock, 1994: 49–55; Pines, 2000; Kominami, 2001; Ames, 2002; Pines, 2002: 89–104; Ishikawa, 2003: 107–57; Satō, 2003: 163–236; Puett, 2006; Ing, 2012: 18–37; Satō, 2014; Zhang Jinfan 2014: 3–40; Tomiya, 2016: 16–74.

[14] On the etymology and origin of *li*, see Zhang Yongjiang, 2017: 117–8.

[15] In fact, the 'Book of Rites' (*Liji*), an important part of the Confucian canon, explicitly equates *li* to reason (*li*): 'Ritual is reason' (Liji, *Zhongni Yan Ju* 6, author's translation).

[16] *Guanzi*, 'Ruler and Ministers II' 8 (author's translation).

system embodies the proper deference that sons should give their father or the dedication of ministers to their ruler, and reciprocally the dignity and humaneness that those in higher positions are meant to strive for in their dealings with those under their care. The same passage of the *Guanzi* argues, for instance, that 'the ruler institutes benevolence, the minister preserves trustworthiness. This is called the *li* of superior and inferior'. Here, we see the association of *li* with moral self-cultivation and the virtues necessary to fulfil one's social role. *Li* is also often evoked in conjunction with righteousness (*yi*) in Confucian texts.[17] Moral self-cultivation is thus considered essential to the proper practice of ritual by many pre-Qin thinkers, and its absence outright dangerous (Sato, 2003: 200–26).

There is a strong practical aspect to *li* as well, its most concrete form being a guide to proper conduct in every public aspect of one's life. As Ishikawa Hideaki puts it, it is supposed to regulate both the inner workings of men and their formal behaviour (2003: 85). That second part is crucial to making social relations clear and predictable. *Li* indeed 'means so to organize and relate the different parts of society as to leave no doubt or equivocation as to their mutual status' (Hsü, 1932: 95). Removing such uncertainty, it was believed, was the only way to domesticate human passions and, within the reassuring cocoon of ritualized behaviour, to guarantee social order (Pye, 1968: 158; Pocock, 1973: 43–4).

In its socio-political function, *li* is therefore demonstrative in nature, with its focus on the performance of the proper actions required of any given situation or relationship as an expression of the inner moral virtues of individuals. The ruler is supposed to show his benevolence by conducting state ceremonies, dispensing justice from his throne, properly receiving guests, and generally acquitting himself of all his public functions in full view of heaven, court, and country. Ministers prove their trustworthiness by assuming their role in the same state ceremonies, by presenting the reports of their activities to the ruler following the right procedure and by respecting the rules of decorum at court. As Roger Ames points out, certain parts of *The Analects* depicting the daily life of Confucius reveal 'the extent to which the appropriate behaviors of a scholar-official participating in the daily life of the court [is] choreographed: the slightest gesture, the cut of one's clothes, the cadence of one's stride, one's posture and facial expression, one's tone of voice, even the rhythm of one's breathing' (2002: 146). Such

---

[17] Confucius says in the *Analects* that 'the gentleman makes righteousness his essence. He performs it according to the rules of propriety. He brings it forth in humility. He completes it with sincerity' (*Analects* XV, 18, slight alteration of the translation by James Legge). Mencius concurs: 'Righteousness is the way, and propriety is the door, but it is only the [gentleman] who can follow this way, and go out and in by this door' (*Mencius* X, 16, translation by James Legge).

formal behaviour is what gives hierarchical social relations their reality and is thus constitutive of the social order (Watanabe Shinichirō, 1996): 106–7; Ishikawa, 2003: 86).

Some scholars have argued that the performance of ritual acts is all that really matters and that the sincerity of the actors is not necessarily important since 'performing the act marks acceptance of the convention. It does not matter how you feel about the convention, if you identify with it or not' (Seligman et al, 2008: 24). In fact, as we noted earlier, the sincere dedication of participants in ritual to the virtues it embodies was considered crucial by seminal Confucian thinkers, who hoped that individuals would eventually embrace 'proper behaviour' spontaneously, without any need for social pressure. Nevertheless, it is still through practice that one demonstrates possession of Confucian virtues and the practice itself remains central to *li*'s function as a means to maintain the hierarchical order. By acting in accordance with the rules of proper behaviour, individuals can not only foster righteousness and suppress any urge they might have to disrupt social harmony, but also manifest their acceptance of their proper place in society. As Xunzi reminds us:

> it is the meaning of ritual principles that there should be rankings according to nobility or baseness, disparities between the privileges of old and young, and modes to match these with poverty and wealth, insignificance and importance. Hence, the Son of Heaven wears the dragon robe of royal red with its ceremonial cap, the feudal lords wear the black dragon robe with its ceremonial cap, the grand officers wear a skirt with an ornamented border at the bottom and the appropriate cap, and knights wear a hat of skin with their clothes.[18]

The three tools of rulership: rectification, coercion, and incentives

Legalist thinkers have as little time for such ritual niceties as they do for the extolment of moral virtues. Shang Yang is the harshest critique of the Confucian conception of *li*, dismissing it alternatively as a '[symptom] of dissipations and licence'[19] and, along with benevolence and righteousness, as one of the 'six parasites' that weaken the state and are bound to bring about its destruction.[20] Han Fei, on the other hand, voids *li* of its moral content but still acknowledges its importance when reduced to simple

---

[18] In 'Enriching the state' (Knoblock, 1990: 122).
[19] *Book of Lord Shang*, 'Discussion about the people' 1 (translation by J.J.L. Duyvendak).
[20] In *Book of Lord Shang*, 'Making orders strict' 3.

rules of courtesy and respect among rulers in the troubled context of the Warring States, noting in particular the importance for small states to not offend mightier neighbours or risk being destroyed.[21] Both thinkers, though, still firmly adhere to the hierarchical conception of society of which *li* is an integral part, and hence are keen to transfer its functions as upholder of the social structure and guide to individual behaviour to the law (*fa*) (Ishikawa, 2003: 182–3).[22] Shang Yang even at one point evokes a 'law of ritual' (*li zhi fa*).[23] This proved quite prescient as the imperial Confucian–Legalist synthesis took the establishment of legal codes as seriously as the maintenance of ritual propriety and infused *fa* with the principles of *li* (Zhang Jinfan, 2014: 24–40).

Yet while they disagree on the right framework to maintain social order, there is more common ground between Confucians and Legalists when it comes to their understanding of the tools at the disposal of the ruler to guarantee the people's adherence to that framework. Han Feizi lists these tools thusly:

> There are three means of governance the sage can use : the first is called profit, the second is called awesomeness and the third is called names. Profit is the means to win over the people; awesomeness is the means to issue orders; names are the principle shared by superiors and inferiors.[24]

We shall examine those three means in reverse order, starting with 'names'.

---

[21] In 'The ten faults' 11 (Han Fei, 2003: 69–72). There is in fact one section of the *Han Feizi*, 'Explaining Lao' (*Xie Lao*), that takes a broader view of *li* that would be recognizable to Confucians. Sarah Queen suggests two possible explanations for such a discrepancy with other parts of the work: either the *Han Feizi* compiles the writings of several authors, or the same author wrote *Xie Lao* late in his life inspired by a greater concern with ethics than he previously had (Queen, 2013: 219–20).

[22] Here too, Xunzi stands close to the middle ground between Confucianism and Legalism, arguing in 'Enriching the state' for different standards for the upper and middle classes of society: 'From the position of the knight up to the supreme position, all must be moderated through ritual and music. The ordinary masses, the Hundred Clans, must be controlled by law and norms of behavior' (Knoblock, 1990: 123). This highlights the penal function of the law, used to discipline those unable to follow ritual norms, that is very prominent in the Chinese tradition (see Ames, 1994: 108–32, and the discussion of punishments later).

[23] In *Book of Lord Shang*, 'Calculation of Land' 5. See Pines, 2000: 23–4 for a commentary on the Legalists' dilemma between adherence to the socio-political functions of *li* and rejection of Confucius and Mencius' conception of it, which is grounded in admiration of an idealized past that the Legalists are eager to leave behind.

[24] *Han Feizi*, 'Violating orders' 1 (author's translation).

Language: rectifying words

The character for 'names' (*ming*) refers to the titles granted by the ruler to various lords and nobles who assume an official function. This should therefore be understood as a reference to the technique of administrative control that Han Fei calls 'forms and names' (*xingming*) (or alternatively 'names and reality', *mingshi*), itself a Legalist version of the doctrine of the 'rectification of names' (*zhengming*), a tool of authority dear to Confucius (Lewis, 1999: 31–3). In different contexts, both thinkers argue fundamentally for the ruler to put great care in making sure that the names of things – or more generally words – match the concrete nature of what they describe. For Han Fei, this is the way to confirm that the official titles of ministers and what they promise to do corresponds to what they actually accomplish. By doing so, the ruler can keep ministers in line and make sure they properly fulfil their role. As Han Fei writes, 'if the ruler of men wishes to put an end to evil-doing, then he must be careful to match up names and results, that is to say, words and deeds'.[25] Only if names are clearly stated can they form the 'common principle' (*tongdao*) of ruler and minister and properly guide the conduct of the latter.

For Confucius, the rectification of names is also the task of the ruler, and one of fundamental importance. For him and other like-minded thinkers,

> giving to things names which truthfully describe them in order to distinguish between right and wrong and to set up a universal standard that will distinguish the true from the untrue, the right from the wrong, the beneficial from the harmful, the logical from the illogical, the just from the unjust, and the proper from the improper

is an essential step to create a well-ordered society (Hsü, 1932: 46–7). In a famous passage of *The Analects*, Confucius states:

> If names be not correct, language is not in accordance with the truth of things. If language be not in accordance with the truth of things, affairs cannot be carried on to success. When affairs cannot be carried on to success, proprieties and music will not flourish. When proprieties and music do not flourish, punishments will not be properly awarded. When punishments are not properly awarded, the people do not know how to move hand or foot.[26]

---

[25] In 'Two handles' 2 (Han Fei, 2003: 31).
[26] *The Analects* XIII, 3 (translation by James Legge).

One understands here that the rectification of names is the ground stone on which the state's effort to guide the people is built. One passage of the 'Commentary of Zuo to the Spring and Autumn Annals' (*Chunqiu Zuo zhuan*) is even clearer: 'Names are used to define what is congruent with duty [(*yi*)]; what is congruent with duty is used to produce ritual principles; ritual principles are embodied in the government; and the function of government is to rectify the people' (Knoblock, 1994: 117). Names, and language more broadly, are thus in the end a powerful tool used by the ruler to teach the people what virtuous conduct is and how to properly perform their differentiated social roles. In this way, the rectification of names is a form of education. For Legalists, education simply means making the law clear and using officials as teachers going through the land to spread knowledge of it (Hsiao Kung-chuan, 1979: 398–9). For Confucians, education is at the heart of government, and it is the duty of the ruler to lead by example and to spread knowledge and understanding of the virtues that make for a good citizen who follows ritual norms (Hsiao Kung-chuan, 1979: 111–3). In either case, though, making sure the language used in those endeavours is correct is a necessary first step.

Strength: establishing awesomeness

The second means of governance evoked by Han Fei is 'awesomeness' (*wei*) – understood here as the quality of being very impressive, without any particular positive connotation. The character can also be translated as majesty, authority, or might and in general refers to the reputation for strength that allows one to receive obedience. This is the meaning of the passage from Xunzi's work previously quoted, stating that the true king's awesomeness 'pervades the country, hence no one in the empire cares to oppose him' (Dubs, 1928: 131). In other words, if the people are properly impressed by the ruler's might, they will not dare deviate from their prescribed social role. Unsurprisingly, Confucians and Legalists disagree on what fosters *wei*. The former argue that seriousness in following the way of virtue and in organizing the state according to its precepts will naturally attract people and effortlessly gain their allegiance, thus granting real and long-lasting majesty.[27] This is also the kind of power that Xunzi has in mind in the earlier quote. Elsewhere, when discussing the 'three kinds of awesomeness', he compares authority gained by following the Way with the ruthless use of force, praising the former and underlining the risks of the latter.[28]

---

[27] See, for instance, *Mencius* II, 10, where he asserts that awesomeness does not come from strong weapons and armours of war but from receiving the support of the multitude by following the Way.

[28] In 'Strengthening the state' (Knoblock, 1990: 219–20).

Yet almost immediately after this comparison, Xunzi also acknowledges the success of the state of Qin in establishing its awesomeness through raw power (Knoblock, 1990: 244–5). In another passage, he criticizes the policies advocated by the philosopher Mozi,[29] arguing that they would impoverish the state and decrease its population, leading to a loss of authority.[30] This amounts to a recognition of the efficacy of the techniques advocated by the Legalists, even though Xunzi still insists that they are unsustainable. What are those techniques, then? Legalists characteristically stress that awesomeness is grounded in material power. We must here invoke the famous injunction to build a 'wealthy state and strong army' (*fuguo qiangbing*), expressed, for instance, clearly by Shang Yang: 'For one who administers a country, the way to consolidate its strength, is to make the country rich and its soldiers strong'.[31] This, the *Guanzi* tells us, is the way to build *wei*: 'What makes a ruler successful is wealth and strength; if his country is wealthy and his army strong, then vassals will obey his rule and hostile neighbours will fear his might'.[32] In fact, the ancient *Book of Change* itself, a central pillar of the whole Chinese system of thought, describes the invention of bows and arrows as serving to 'awe all-under-heaven',[33] and thus sees weapons as means of displaying the majesty of the ruler who made them (Wang Gungwu, 1984: 9).

Wei is in this way close in meaning to the modern international relations concept of 'prestige', described by classical realists like Martin Wight as the 'halo round power' (1978: 97) or more prosaically by Robert Gilpin as 'the reputation for power, and military power in particular' (1981: 31). This reputation is acquired most effectively through victory in battle even if victory is a means and not an end, a point on which 20th-century Western scholars like E.H. Carr (2016: 102–3) find themselves echoing Shang Yang, who rhetorically asks: 'How does one's reputation become respected and one's territory wide so that one becomes king? By prevailing in war'.[34]

Yet Legalists also emphasize the importance of creating the stable expectation of punishments for offences against the social order or for failures

---

[29] Mozi was another major thinker of the early Warring States period. Although his philosophy was later eclipsed by Confucianism and Legalism, the sophistication of his arguments about the quasi-religious nature of 'heaven' (*tian*), about the necessity for unified and objective moral 'standards' (*fa*) that are of concrete benefits to the people, or about the concept of a 'universal love' (*jianai*) that does not discriminate based on ties of kinship or social classes posed a challenge that all rival philosophers had to respond to. He thus provided an important impetus to the development of other schools of thought. For more on Mozi and his school, see Schwartz, 1985: 135–72; Graham, 1989: 33–53.
[30] In 'Enriching the state' (Knoblock, 1990: 128).
[31] *Book of Lord Shang*, 'Unifying words' 2 (translation by J.J.L. Duyvendak).
[32] *Guanzi*, 'Explaining the situation' 18 (authors' translation).
[33] *Yijing*, 'Xi Ci Xia' 2.
[34] *Book of Lord Shang* 'Policies' 2 (author's translation).

to fulfil one's duty in order to reinforce the ruler's majesty. Punishments (*xing* or *fa*) are, along with rewards, the 'two handles' central to the philosophy of government of Han Fei. Only if the ruler keeps a monopoly on them, he argues, can he impress his awesomeness on his ministers (Han Fei, 2003: 29). Shang Yang, keener on punishments than on rewards, agrees that 'punishment produces force, force produces strength, strength produces awe, awe produces virtue [among the people]'.[35]

The use of coercion to compel individuals to properly fulfil their social role may seem incompatible with the Confucian emphasis on rule through example and cultivation of virtue. In fact, as Benjamin Schwartz notes:

> the most utopian variant of Confucianism may dream of a society in which harmonious relations among humans are maintained wholly by the uncoerced obedience of the customary rules of morality (*li*), but other variants of Confucianism seem to accept the existence of the principle of evil in human society which makes it regrettably necessary to control certain elements of society and certain modes of behavior through the use of physical force. (1996: 70)

Xunzi was one of those realist Confucians who advises in 'Regulations of the king' that the primary distinction in adjudicating affairs of state is that 'those who come forward with good intentions should be treated with full ritual courtesy; those who come forward without good intentions should be handled with punishments' (Knoblock, 1990: 95). In fact, Confucius himself notes the necessity of correct punishments to guide the people in the passage of *The Analects* quoted previously in connection with the rectification of names.

Elsewhere, he also acknowledges that it is the responsibility of the ruler to send 'punitive expeditions' (*zhengfa*) as well as to maintain ritual propriety in a well-governed empire.[36] What Confucianism does, then, is not so much reject the use of force but colour it with moral disapprobation. A virtuous ruler uses coercion only when he must do so to preserve order against those who harm it. Punishment is not simply a natural consequence of a duty unfulfilled, as Han Fei understands it, but retribution for the moral failure of having been shown the right way but choosing not to follow it. Both Legalists and Confucians agree, though, that punishments are a means to an end of order preservation. If they are widely understood to be reliably and

---

[35] *Book of Lord Shang*, 'Elimination of strength' 8 (translation by J.J.L. Duyvendak).
[36] In *The Analects* XVI, 2: 'When good government prevails in the empire, ceremonies, music, and punitive military expeditions proceed from the Son of Heaven' (translation by James Legge).

fairly meted out by a ruler who has proven his strength, his awesomeness alone will suffice to ensure that all know their place and avoid breaking rules.

Benefits: incentivizing obedience

The final tool of the ruler evoked by Han Fei is the provision of 'profits' or 'benefits' (*li*) that allow him to win the people over. This is, in his thought, the necessary pendant to the threat of punishments for bad behaviour. Since it is only natural for individuals to follow their self-interest, incentivizing good behaviour with rewards in the form of either economic gains or social honours will consolidate the ruler's position:

> The two handles are punishment and favor. What do I mean by punishment and favor? To inflict mutilation and death on men is called punishment; to bestow honor and reward is called favor. Those who act as ministers fear the penalties and hope to profit by the rewards. Hence, if the ruler wields his punishments and favors, the ministers will fear his sternness and flock to receive his benefits.[37]

Confucians take a very poor view of such ministers swayed by self-interest. The Master himself puts it bluntly: 'The mind of the superior man is conversant with righteousness; the mind of the mean man is conversant with gain'.[38] Xunzi concurs: 'Those who put first what is just and later matters of benefit are honorable; those who put first what is beneficial and later what is just are shameful'.[39] That the lure of profits is needed at all is thus the unfortunate consequence of there being plenty of lowly individuals incapable of following ritual norms of their own accord – or of being taught to do so. Its use comes again with a strong hint of moral condemnation.

What is very much approved of by Confucians, though, is the ruler providing benefits to the people (*limin*) out of the goodness of his heart. Indeed, such generosity is considered a necessary feature of virtuous government and the very guarantee of the prosperity of the state (Hsiao Kung-chuan, 1979: 109–10; Ames, 1994: 157–9). Manifestations of benevolent leadership can thus include providing monetary benefits and marks of honour. Among Confucius' many recommendations in the 'Doctrine of the mean' ('*Zhong Yong*'), part of the *Book of Rites* (*Li Ji*), are to 'encourage his relatives to love him' by 'giving them places of honor and large emolument', to 'encourage the body of officers' by 'according to them

---

[37] In *Han Feizi*, 'Two handles' (Han Fei, 2003: 29).
[38] *The Analects* IV, 16 (translation by James Legge).
[39] In 'Of honor and disgrace' (Knoblock, 1988: 189).

a generous confidence, and making their emoluments large', and to 'cherish the princes of the states' by among other things '[sending] them away after liberal treatment, and [welcoming] their coming with small contributions'.[40]

In such cases, then, and especially when it comes to the encouragement of the body of officers, the aim is still to obtain good service through generous rewards even if the rationale for doing so is different. Whether it is justified as a demonstration of virtuous government or as a savvy exploitation of the instincts of men, then, the use of the wealth of the state to produce incentives for good behaviour is well established in traditional Chinese modes of rulership.

Conclusion

To summarize the argument of this chapter, our ideal type of hierarchical order based on the Confucian–Legalist synthesis is made up of the following constitutive elements: first, a fixation with achieving order; second, a conviction that such order is only possible when inevitable social inequalities are rationalized and fixed in one overarching hierarchical structure with one head; third, the justification of the exalted role of said head based on his moral superiority; fourth, the use of rituals as the master framework that gives reality on a day-to-day basis to the hierarchical order and fosters the ethics necessary for its maintenance; fifth, the conscious use of the tools of state power to maintain that framework in place by educating the people through the use of 'correct language', by deterring norm breaking through the demonstration of the state's might, and by offering positive incentives for the proper fulfilment of one's social role.

It should be emphasized here that rituals are truly the focal point of this structure, the glue that holds it together, and the mechanism that rationalizes social inequalities. The maintenance of ritual propriety is the concrete manifestation of the 'rule through virtue' (*dezhi*) to which Confucians aspired. The use of the three tools of state power described earlier is aimed at ensuring the widest possible conformity to ritual rules. Allowing individuals to demonstrate adhesion to social conventions and dedication to becoming good citizens is core to ritual's social function. The internalization of the underlying value can come later and may never be achieved by those incapable of becoming 'gentlemen' (*junzi*) in the Confucian parlance. In any case, the dedicated practice of ritual is the only way to try to reach that enlightened state. Or, as Albert Galvany puts it with the more cynical tone appropriate to his study of Legalism:

---

[40] *The Book of Rites*, 'Doctrine of the mean' 21 (translation by James Legge).

once the individual has been duly inserted into a context of unending reiteration and reinforcement of the liturgical codes, he would end up behaving 'spontaneously' although, in this case, it is not so much a matter of unconditioned autonomy as of programmed automatism deriving from the internalisation of conditioning factors imposed by these same ritual forms through a complex and meticulous process of instruction. (2013: 95)

In that sense, the hierarchical order is truly one that is 'ruled through ritual' (*lizhi*).

The next five chapters will apply this general framework to China's foreign relations over the course of its history from imperial times to the present day. First, I will use it to highlight certain important and enduring patterns in the Chinese empire's pursuit of a hierarchical order, and to understand how the shock of China's forced entry into a modern international society dominated by the West affected its world view. In the final three chapters of this book, I will look more closely at different elements of my ideal type – order and hierarchy, morality and ritual, and the use of the three tools of rulership outlined previously – as they apply to the foreign policy of the People's Republic, and in particular to the 'new era' dominated by the figure of Xi Jinping.

3

Statecraft in the Long Imperial Era

To demonstrate how China's imperial past still shapes its foreign policy today requires first determining precisely which ideas and practices have carried over and in what form. The previous chapter explored how the aspiration to establish a hierarchical world order coursed through the foundational texts of Chinese political philosophy – and outlined the analytical framework for the rest of this book in the process. This chapter and the next examine how their ideas translated into practice and in what shape they were inherited by Chinese statesmen of the modern era. Here, we conduct a broad overview of Chinese statecraft over the course of the long imperial era, aiming to highlight what elements of the ideal of hierarchical order shone through most frequently and consistently in the imperial court's dealings with the outside world.

We will emphasize three points in particular. First, Chinese statesmen remained steadfastly attached to the idea that maintaining an all-encompassing hierarchy centred on the Son of Heaven was the only path to order and that his superior moral qualities justified his exalted position. They did not falter even when faced with situations where the empire's ability to assert its superiority was either in doubt or simply non-existent, and where the emperor strayed very far from Confucian virtues. In such cases, they employed various rhetorical techniques to reconcile reality with their ideal of hierarchical order. Second, the role of ritual in maintaining this order went much beyond the reception of tribute and the granting of imperial titles to forge suzerain–vassal relations with other polities, although these were indeed the most common and favoured ritual institutions. A large part of this chapter will be dedicated to an analysis of the broader universe of Chinese techniques of 'rule through ritual' (*lizhi*), and to their purpose and function. Third, it was well understood throughout the imperial era that the power to 'rectify names', to awe through military might, and to offer economic benefits to those who followed ritual rules were essential tools for obtaining compliance with the Chinese vision of hierarchical order.

Order and hierarchy

Chinese statesmen and thinkers' preoccupation with preserving order was

> expressed throughout the imperial era (221 BCE–1912 CE) not only in China's highly refined bureaucratic institutions and methods of social and economic organization but also in Chinese philosophy, religious and secular ritual, standards of literary and artistic achievement, and in various comprehensive systems of classifying all natural and supernatural phenomena. ... The famous nineteenth-century statesman, Zeng Guofan, put the matter succinctly: 'The mind of Heaven hates disorder'. (Smith, 2012: 3)

The stated purpose of the policies adopted by the imperial court was hence ultimately to spread order throughout the known world and to 'pacify all-under-heaven' (*ping tianxia*), as a common expression would have it.[1]

This pacification was inseparable from the desire to obtain the recognition by surrounding polities of China's superiority. Indeed, China's imperial rulers were convinced not only that it was natural for great polities to receive deference from smaller ones, but also that their own state was the greatest of all and therefore undoubtedly superior to any other. As Benjamin Schwartz puts it, 'the traditional Chinese perception of world order was not based simply on a devotion to the abstract doctrine that the world ought to be organized hierarchically about some one higher center of civilization but on the concrete belief that Chinese civilization was that civilization' (1968: 286).

There is no denying the persistence of dismissive or contemptuous views towards surrounding 'barbarians' (*yidi*), and the expectation of obedience on their part, that was shared among the Chinese elite throughout its imperial history.[2] Those barbarians were routinely compared with 'birds and beasts' in pre-Qin texts already – although that subhuman status could also be applied to lower strata of the Chinese populace as well (Hori, 1993: 37–41, Pines,

---

[1] Said expression is the end of a chain syllogism in the 'Great learning' ('*Daxue*', part of the *Book of Rites*) that has been endlessly quoted and referred to. The chain starts with the investigation of things and personal self-cultivation, and ends with the pacification of all-under-heaven, with the regulation of the family and the governance of the state in between.

[2] The proper translation of *yidi* (and of many other classical terms) is the topic of much debate and criticism (see, for example, Beckwith, 2009: 355–62; Rawski, 2015: 189–95). In this book, we will use their generally accepted translation while noting here that the English meaning of the word 'barbarian' is not necessarily reflective of the way ancient Chinese saw their neighbours, although their sentiment of superiority was very real.

2005: 63–9). That did not make them unredeemable or inherently worthless, but such epithets indicated a strong sense of superiority that would prove unshakeable. One very concrete manifestation of this sense of superiority was the fact that successive dynasties most often placed barbarian vassals underneath Chinese nobles with equivalent titles in any ranking system they created (Kaneko, 2001: 39–41).

As we outlined in Chapter 1, even the most powerful dynasties were not always in a position to assert their superiority over surrounding polities. Various techniques were then employed to preserve at least the appearances of adherence to Sinocentric hierarchical principles. When interactions with barbarians did not follow said principles, such as in Ming Yongle's diplomacy with the powerful Timurid Empire in Central Asia, Chinese chroniclers made sure that historical records ignored all breaches of proper form (Fletcher, 1968: 211–2, 214; Rossabi, 1976: 17, 27). Reversely, the translation of the correspondence received from foreign polities that did not use the Chinese script was regularly the occasion to modify any formulation that could be read as disrespectful to the Son of Heaven (Serruys, 1967: 451–3, Bielenstein, 2005: 6). One noteworthy example is the modifications made by the Qing government, before they were officially published within the empire, to the text of the treaties of Nerchinsk (1689) and Kyakhta (1727), concluded with Russia on an equal basis for the sake of border security. All formulations that indicated equality had been removed so as not to hurt Chinese sensibilities, transforming the treaties into domestic regulations whereby the Qing gave orders to its small 'outer vassal' (*waifan*) without making any concessions deviating from normal hierarchical interactions (Yoshida, 1984: 291–4).

There were cases, however, when a neighbour was so mighty and threatening that his power had to be acknowledged in official documents. This was notably the case in the confrontation between the Han and the Xiongnu nomadic federation to its north. The word used to describe this adversary was 'enemy state' (*diguo*), which implied equality, but only as a foe who was rejecting the will of heaven by refusing to acknowledge Chinese superiority (Hori, 1993: 69). Even when faced with equally or more powerful Inner Asian neighbours such as the Northern Wei, the Liao, or the Jin, occupying parts of China proper and making evident efforts to adopt at least some Chinese norms and customs, the 'truly' Chinese Southern and Song dynasties still looked down on them and evinced in domestic writings a scorn only fuelled by their incapacity to 'expel the barbarians' and reunite the realm (Danjō, 2016: 63, 149–50, 163). The next two conquest dynasties of the Yuan and the Qing also had to adopt what Danjō Hiroshi calls the 'shell of a Chinese dynasty', regardless of their degree of acculturation underneath, in order to have any chance of being accepted by their Chinese subjects (2016: 169–71). The Qing in particular, under whom the Chinese empire came to durably encompass all of Inner Asia as well as China proper,[3] made great efforts to reconfigure the traditional distinction between superior Chinese and inferior barbarians in order to include their Inner Asian subjects in the civilized realm regardless of their different ethnicity and culture (Danjō, 2016: 242–6). However, they still sought to demonstrate their ability to obtain submission from 'outer barbarians' beyond their borders.

The Chinese belief that maintaining world order meant interacting with surrounding polities according to hierarchical principles thus remained consistent throughout imperial times, but was frequently challenged by the reality of barbarians' equal or superior power. In practice, the enduring Chinese concern with hierarchy and sense of superiority was a fixed ideal that often had to be adapted to less than ideal circumstances. The appearances of hierarchical relations with the outside world needed to be preserved within the empire and in the Chinese written realm, while conquerors could be accepted if they took on a 'Chinese shell' and the mission to 'pacify all-under-heaven'.

A claim to moral superiority

The Confucian basis of the imperial model of moral rulership was laid around the middle of the Han dynasty – the founding dynasty of the Qin had made no efforts to present themselves as anything other than overwhelmingly powerful – and 'survived basically intact for two thousand years' after that (Loewe, 1986: 103). If the Son of Heaven by right stood at the top of a hierarchy that encompassed not only his empire but the whole known world, it was because his 'all-wise example and virtue [*de*] ... not only reached throughout China proper but continued outward beyond the borders of China to all mankind and gave them order and peace' (Fairbank, 1968: 8). The descriptions in official documents of the emperor's relations with foreign rulers and with private merchants and scholars coming to Chinese shores were thus always couched in the language of benevolence (*ren*), generosity (*hui*), and grace (*en*) granted to grateful recipients who could not help but admire (*mu*) such all-encompassing virtue (Danjō, 2013: 428).

Exerting moral leadership towards all-under-heaven supposedly meant following Confucian precepts for good and gentle government towards all, be they Chinese subjects or foreign polities, but Chinese rulers and literati could prove very flexible in adapting the discourse of benevolence

---

[3] China proper means here the area populated in majority by ethnic Chinese and centred on the Yellow River basin in the north and the Yangtze River basin in the south, sometimes together called the 'Nine Provinces' after the territory under the control of the Qin, the first unifiers of the empire.

and righteousness to their sometimes difficult circumstances. If it was relatively easy to praise the virtue of a wise and good-humoured emperor reigning over a realm at peace with enough wealth and power to deter any significant threat from outside, such situations were quite rare indeed. In fact, even a ruler as exalted and admired as Qing Qianlong could be ruthless with those whom he suspected of disloyalty at court. He also ordered the straight-out extermination of the Dzungars, a tribe that had long been a thorn in the empire's side (Perdue, 2005: 283–6; Elliott, 2009: 22–3). Most emperors were neither as powerful nor as successful, and some had no interest in playing the part assigned to them by Confucian models of rulership. Several successors to Khubilai Khan, founder of the Mongol Yuan dynasty, showed little interest in governing or acting as a moral example in the Chinese mould. Some Confucian scholars responded by arguing that such lack of virtue could be ignored as long as the emperor left the administration of the realm to 'authentic scholars' – presumably those making such arguments – who did know Confucian principles and could fulfil governing duties on his behalf (Langlois, 1981: 184). More generally, Confucian writings implied that the 'sage' (*shengren*) who called scholars to serve as officials did not necessarily need to possess strong moral qualities himself, but simply the power and ability to mobilize the literati class to provide virtuous governance (Dardess, 1984: 94). In other words, the principle of ruling through moral superiority was more important than the person of the ruler himself.

Equally revealing of great flexibility for the sake of the maintenance of that principle is the case of the early Tang emperors Gaozu, Taizong, and Gaozong, who, unlike the late Yuan, are regarded as among the most successful and benevolent rulers in Chinese history. When it comes to foreign policy and the unprecedented expansion of their empire, their virtue and righteousness were interpreted – in a fashion that Han Fei would have much approved of – as the ability to correctly read the complex politics of the Inner Asian steppe, take the most efficient and appropriate approach to achieve their goals, and establish their authority or parry threats. As Wang Zhenping writes:

> this line of thinking argued that policies suitable to the specific circumstances of time and space were manifestations of the abstract moral principles of virtue and righteousness. State actions guided by these policies were themselves virtuous deeds because they exemplified the supreme morality in politics: acting on full consideration of the circumstances and the consequences. (2013: 10)

Wang points out that 'appropriateness' is in fact encompassed in the meaning of *yi*, just as righteousness is. Finding virtue in adaptability as the

Tang did was thus not an aberration but the invocation of a well-anchored tradition looking approvingly on the ability of a ruler to adapt to the messy conditions of the real world and to make the best of any given situation (Wang Zhenping, 2013: 258; see also Pan Yihong, 1997: 28–9).

We can find examples of such reasoning in later periods as well. Zhao Yi, a Qing-era scholar commenting on an instance during the Southern Song when the emperor had to accept to receive an envoy of the powerful Jin to their north on equal footing, argued that 'the teachings of true principle cannot always be reconciled with the circumstances of the times. If one cannot entirely maintain the demands of true principle, then true principle must be adjusted to the circumstance of the time, and only then do we have the practice of true principle' (quoted in Schwartz, 1968: 280).

Understood in this way, then, the virtue of the emperor amounts to little more than success in his endeavours, and is to an extent self-justifying: as long as he can maintain himself in power, strengthen the state, and receive the allegiance of foreigners, he must be virtuous; reversely, meeting with foreign policy failure or, more dramatically, losing the throne are signs of his moral failings. No case illustrates better the appeal of generating a virtuous image through foreign policy success than that of Ming Yongle. Having usurped the throne by murdering his nephew, he sought to gain legitimacy not only by promoting the production of Neo-Confucian works at home, but also by launching massive campaigns (including the famous voyages of admiral Zheng He) to attract or compel foreign envoys to come and bow in front of him (Danjō, 2016: 211–16). Such examples show that, just like the Chinese elite's preoccupation with order and the maintenance of hierarchy, their concern with maintaining at least the pretence of the moral superiority of the emperor and his court remained consistent during the long imperial era despite circumstances that often made this task quite difficult.

Ritual

Ritual was meant to be the mode of interaction that gave concrete shape to the all-encompassing hierarchy ruled over by the Son of Heaven and demonstrated that his virtuous power was effective and accepted by others. Within the imperial court and throughout the empire, it was an essential medium of politics and the means to signify various actors' social status. Efforts by court officials or local elites in different regions to gain status, or to undermine that of rivals, took the shape of:

> 'vigorous debates … about what is essential and what is dispensable in a particular ritual; about who must do what for it to count as having been executed properly; about just wherein its import or function

lies; and about whether, and if so, how past practice may be amended, improved, or definitively returned to.' (Laidlaw, 1999: 406)[4]

Ritual was, in other words, a common language that all Chinese elites and officials spoke. Even if the meaning of many words (or behaviours) were reinterpreted time and again, some disappearing and new ones being elaborated, that language remained the same over China's long imperial history.

That language was also the one that governed relations with foreign polities. To understand how exactly ritual was used to maintain order, we must conduct an overview of the different modes (or vocabularies) of ritual interactions between the court and those foreign polities, starting with the most common ones of tribute and investiture before shifting to the fictive kinship ties common in relations between the Chinese empire and powerful Inner Asian neighbours. We will then consider Chinese customs in court and diplomatic rituals more broadly before outlining the two fundamental purposes of the 'ritual order' that China sought to maintain through all those practices. This extended discussion aims to correct the often too narrow vision adopted by international relations scholars looking at imperial China's foreign policy, who tend to limit themselves to a simplistic discussion of the so-called 'tribute system', obscuring the complexity and purpose of the wider range of Chinese ritual practices. Offering a more comprehensive look will allow us to better understand the central role of ritual in China's traditional vision of order to lay the ground for the discussion of the modern era that follows.

The typical mode of interaction between the Son of Heaven and foreign rulers or their representative was a state ceremony involving gestures of deference to the Chinese throne and the presentation of tribute (*chaogong*) in the form of local products, repaid with lavish presents. During their first visit or through an envoy later sent to their court, foreign rulers presenting themselves to the emperor were then often bestowed a title (*cefeng*) establishing a lord-servitor (*junchen*) relation.[5] It was through such ritual behaviour that the foreign polity was symbolically included in the imperial domain, and the repetition of these ceremonies at regular intervals – most importantly, after a leadership succession had occurred on either side, since as we noted in Chapter 1, the lord-servitor bond was a personal one between

---

[4] On ritual as a form of negotiation of power relations, see Cannadine, 1987; Bell, 2009: 171–223.
[5] Tribute and investiture often went together, but not always. For instance, Japan stopped accepting investiture during the sixth century, even as it continued to send tributary embassies (Nishijima, 1983: 600).

the Chinese emperor and foreign rulers even if most titles were hereditary – was meant to guarantee the maintenance of order by periodically reaffirming the relationship and the allegiance of one side with the other.

Such state ceremonies involving tribute bearing and investiture were the model of predilection for foreign relations across dynasties because it most clearly and firmly symbolized their hierarchical relationship with foreign counterparts and most directly reflected the virtues that China and smaller neighbours were supposed to cherish – 'caring for the small states' (*zi xiao*) for the former and 'serving the large state' (*shi dai*) for the latter (Li Yunquan, 2006: 39; Motegi, 2009: 45; Chen Kanling, 2015: 44). This model still prevailed in the interactions between the Chinese court and smaller countries in times when the empire itself was divided and weaker, such as the Northern and Southern dynasties and Song periods, even as relations between the rival imperial courts themselves followed different norms (Hori, 2006: 227–8). It is therefore no surprise that many scholars have taken tribute and investiture as the centre of their analysis of traditional Chinese foreign relations.[6]

No matter how important they were, though, these two sets of practices did not represent the totality of China's interactions with neighbours. The main alternative to the typical form of lord-servitor ordering was what Danjō Hiroshi calls a 'patriarchal clan order', which sought to maintain a form of ritualized hierarchical relations with some Inner Asian barbarians who were too powerful to be awed or forced into submission (Danjō, 2016: 119–20). The practices associated with it included 'peace through kinship' (*heqin*) and 'oath pacts' (*mengyue*). They aimed to establish real or fictional ties of kinship between the Chinese emperor and other rulers that would still confirm the former's superior position, even if the distance in status between the two sides in those family-like relations was much less great than in the more rigid lord-servitor bond.[7]

---

[6] Nishijima Sadao (1983: 415 ff.) is the one who introduced the idea of an 'investiture system', while the seminal works on the so-called 'tributary system' are an essay by John Fairbank and Teng Ssu-yu (1941), an essay by Mark Mancall (1968) in a volume on the *Chinese World Order* edited by the same Fairbank, and, more recently, the opus by Hamashita Takeshi (1997). Even if tribute was indeed a crucial Chinese foreign policy tool, the term 'system' in most cases certainly overstates the extent to which the Chinese thought of it as a coherent and comprehensive framework – except perhaps during the early Ming, who truly sought to conduct all foreign interactions through such means (Danjō, 2013). Combining the two, Li Baojun and Liu Bo (2011) propose the idea of a 'tribute-investiture order'.

[7] One clear example of the difference comes from relations between the conquest dynasties of the Song era, the Western Xia, the Liao, and the Jin. When the Xia envoy reaches the Jin court, which had just vanquished the Liao, assuming that previous customs would continue, he was sternly told to show more deference: 'Xia and Liao were as nephew and uncle; therefore rituals expressing kinship were allowed. Today Xia is simply a subject

Heqin is the name of the policy adopted by the early Han emperors regarding their powerful Xiongnu neighbour. It consisted of a pact (*yue*) whereby the Son of Heaven and the Chanyu, the Xiongnu leader, became elder and younger brothers (*xiongdi*), while the former gave to the latter a princess from his clan in marriage and made annual payments of fixed quantities of silk, wine, rice, and other goods (Hori, 2006: 16). The annual payments were essentially a bribe to ensure peace between the two entities, and in practice hinted at a relation of subordination of the Han emperor to the Chanyu, who posed a threat the Chinese did not know how to deal with. Yet by positioning himself as the elder brother in their relationship, the Son of Heaven still sought to preserve – barely – his superior status in the family-like ritual bond.[8]

Various elements of the same policy were employed by later dynasties. Particularly noteworthy are the covenants (*meng*)[9] of the Tang and the Song aiming to establish their relations with powerful neighbours that they could not bring to submission. For the Tang, those neighbours were Tibet and the Turks at various points, and the Uighurs after the beginning of the An Lushan rebellion that fatally weakened the empire. Covenants with the leaders of those polities established fictive kinship ties of uncle and nephew (*jiusheng*), father and son (*fuzi*), and elder and younger brothers respectively (Kaneko, 1974: 32; Twichett, 1979: 436; Pan Yihong, 1997: 255, 276–7, 293; Danjō, 2016: 120).

Although all those covenants preserved the superior status of the emperor within fictive kinship ties, they were very close to equal relationships. The pretence of Chinese superiority was almost totally gone in the case of the Song's 'Covenant of Chanyuan' with the Liao. There too, the Song emperor was allowed to keep his status of elder brother to the 'younger' Liao emperor, but only temporarily as their relative ranking was meant to adapt to the age and generation of various members within the fictive family and was carefully tracked through frequent exchanges of ritual letters of greetings (Wright, 1996: 61–2, 65, 85; Mote, 1999: 70–1). Furthermore, in a manner similar to the Han's *heqin* pact with the Xiongnu, the covenant also stipulated the payment of considerable amounts of silk and silver, which were called gifts by the Song but tribute by the Liao. The situation became even more perilous for the Song's self-esteem when the Jin conquered the Liao (and

---

state of the Great Jin; therefore rituals appropriate to lord and servitor are to be observed' (quoted in Mote, 1999: 251). It should be noted here that the expression of ties among rulers and nobles as fictional kinship was a custom shared by the Chinese and Inner Asian nomads (Skaff, 2012: 224–37).

[8] There is in fact no word in Chinese that could simply translate as 'brothers' on neutral, equal footing; the distinction between elder and younger is an intrinsic part of that relationship.

[9] On covenants and the 'solemn ceremony' conducted to seal them, see Wright, 2005: 73–4.

pushed the Chinese court to flee southwards), as its covenant with the new neighbour concluded in 1141 not only included heavy yearly payments but also reduced the Chinese emperor to the status of vassal ritually invested by the Jin in a strict lord-servitor relation (Tao, 2009: 684).

This was the last time that a Chinese emperor had to submit to such humiliation, but only because future conquest dynasties would take possession of the whole of China. The last one, the Qing, elaborated its own way to periodically reaffirm its rule over the people of Inner Asia through rituals managed by a new institution created especially for that purpose, the 'Court for the Administration of the Outer Regions' (*Lifanyuan*).[10] One of those was a form of tribute, repurposed here to regularly reaffirm lord–vassal relations within the empire. Another one, the 'Pilgrimage to the Emperor' (*chaojin*), was an original creation but remained well within the realm of practices recognizable to Chinese Confucians. It involved the visit by those Inner Asian high nobles who had been invested by the Son of Heaven to rule over their people and who then periodically came to renew their allegiance to the Chinese throne and to pay their respect in a tightly directed ceremony. The only truly unique Qing ritual institution was the 'Imperial Hunt' (*weilie*, literally 'surround and hunt'), which descended directly from Inner Asian traditions of bonding among social elites through hunting in groups. This activity was meant to keep participants ready for warfare, and was also common among previous conquest dynasties, although in a less regularized and institutionalized form (Elliott and Chia, 2004: 66–8). These hunts hence had little to do with the Chinese heart of the empire, but were still conducted under the similar logic of periodically reaffirming, through ritual, the inclusion of non-Chinese polities into the domain ruled from Beijing.

Tribute and investiture were thus not the only ritual forms used by Chinese emperors to maintain the hierarchical order within their domain and with neighbours – or at least to preserve appearances as much as possible when it came to covenants. The various specific practices discussed earlier are to be placed in the broader framework of ritualized diplomacy through travelling envoys and of the ceremonial calendar of the imperial court, which also gave plenty of occasions to symbolically express the relationship between rulers. Indeed, it is perhaps through regulations for the reception of envoys and the organization of court ceremonies in general that the Chinese vision of hierarchical order can be grasped most comprehensively, as they revealed the overall ranking system imagined by the court.

---

[10] Di Cosmo (1998) offers an excellent introduction to the *Lifanyuan*. The following discussion of the associated ritual practices is based on Chia Ning (1993).

During the Han, for instance, visitors were granted seals whose type, shape, material, and colour indicated their status in the eyes of the Chinese court (Kurihara, 1969: 201–7; Kaneko, 2001: 38–9; Danjō, 2016: 176–7). The Tang organized other polities according to different grades that determined the manner of their reception, privileging the local rulers of non-Chinese parts of the empire over foreign ones (Skaff, 2012: 136). Similar status-based distinctions were made at the Song court, which received envoys very differently according to the status of the rulers they represented, with the Liao and later the Jin accorded most honours, followed by the Western Xia and the Korean kingdom of Goryeo, and then by all other 'minor foreign states' (Franke, 1983: 120). As for the Ming, they signified the relative status of various tributaries by bestowing different kinds of dresses and qualities of seals to them (Danjō, 2013: 362–70).

Major state ceremonies, such as those for the emperor's birthday or to mark the New Year, provided the fullest picture of the way Chinese statesmen literally 'ordered' the world in pyramidal form, with visiting foreign rulers or representatives rigorously ranked and organized (Kataoka, 1998: 241–3; Danjō, 2016: 118–9; Zhang Yongjiang, 2017: 125–6). In matters of protocol, then, 'all foreign countries were ranked in relation to each other [to decide] their precedence at the Chinese court' (Bielenstein, 2005: 8). The keys to such ranking were entirely in Chinese hands, and were based in large part – but not entirely – on the position accorded to various polities in the Chinese ranks and titles system, which is discussed later.

What united the different practices described previously was a common logic of inclusion in an order overseen by the Son of Heaven and governed by ritual. Actions taken by other polities that did not conform to Chinese expectations or endangered the smooth enactment of these practices were described as 'not in accordance with ritual' (*shili* or *wuli*) and opened the offender to retaliations meant to bring his behaviour back in line with the Chinese rules of propriety that guaranteed order (Chen Kanling, 2015: 45–6). This is why, among the many frameworks that have been used to describe China's traditional vision of international order,[11] we prefer those that focus on 'guest rituals' (*bin li*) (Chun, 1989; Hevia, 1989; 1995; Lee, 2013, Brook, van Walt van Praag, and Boltjes, 2018: especially 58–64), the 'ritual system' (*lizhi*) (Iwai, 2005), or perhaps most appropriately as a general framework meant to cover all-under-heaven, a 'ritual order', or order of 'rule through ritual' (*lizhi*) (Huang Zhilian, 1992; Huang Zhilian 1994; Danjō, 2013: especially the concluding chapter; 2016; Chen Kanling, 2015; 2017).[12]

---

[11] Chen Zhigang (2010) lists eight conceptions in total.
[12] Other works emphasizing the importance of rituals in Chinese foreign relations include Li Yunquan, 2004: Ch. 4; 2011; Skaff, 2012: Ch. 5.

Such a characterization allows us to focus on the fundamental role of ritual as the backbone of the hierarchical order China envisioned rather than on its particular manifestations. A broader view also more clearly highlights the twin purposes that ritual served.

First, the ability to conduct ceremonies that involved foreign participants regularly reaffirmed the Son of Heaven's place at the top of the hierarchy. As Iwai Shigeki puts it, to demonstrate his supreme status, the Chinese ruler needed to periodically 'direct' ceremonies involving foreign rulers or envoys and 'actualize' their superior-to-inferior relations (2005: 126). Such performances were what gave the emperor's claim to rulership its reality since 'the power of the superior [lied] in his capacity to generate conditions necessary for the inclusion of inferiors' (Hevia, 1995: 125). The fact that inclusion happened on the emperor's own ground, in his reception hall, was also crucial. His power 'was made manifest by the fact that others were made to move towards [him]' (Ringmar, 2012: 13). The Son of Heaven's role as master of ceremony in his capital, assigning their ranked 'proper place' to all other participants, demonstrated his authority over all those who came to him. In other words, if as stated previously ritual was a language, the Son of Heaven's decisive role created a narrative, in that language, of Chinese superiority and others' obedience. Successful performance of the rituals demonstrated China's narrative power and the inclusion of new foreign participants increased it.[13] Tribute and investiture were the most prized means of international interactions because they ensured that purpose would be fulfilled. Inclusion in the 'patriarchal clan order' through covenants was an unreliable alternative, associated in the Chinese mind with instability and negative circumstances (Pan Yihong, 1997: 248). It is therefore not surprising that the pacts concluded were not infrequently breached or undermined in the hope of gaining a military advantage (Pan Yihong, 1997: 249, 257; Wang Fei-ling, 2017: 89–90). The humiliating peace agreement with the Jin was particularly reviled (Tao, 2009: 681). On the other hand, some covenants were in fact respected and accepted as stable frameworks for inter-state relations. The Covenant of Chanyuan, notably, lasted for a century (Mote, 1999: 71).

This is surely because such pacts did fulfil the second purpose of ritualized interactions between polities, namely, to offer a stable framework within which changes in the Middle Kingdom's international environment (shifts in the international balance of power, events on the empire's borders, and domestic developments in surrounding polities) could be dealt with in a flexible manner that still broadly conformed to the Chinese world view

---

[13] On international orders as performed narratives (or scripts) in general, see Ringmar (2012).

(Franke, 1983: 122; Wills, 2012: 476–7). As long as ritual propriety was maintained, and the status of the other side in any relationship clearly established, Chinese officials could adapt to circumstances. Such was the case, for instance, when they accepted to modify the audience ritual to accommodate the demands of the British envoy George Macartney in 1793 (Hevia, 1995: 105–6). Even when they had no choice but to accept an equal relationship, as was the case in Song–Liao relations, audience rituals could be adapted by sitting both parties facing each other east–west instead of north–south, replacing two points of the compass that had a hierarchical connotation by two that expressed equality (Schwartz, 1968: 280).[14]

In fact, as James Hevia points out, since 'concrete practical performance' was so central to the operation of rituals, the texts that dealt with them could provide only general guidelines, based on a description of precedents, that left to participants the agency to translate them into actions in a way that fitted the needs of the moment (1995: 217).[15] Those precedents were described in great detail but, as Frederick Mote writes, 'the Chinese did not spend much time formulating general statements of principle regarding interstate relations' (1999: 380). Rules governing interactions between polities were not, and could not, be stated absolutely. They were instead contingent on the nature of the relationship between the two parties and their relative status. The space left for practitioners to interpret guidelines and precedents means that rituals were not organized according to an overall systematic logic, and varied from one relation to the next and over time (Kawashima and Hattori, 2007: 5). For instance, the relationship between Northern and Southern dynasties in the fifth and sixth centuries changed from tribute paid by the South to the North to one of exchange of envoys on an equal footing as the Northern dynasty weakened (Hori, 2006: 231–2).

The willingness of Chinese statesmen to compromise when circumstances demanded it, even as they sought to maintain the principal of ritual inclusion in the imperial domain, is perhaps best manifested in the way the Tang and the Song responded to the growing number of merchant ships coming to Chinese shores as a consequence of the growth in maritime trade that accompanied the shift of the Asian economy from land to sea.[16] This response shaped the practice of the Ming and Qing after them. Seafaring merchants

---

[14] See Perdue, 2010: 352–3 for a similar discussion of the acceptance of equality by Qing Manchu officials in their negotiations with Russia.

[15] As Lee Ji-Young notes, this flexibility was equally useful for surrounding polities, who could participate in rituals without necessarily interpreting them in the same way as the imperial court did (2013: 315–6).

[16] On this historical shift in the centre of gravity of the Asian economy, see Sen, 2003: 151–82; von Glahn, 2016: Ch. 6.

were depicted as yet more barbarians attracted by the emperor's virtue, who should be treated with generosity and grace. After having abandoned attempts to ban trade outside tributary missions during the Song and then the Ming, the imperial court sought to establish a ritual relationship with them too. The Tang had done so by labelling some of their goods as gifts to the throne, to be repaid by tax exemptions and by letting foreigners manage their own affairs on Chinese soil (Danjō, 2013: 431–2). The Song then revived the system of private 'mutual trade' (*hushi*) originally developed for the Inner Asian frontier, implementing it at designated ports while institutionalizing the custom of offering, through local representatives, lavish banquets to visiting merchants to symbolically welcome them in the imperial domain (Danjō, 2013: 433–4).[17]

In that case, the twin purposes of rituals worked in harmony. They allowed the Chinese court to creatively adapt to a new situation – the multiplication of foreign private merchants visiting the coast – while still actualizing the hierarchical relation between the Son of Heaven and any individual who came to his shore, even if he was no state representative. Another example of a case where ritual fulfilled its twin purposes well is the treatment of incidents on the empire's borders with small tributary states like Korea and Vietnam. As Kim Jaymin (2015) notes in his study of Qing Qianlong's decisions in that regard, the emperor was free to respond to crimes committed by foreign citizens against Chinese ones on a case-by-case basis, justifying whatever action he took based on his evaluation of his vassals' respect for ritual propriety. In that case, ritual norms gave him both flexibility – since he was sole judge of how virtuous the behaviour of neighbours was – and multiple occasions to demonstrate his narrative power by defining the state of his relation with vassals at any one time. In other cases when the empire was not obviously more powerful than neighbouring polities, the flexibility of ritual allowed for the negotiation of some modus vivendi, but this did not extinguish the urge to shift towards the mode of tribute and investiture that would clearly demonstrate Chinese superiority. In short, ritual's flexibility allowed the imperial court to adapt when it needed to, but its ultimate aim was still to demonstrate dominance wherever it could.

---

[17] The original *hushi* of the Inner Asian borders were not loci to forge a ritual bond between barbarians and the emperor but rather a pragmatic means to placate them and facilitate their entrance into the ritual order by more traditional means (Matsuda, 1986: 161–8; Danjō, 2013: 427–8). For an extended discussion of the place of coastal *hushi* in the ritual order, see Danjō, 2013: 438–42. Iwai Shigeki (2007) also points out the importance of the coastal *hushi* during the Qing as loci to conduct 'quiet diplomacy' with non-tributary states through local officials and private intermediaries, thus sidestepping delicate issues of ritual propriety in inter-state relations.

Tools of rulership

It was traditionally presumed that foreigners would come of their own will and eagerly seek inclusion in the Sinocentric ritual order since ritual was the quintessence of civilization itself. This expectation again originates in the seminal pre-imperial period. As Yuri Pines points out, 'the idea of transformability of savageness into civilized behaviour permeates [Warring States] Confucian thought' (2005: 74). The question, then, was how to achieve such a transformation of barbarian 'birds and beasts' into followers of ritual propriety. We will here discuss how the imperial court used an elaborate system of titles and ranks, the awesomeness that comes from superior military power, and the lure of profits to guide foreigners into behaving in accordance with its expectations.

Language

The 'rectification of names' took a very concrete meaning in China's foreign relations through the comprehensive ranking system managed by the imperial court, into which invested foreign rulers were integrated. The very act of granting a title to a non-Chinese power holder established the ritual connection between him and the Son of Heaven, but titles themselves were not uniform and indicated recipients' ascribed rank and status in that system, which was meant to accord with the 'real' nature of his relations with China. Indeed, such status allocation was considered the foundation for proper ritual interactions. Even polities that did not receive investiture were still classified one way or another – near rivals in Inner Asia as fictive kin, simple tributaries as tributary countries (*chaogong guo*), and in the late Qing countries that sent merchants but never an official embassy to the court as 'mutual trading countries' (*hushi guo*) (Danjō, 2013: 443–4). The designation of the Xiongnu as an 'enemy state' (*diguo*) during the Han proceeded from the same desire to give them a status that correctly reflected the nature of their relationship to China so that they could be treated appropriately in diplomatic interactions – even if that status was that of an adversary outside of the civilized realm.

The centrepiece of China's classification efforts was its titles and ranks system, which was maintained throughout the imperial era even as each dynasty developed its own version of it. Under the Han, the titles allocated to barbarians were part of a system of 'ranks of nobility' (*juewei*) covering both the imperial domain and its foreign relations, with 'king' (*wang*) and 'marquis' (*hou*) as the most important ranks in the latter case (Danjō, 2016: 74–5). In the later Han and in the period of division that followed, some rulers from Inner Asia and even from Korea and Japan started to receive not only 'ranks of nobility', but also 'official ranks' (*guanwei*) previously reserved for

Chinese officials (Tanigawa, 1979: 96–100). There was certainly an element of 'ranking inflation' at play here, as visitors were given grander and grander titles in order to attract them to various courts with competing claims on a splintering empire (Nakanishi, 2013: 91). Yet these additions to foreigners' titles were also an effort to make names accord with a reality where the Chinese heartland was increasingly relying on barbarians living on its borders to defend it, barbarians who in some cases came to be considered part of the Chinese realm (Tanigawa, 1979: 102).

The Tang, who greatly extended this realm to include much of Inner Asia, confirmed the merger of the official and nobility ranks system. The rulers of the non-Chinese prefectures within the empire were given both official titles such as 'military governors' (*dudu*) or 'provincial governors' (*cishi*) and the nobility rank of king, which they shared with other polities outside the empire (Hori, 1993: 210; Kaneko, 2001: 53–61). Not all kings were equal, though. The Tang made further distinctions of ranks between 'country' (*guo*) and 'prefecture' (*jun*) rulers. Some titles were also preceded by a polity's name, indicating a stable long-term relation, or by a moral epithet that indicated a more fragile and temporary bond based on only one ritual interaction (Kaneko, 2001: Ch. 5 and Ch. 8).

Following dynasties continued to use 'king' as the standard title for invested vassals, even as they made adjustments to the overall Chinese ranking system (Danjō, 2013: 353–4). Titles could be updated from one category to the other as the nature of a polity's relation with the court changed. This included downgrades, as happened to the Vietnamese king, demoted to a high-ranking military title in the 16th century in sanction of what the Ming court deemed repeated instances of duplicitous and improper behaviour (Wang Gungwu, 1998: 330). The Qing also developed their own system of ranks to grant to the nobility of their Inner Asian territories, reusing old local ones such as 'khan' (*han*) as well as traditional Chinese titles like 'king' and inscribing them on seals in both Chinese and Inner Asian scripts (Yan Ziyou, 1999; Zhang Yongjiang, 2017: 131).

This quick overview reveals a deep concern with the ranking of non-Chinese polities, a concern that parallels the care put into organizing the domestic bureaucratic and nobility hierarchy, and shows what could be called China's 'urge to classify' those it interacted with. The aim was to have their ascribed status accurately reflect their position vis-à-vis the court and serve as a guide for stable and proper relations. Successive dynasties attached great importance to the creation of a rational system of status attribution through titles, in the hope that it would be widely accepted as a guide to ritual interactions. Such hopes may have been warranted when it came to other states in the 'East Asian cultural sphere' evoked in Chapter 1 – Korea, Japan, and Vietnam, and later the Ryukyu Kingdom – who had embraced many elements of Chinese culture and the values by which the ranking system was inspired, or to the conquest dynasties who had adopted at least the trappings of Chinese rulership. Chinese expectations were, however, more likely to be disappointed when it came to less Sinicized polities. Indeed, officials who had to deal with such places often expressed their dismay at the lack of respect for ritual etiquette of their interlocutors and their inability to reciprocate Chinese efforts to adopt the correct language for inter-state communication (Franke, 1981: 118). The Han, who were facing this problem when dealing with the Xiongnu, included in the *heqin* policy 'an "indoctrination" campaign, whereby the Han would send rhetoricians to [them] to explain the rules of proper conduct' (Di Cosmo, 2002: 193). One could also mention similar efforts at education undertaken by the early Ming towards the Japanese who were requested to come and pay tribute to the new rulers of China (Li Kangying, 2010: 106).

In most cases, though, no such proactive measures were taken. Chinese officials simply ignored minor ritual improprieties and made sure to offer sufficient guidance to all the visitors who came to the imperial court so that even the most uncultured barbarian would know how to behave in front of the Son of Heaven.[18] For more serious violations or outright challenges against the ritual order, more radical measures were readily taken.

Awesomeness

Military force was indeed always available and Chinese rulers did not hesitate to use it to awe recalcitrant neighbours into submission. The necessity to support order with the full might of the state against any who would harm it is fully recognized in classical Chinese writings. The Wuzi, for instance, one of the 'seven military classics' compiled mostly during the Warring States period, opined that 'the enlightened ruler ... will certainly nourish culture and virtue within the domestic sphere while, in response to external situations, putting his military preparations in order' (Sawyer, 1993: 206). A passage of the 'Commentary of Zuo to the Spring and Autumn Annals' (*Chunqiu Zuo zhuan*) helps put that admonishment in context through the Sino–barbarian distinction, declaring that 'the Middle Kingdom is put at ease through virtue, the four barbarians are awed through punishment'.[19]

This second quote puts in relation the two key terms that define the Chinese understanding of the use of military force as highlighted in Chapter 2, namely, 'awesomeness' (*wei*) and 'punishment' (*xing*). The declared purpose of 'punitive' military expeditions was to demonstrate the power

---

[18] See Hevia, 1995: 98–101, 157–8 for an account of such efforts towards the visiting British embassy.
[19] In '25th year of Duke Xi' (author's translation).

of China's ruler, to thoroughly impress the barbarians and thus to create the conditions necessary for the inclusion in the ritual order of polities insensitive to the charms of Chinese civilization. Indeed, it was commonly accepted that the empire 'could not depend on virtue and moral superiority [alone], but needed to use force against recalcitrance and barbarism' (Wang Gungwu, 1983: 49).

The declared purpose of maintaining a 'wealthy state and strong army', as the Legalist injunction goes, was thus truly to awe all-under-heaven into submission. This is, for instance, how a successful campaign to today's Xinjiang was celebrated in the Han historical records:

> [Two Chinese generals] eventually succeeded in carrying out expansion to the far west and in bringing foreign territories into submission. Overawed by military strength and attracted by wealth, none [of the rulers of the states in the Western Regions] did not present strange local products as tribute and his beloved sons as hostages. They bared their heads and kneeled down toward the east to pay homage to the Son of Heaven. (*Book of Later Han*, quoted in Yü Ying-shi, 1986: 413)

Such expeditions were typically cast as punitive in nature, since in the logic of the ritual order, the use of force was a measure of last resort taken when the counterpart had committed an act counter to ritual propriety, or outright rejected it. The purpose of punishment was in most cases not the elimination of those unwilling to respect ritual norms, but rather to 'bring them back to the fold' by force and to re-establish the empire's awesomeness. Once that task was accomplished, the Son of Heaven was supposed to promptly 'leave punishments behind and return to the rites' (*quxing guili*) (Chen Kanling, 2015: 45). For instance, a poem included in the classical *Book of Odes* (*Shijing*) praises a general who has 'punished' a tribe called the Xianyun and thus 'awed' another one into submissively coming to court.[20] In a similar vein, the task of the several garrisoned 'Protectorate-generals' (*duhufu*) set up by the Tang to supervise their outlying prefectures was to be a reminder of the empire's might, to 'pacify' the various barbarians and to 'take punitive actions' when necessary (Pan Yihong, 1997: 198).

During the Ming, all accounts of military expeditions on the south-western edge of the empire likewise described their purpose as the 'pacification' of the region for the benefit of its inhabitants and the re-establishment of the harmony of all-under-heaven (Wade, 2000: 40–2; 2015: 86–7). The first Ming emperor, Hongwu, also threatened punishment against Korea for breaches of ritual norms, even if he did not actually dispatch an expedition

---

[20] In 'Gathering white millet' 4.

(Fuma, 2007a: 315–25). His successor, Yongle, not only invaded Vietnam, invoking multiple breaches of propriety to justify doing so, but also sought to rule the seas of South-East Asia through his admiral, Zheng He, who proved ready to coerce recalcitrant kings into coming to pay allegiance to his master (Wade, 2005: 511; Fuma, 2007b: 6–8). Yongle also threatened retaliation on those who did not respect ritual propriety, demanding reparation to a Javanese king who had killed Chinese envoys by invoking the recent intervention in Vietnam as an example of the punitive expedition that might be sent if he did not comply, while also warning a Burmese king seeking to form trouble on the south-western border of invasion if he did not cease and desist (Wang Yuan-kang, 2011: 161–2).

In this domain at least, the Qing fully adopted Ming customs (even if they did not mount any maritime adventure). The Qianlong emperor launched another 'punitive expedition' against Vietnam to re-establish the properly invested king who had been dethroned – he eventually settled, after a disastrous campaign, for having the usurper come and participate in his birthday ceremony and pledge loyalty instead (Fuma, 2007b: 2427) – and kept 'an iron fist always ... in reserve behind the smooth ritual mask' in relations with Inner Asian vassals (Perdue, 2005: 548). In fact, coming to pay tribute and to make pilgrimage to the imperial court became under the Qing a legal obligation for these polities, and failure to fulfil their ritual obligations was considered a crime (Chia Ning, 1993: 84). Efforts to preserve the Son of Heaven's awesomeness through the threat, and sometimes actual launch, of military campaigns and other punishments are thus a clear theme running through China's imperial history, from the first dynasty to the last.

Profits

To complement the use of force, Chinese statesmen were also keenly aware that they could also bring 'uncivilized' foreigners into the ritual order through the lure of profits. Talking about the northern barbarians, the Han dynasty scholar Dong Zhongshu argued that 'while gentlemen can be moved by principle, greedy people can be moved only by profit. People like the [Xiongnu] cannot be converted by humanity and justice, but can only be appeased with high profit' (quoted in Yang Lien-sheng, 1968: 28). The last pillar of the *heqin* policy was thus to use what another Han official, Jia Yi, called the 'five baits' consisting of clothes, food, women, slaves, and high honours to make the nomads soft and dependent on Chinese largesse in order to obtain their submission (Yü Ying-shi, 1967: 36–7).

In fact, all those who came to court to pay tribute were richly rewarded with gifts often vastly exceeding the value of the tributary goods. All dynasties thus followed Han Fei's advice to use rewards in conjunction with punishments to shape the behaviour of subordinates. To come back to the passage of the *Book of Later Han* quoted earlier, the author says of the rulers of the Western Regions: 'Those who were submissive from the very beginning received money and official seals as imperial gifts, but those who surrendered later were taken to the capital to receive punishment' (quoted in Yü Ying-shi, 1986: 413). The use of economic benefits to entice foreigners reached a high point during the early Ming with the tributary trade system under which no trade was allowed outside of official missions to the court (a policy the Song also briefly tried to adopt). This had several purposes, but one of the motives invoked in Chinese texts is indeed to ensure the submission of foreigners seeking Chinese riches (Wills, 1984: 19; Li Kangying, 2010: 110). The venality of uncivilized barbarians was again quoted by a Ming official arguing that those against the reception of tribute missions from the dreaded Mongols '[did] not realize that (this breed of) dogs and sheep desire profits and long for Chinese wealth' (quoted in Serruys, 1967: 60).

By Qing times, private trade had become a much more important medium of economic exchanges than tributary missions. This did not mean that the imperial court had abandoned the aim to use the lure of profits to support the ritual order. Indeed, both on the Inner Asian frontier and on the coast, it used its regulatory authority so that 'close supervision of borders, cooperation with merchants, and restrictions on trade served as useful tools for gaining "barbarian" obedience' (Perdue, 2005: 554; see also Fairbank 1978: 32). Ironically, those same restrictions were eventually invoked by the British to justify the aggression that would mark the beginning of the end of the dynasty and of the entire imperial system.

Conclusion

This chapter has sought to examine, inevitably only superficially, 2,000 years of Chinese imperial history through the filter of the ideal type of hierarchical order outlined earlier. In the ideal vision of that order, the Son of Heaven would be the perfect embodiment of Confucian virtue, his benevolence would naturally attract surrounding polities to bring tribute and receive titles from him, every foreign ruler would accept his assigned place in the Chinese ranking system, and the empire's awesome power and boundless wealth would be enough to prevent anyone from disturbing the peace and harmony of 'all-under-heaven'. Yet centuries of adapting to circumstances that very rarely allowed this utopia to come close to realization reveals that Chinese statesmen were attached to the principles underpinning it but highly adaptable in practice.

First, the requirement that the Son of Heaven be uniquely virtuous was absolute, even when the titleholder himself did not conform to the ideal of the Confucian sage king. In such cases, Chinese literati could find ways to redefine what virtuous leadership meant to fit their circumstances and preserve the moral legitimacy of the imperial court. China's place at the top of the hierarchy and superiority over any neighbour was similarly a given, but pragmatic adaptations to an unfavourable balance of power could be made, in which case the imperial court would accept some symbols of equality while preserving the appearances of hierarchical relations within the empire and in the world of Chinese writing. Second, concrete interactions between rulers were meant to give concrete shape to the hierarchical order and build a narrative of Chinese superiority and others' obedience. The exact modalities of each individual relation were, however, open to negotiations. Ritual could even accommodate equal interactions when necessary, although the Chinese never did so more than grudgingly. Such cases where ritual could not fulfil its primary function of demonstrating Chinese superiority highlighted its secondary one, namely determining and clearly expressing the status of each side in a relationship. This was believed to be a necessary condition to the establishment of a stable framework for relations between rulers.

Third, the Chinese were inhabited by an urge to classify all foreign polities with which they interacted within an overall ranking system, which they hoped would serve as a guide to ritually proper interactions, but sought to accord this classification with the 'real' nature of each relationship and did not let titles completely dictate how they would treat individual foreign rulers. Any failure to comply with ritual norms was seen in classical Confucian fashion as signs of wickedness, and therefore justified whatever punitive measure the imperial court took in response. In practice, though, responses varied greatly from one case to the next and over time, from isolation to education and from economic incentives to threats and coercion. The wealth and power of the state were in any case understood as necessary means to protect the ritual order through the kind of awesomeness that would deter potential offenders (Huang Zhilian, 1994: 121).

In all these respects, attachment to the underlying principles of the hierarchical order was accompanied by a great deal of flexibility and pragmatism in the pursuit of its realization. Even as Chinese statesmen idealistically kept these principles as their lodestar, they remained realistically attuned to the prevailing balance of power, to what was achievable, and to what was expedient to secure the empire's borders and expand its territory, or at least its influence. Since this attachment was so deeply anchored, its survival into the modern era despite the major transformations affecting China and its environment should not be surprising. It is to those transformations that we turn our attention next.

4

China's Forced Entry into International Society and the Transformation of the Ideal of Hierarchical Order

The ritual order, as it existed in one form or another during the whole imperial era, eventually came to an end around the turn of the 20th century under the combined assault of European colonialism and Japan's Westernization and turn to imperialism. Internationally, the transition to a diplomatic system based on bilateral treaties was not sudden or absolute – Hamashita Takeshi speaks of an 'era of negotiation' between tributary and treaty relations from 1830 to 1890 (1997: Ch. 7; 2003) – but eventually all East Asian states still free from colonial rule had to adopt the Western style of relations between nation states. China itself had to abandon its traditional view of itself as the centre of a world order governed by ritual and adapt to the new realities of the expanding Western international society. This involved reconfiguring its domestic state structure on Western lines as well, culminating with the Xinhai revolution of 1911, which aimed for the establishment of a constitutional republic. Eventually, Confucianism itself, now seen as the cause of China's decline and the source of its woes, was rejected and replaced by nationalism and Marxism-Leninism as the two new ideological pillars of the 'new China' that eventually emerged in 1949.

Our aim in this chapter is to identify what remained, after these revolutionary changes, of China's traditional world view and of its attachment to the core principles underlying its traditional vision of order. The following pages show how China's pessimistic assessment of the international society dominated by Western imperial powers gave rise to a new sense of mission, aiming to establish a more just, though still hierarchical, international order that would see China recover its rightful place as the leader of Asia. This claim was still framed in moral terms, as China favourably compared itself with Western imperial powers thanks to its 'inherent virtues' and advocacy for the liberation of Asian nations. This chapter also discusses how, despite the necessity to abandon traditional tools of statecraft and embrace the norms of modern diplomacy, China remained focused on matters of international status in its interactions with international society. In all those respects, the late imperial and republican era was a pivotal period during which the traditional Chinese vision of order was transformed, leaving its essence intact but adapted to the modern society of sovereign states. In its new shape, this vision would continue to guide the successive generations of statesmen of the PRC. This is why examining the period of transition of the turn of the 20th century is crucial to understanding Chinese foreign policy today.

One exception, though, is the use of the traditional tools of rulership identified in Chapter 2. A country under attack from foreign invaders and beset by deep internal divisions was at the time in no position to teach, coerce, or induce anyone to support its status claims. The Chinese were painfully aware of this fact, of course. Guided by their very pessimistic assessment of modern international society as an arena of raw power competition, they were driven more than anything by the desire to rebuild their country's own wealth and power. As Orville Schell and John Delury put it, 'What "liberté, egalité, fraternité" meant to the French Revolution and to the making of modernity in the West, "wealth, strength, and honor" have meant to the forging of modern China' (2013: 8). While the Republican period can tell us little regarding how China's wealth and power would come to be used in the modern era, we will discuss this theme at length in a later chapter. For now, though, let us examine how Chinese statesmen and scholars of the late 19th century reacted to their country's diminished stature in the expanding Western international society.

Order and hierarchy

One of the most significant intellectual developments that accompanied China's traumatic collision with Western great powers was to alter its understanding of order. Order traditionally was something to be preserved. It became something to be achieved. Chinese scholars and intellectuals had looked to the distant past of China's high antiquity, idealized and immortalized in the Confucian canon, as the model of the perfect society that later periods could always look back to for inspiration and guidance. This meant that the basic formula for achieving stable order had already been set out and could in theory simply be replicated. Even as successive dynasties brought in their own sets of reforms to meet the needs of their present conditions, they also presented their founding as a return to order after the corruption that had brought their predecessors low and the chaos that inevitably accompanied a period of transition – not as the occasion to build something entirely new. Thus, Zhu Yuanzhang, founder of the Ming, saw his task as '[restoring] social order to the empire' after the degradation of the late Yuan and 'cloaked even his innovations under the mantle of a return to the Chinese essence' (Farmer, 1995: 2–3). The Qing, when they seized power, then made sure to 'pointedly [adhere] to the institutional structure of the Ming dynasty' to which they made 'no major changes' (Mote, 1999: 823–4) – except for the establishment of the *Lifanyuan* as a centralized colonial administration to rule over its Inner Asian territories.

This tendency to understand order as something that already existed and needed to be maintained or restored rather than created from scratch was shattered by the combined forces of the Western ideas introduced in the late 19th century and of Chinese intellectuals' sense of national crisis and pessimistic assessment of the international society they were thrown into. Kang Youwei (1858–1927), one of China's most famous and influential early reformers, embodies the new line of thinking well. The influence of Western concepts of progress and evolution on his generation were evident first in his programme of revolutionary reforms, which aimed to 'protect the state' by transforming it into something new, akin to a Western constitutional monarchy with Confucianism as a state religion and a modern bureaucratic and education system (Hao Cheng, 1980: 285–7). They were evident as well in his vision of a world order evolving in three stages from the age of 'disorder' (*juluan*) through an age of 'small peace' (*xiaokang*), and eventually towards an age of 'great unity' (*datong*), where the human suffering Kang saw all around him would finally be extinguished (Hao Cheng, 1980: 288).

In both aspects of his work, he was heralding a 'tidal change in Chinese thinking' by 'projecting a new future' resulting from an inescapable process of historical development (de Bary, 1988: 93). As Wang Hui points out, this amounted to a transformation in the Chinese understanding of time. Gone are concepts of cycles of decay and renewal, of transformation and change as a natural process without predetermined end point or purpose, to be replaced by a 'linear concept of time that extends into the future' and by a teleological understanding of national and international development (Wang Hui, 2004: 63). Nationally, the end goal for Kang and his contemporaries was to obtain the wealth and power that would allow China to resist foreign aggression (Schwartz, 1964).[1] More broadly, though, as Kang's 'three ages'

---

[1] The influence of the idea of evolution and of stages of development leading to the transformation of China into a strong country was evident in the thinking of its most famous revolutionary leader, Sun Yat-sen, who thought that his country would need to go through three phases of rule through 'military law', through 'provisional constitutional law', and finally through 'constitutional law' to achieve this goal. A similar project was later adopted by leaders of both the Chinese Communist Party and the Chinese Nationalist Party (Hirano, 2007: 341). This goes to show the decisive impact of the changing conception of time and progress described here.

discourse shows, the aspiration to achieve world peace and order had not disappeared from Chinese minds, but had receded into an uncertain, or even utopian, future.

The state of the international society that Chinese intellectuals of the late Qing were discovering was in their eyes quite dire, and this pessimistic assessment was an important reason for the change in their understanding of time. The analogy that quickly came to their minds was the Spring and Autumn and Warring States periods before the unification of the Chinese empire (Hao Yen-p'ing and Wang Erh-min, 1980: 189; Lin Xuezhong, 2009: 210–11). The former period was associated in the Chinese imagination with the progressive breakdown of the refined order that had been overseen by the Zhou dynasty, and the latter with the chaos and disorder that followed said breakdown, as the titular warring states competed for advantage without restraint, using any and all means at their disposal. Such analogies thus had a highly negative connotation, underlining the brutishness of the world China was now facing (Cohen, 1967: 143; Suzuki, 2009: 61). It is unsurprising that Kang Youwei, along with many other intellectuals, described an 'age of disorder' from which they wished to escape.

Such is the form in which the Chinese preoccupation with order survived the shock of the forced entrance into the modern international society, then: as an aspiration, something to achieve at some point in the future through a linear process of evolution and progress that could free the world from its current troubled state. Bringing about this evolution was for Kang's disciples – although not for the man himself – only achievable through a process of struggle against the powerful Western states that were dominating international society and exploiting weaker preys. This negative view underlines how empty the promise of sovereign equality ringed to Chinese ears and how harshly hierarchical they perceived international society to be.

That promise was part of the rhetoric of the Western emissaries who came to Asian shores throughout the 19th century. Said emissaries were convinced of the superiority of their civilization over any non-Western one and 'self-consciously declared [its standards] to represent universal values' that all should aspire to (Gong, 1984: 52). They thus looked down on the people of Asia, thinking of themselves as educators or missionaries coming to impose the Western 'standard of civilization' on inferior and unenlightened barbarians. As Gerrit Gong writes, the idea of a 'standard of civilization' emerged in 19th-century Europe as the criteria by which imperial powers judged who outside the continent was 'worthy' of joining their society of states as legitimate, sovereign, and equal members – and which they used as an excuse to coerce, dominate, or conquer polities that did not fulfil it. The standard encompassed the guarantee of foreigners' rights, an effective state bureaucracy, adherence to Western-style principles of diplomacy and laws both domestically and internationally, and the abandonment of practices Europeans found offensive, like polygamy (Gong, 1984: 14–15).

The late Qing's political elite, whose predecessors had for millennia looked down on many of their own neighbours as unenlightened barbarians, in fact realized fairly late that Western powers were applying a similar logic towards them. The first 'unequal treaties' that the Chinese government would later do everything to revise or abrogate were at the time of their conclusion seen as just another round of pragmatic concessions made to appease turbulent barbarians at the far edge of the empire, who posed no real threat to China's understanding of order or to the supremacy of the Son of Heaven (Swisher, 1958: 26; Shih Chih-yu, 1990: 97). More than the Opium Wars, the event that decisively reshaped China's world view was the Qing's defeat against Japan – one of the aforementioned peripheral barbarians – in 1895. That such a 'small' neighbour could defeat the great empire by utilizing Western knowledge made the Chinese intelligentsia question many of their most fundamental assumptions and greatly popularized Western thought as a means to understand the current state of the world (Paine, 2003: 296–7). When the great translator of Western works, Yan Fu, released his abridged version of Thomas Henry Huxley's *Evolution and Ethics* three years later, then, its impact was immense and converted many readers to the particular version of evolution theory that is social Darwinism (Schwartz, 1964: 99; Satō, 1996: 122–3).

What they saw when they looked at the world thereafter was a harsh environment where conflict was frequent, struggle for existence among states was the norm, and where the laws of natural selection would weed out the weak (Satō, 1992: 87). Power was here the true organizing principle of a hierarchical world order where the strong prevailed and the weak suffered. The leading reformist Liang Qichao, in particular, greatly popularized this view. He described competition for survival as the only path to development and progress and argued that the only way for China to claim its rights as a sovereign state was to strengthen itself – acquire wealth and power (*fuqiang*) – and fight for them (Xu Jilin, 2012: 187–8). There was no talk here of reaching an age of order, peace, and unity, as Liang was entirely focused on the more urgent task of saving China from its predicament and climbing the hierarchy of power (Satō, 1996: 127–8).

What about the idea of the sovereign equality of all states enshrined in international law, then? Western emissaries had long insisted that adhering to the 'standard of civilization' would enable China to benefit from the protection of that principle. According to this narrative, despite the disparities in the size and power of European states, their common adherence to international law made them equal in practice, ensuring their independence in the conduct of domestic affairs and foreign policy and guaranteeing reciprocity in the legal agreements they willingly entered into. All unequal conditions imposed through treaties on non-Western states were simply designed to protect the legitimate interests of the citizens of civilized states against the predations of less enlightened rulers, and would be amended if those rulers changed their ways.

Even within Europe, of course, the legal equality of states, the nominal organizing principle of international life, was in reality frequently undermined by hegemonic behaviour from one or several great powers (Watson, 1992). For countries like China, it was even more difficult to take at face value the promise of protection from international law once they fulfilled the requirements of a 'civilized state' due to their exposure to the coercive mode of behaviour adopted by imperial powers outside Europe. As Yamamuro Shinichi nicely puts it, Western states appeared in Asia like the Roman god Janus with two faces (2001: 279). They presented themselves both as teachers and as brutal invaders, both as 'civilized countries' and as 'strong powers'. Asian polities' assessment of the meaning of international law and its potential role as an organizing principle of world order was shaped by this duality. On one hand, international law embodied the shared principles and values, like sovereign equality, reciprocity, and good faith, which allowed European states to deal with each other with a certain degree of decency. On the other hand, though, international law could be the means through which imperial powers imposed their will on others and consolidated the gains obtained by force. This led many Chinese intellectuals of the turn of the century to see it only as a means to regulate relations between countries of equal strength. In situations of great disparities, it became a tool to be used by the strong and endured by the weak (Cohen, 1967: 141–3; Satō, 1996: 50). Equality – defined entirely in terms of power – was thus not something prescribed by international law but a prerequisite to its application.

This seemed to reduce international law to near irrelevance since equality could only be secured through military and economic might, but in fact the perception of international relations as a brutal arena of power competition did not necessarily preclude a role for it. Indeed, many intellectuals argued that, if the goal was to strengthen China's international position, international law was an indispensable tool to do so – or in other words that mastery of it was a source of power in itself (Satō, 1996: 52; Svarverud, 2007: 138). By the end of the Qing, the prevailing view among Chinese elites was along those lines, accepting the central role of international law in international life as a given fact and arguing for its pragmatic use to secure the country's international position – a view that Liang Qichao himself eventually embraced (Svarverud, 2007: 211, 263). In the first years of the Republic after the Xinhai Revolution of 1911, then, Chinese diplomatic actions seeking treaty revision or asserting its international status were typically justified by invoking principles of international law (Zhang Yongjin, 1991a: 192). Yet this remained a pragmatic embrace, based on the utility of said principles for demanding equality with imperial powers. It did not necessarily reflect a change in the assessment of an international society governed by power competition.

Whatever faith Chinese elites had in international law's guarantee of equality and sovereign independence and in its capacity to moderate power politics was dashed by the failure of China to recover the Shandong peninsula from Germany at the post-First World War Paris Peace Conference, despite its manifest efforts to adhere to the Western standard of civilization and its support for the Allies during the war. This was seen as proof that international society remained a realm of competition and power struggle and that adherence to international law could not protect Chinese rights in the face of the superior might of the great powers sitting at the top of the international hierarchy (Zhang Yongjin, 1991a: 96).

China's pessimistic assessment of the gap between Western states' rhetoric and their actions should, however, not eclipse the fact that it had by then fully accepted the norms of international legitimacy described in Chapter 1, namely, that international society was one of sovereign states with certain legal rights and obligations in their conduct towards each other. As part of this package, it had embraced the legal principle of equality, understood as the basic right to independence, autonomy, and equal status in diplomatic and legal matters (notably treaty making) for all nations big and small, even if this did not preclude differences in social status and rights and responsibilities outside the realm of international law (Lin Xuezhong, 2009: 215). What China rejected was the notion that imperial powers truly respected the norms of legitimacy, and thus that the harsh hierarchical nature of international society was much mitigated. This opened the way for it to invoke its own respect for the same norms as part of its claim to moral superiority. This begs the question, though, of whether the acceptance in theory of the principle of sovereign equality had been reflected in a concrete change of attitude towards China's neighbours and in a new understanding of the nature of its relationship with them.

During the 'era of negotiation' of the late 19th century, the Qing had fought to preserve their tributary relations with East Asian neighbour states while adapting to new circumstances. They (unsuccessfully) went to war with France over Vietnam after their proposal for an arrangement whereby the country would be both French protectorate and Chinese vassal was rejected, and more successfully negotiated a similar arrangement with Britain for Burma (Motegi, 1997: 56–61). They sought, although not very vigorously, to negotiate with Japan to prevent its absorption of the Ryukyu kingdom (Motegi, 1997: 69–71). In Inner Asia, though, they fought more ferociously and with more success to establish 'Chinese sovereignty' in a modern sense on the territories conquered early in the dynasty (Hirano, 2007: 299–300). With the exception of Outer Mongolia (now the Republic of Mongolia), these territories are today internationally recognized parts of China, regardless of controversies over its treatment of the populations of Tibet and Xinjiang.

Yet it is in its evolving policy towards Korea, its closest tributary, that China's efforts to reconcile its deeply anchored sense of superiority with changing international norms are the most apparent. Under pressure from Japan and Western powers, the imperial court initially argued that, as its vassal, Korea was autonomous but not independent, free to conduct its own domestic and foreign affairs as it pleased and to conclude treaties with imperial powers as long as it did so in consultation with China and without prejudice to its tributary obligations (Kawashima, 2004: 356–8). In fact, the Qing encouraged a reluctant Korean court to open its door to trade with the West to avoid a damaging attack (Wright, 1958). As the pressure from imperial powers grew, these efforts to influence Korea became more and more overt to the point that Chinese policy itself started to resemble a form of colonial domination. This included an armed intervention to put down a soldier's mutiny egged on by some in the Korean court, greater direct control asserted over said court, the conclusion of a trade agreement reaffirming China's privileges and superior status, and the inclusion of a similar clause in some treaties signed with Western powers. All this was, however, still justified in the traditional terms of harmonious relations between vassal and suzerain (Lin Ming-te, 1991; Hirano, 2007: 306, 308–9; Suzuki, 2009: 167–72).

This policy came to an abrupt end with the defeat against Japan in the 1894–5 war, largely fought over control of Korea. Yet even after losing its direct influence, China sought to preserve its hierarchical relation with its neighbour within the constraints of the modern legal forms that it was forced to adapt to. It argued that Korea was hardly independent due to continued foreign control of its government and aimed for an arrangement similar to the one concluded with Britain over Burma, while insisting on demonstrating the two sides' unequal status in matters of diplomatic protocol (Okamoto, 2009: 169–71). China eventually relented and accepted to sign an equal treaty in 1899 that recognized Korea's independence and granted each side similar trading and diplomatic privileges. Okamoto Takashi attributes this course correction to the mounting sense of crisis in the Qing court that resulted in the abortive Hundred Days' Reform movement (2009: 172–3). Relations with Korea became in that context a test case for the adoption of modern diplomatic customs.

This was, however, not a sign of a deeper shift in China's perception of its position relative to its neighbours, as Chinese efforts to preserve the rights of its merchants on the peninsula a few years later show. After Japan's annexation of Korea, which occurred only a year or so before the Xinhai Revolution, the new Republican government conducted a dogged negotiation to secure for residents of the Chinese concessions, which had been established in the 1880s and were to be abolished, the same rights of property ownership and same taxation regime as that enjoyed by Western imperial powers. As Kawashima Shin points out, this reveals the true nature of the claim to equality that animated China's quest to revise the unequal treaties. Namely, what China sought was equality with the great powers, not with smaller states like Korea. The special and non-reciprocal rights of the great powers on Korean territory signified the unequal nature of their relationship. By insisting on similar rights for itself, Republican China demonstrated the weight it attached to obtaining equality with the states with the highest status in international society, while showing it still saw its relation with its own neighbour in hierarchical terms despite the extinction of their ritual vassal–suzerain bond (Kawashima, 2004: 377).

China's policy towards Korea thus illustrates how it sought to redefine its role from overseer of the traditional Chinese world order to a modern great power. It eventually had to abandon any pretention at imperial domination and came to embrace the principle of legal equality in its treaty making with states big and small, perhaps making virtue out of a necessity (Zhang Yongjin, 1991b: 13–4). Yet in practice, it sought an equal status with the existing great powers. It understood that this implied not only striving for similar wealth and power, but also being similarly proactive in defending the rights of its citizens abroad. It also kept a sense of superiority over its neighbours. One sign of this is the fact that, even after Japan had acquired wealth and power, defeated Russia in 1905, and been reluctantly acknowledged as a great power by the West, Chinese diplomats still described it as a 'small country' (*zuierguo*) (Kawashima, 2006: 24).

The distinction between nominally equal countries with whom China had diplomatic relations and tributary states was clearly made, for instance, in a draft history of the Qing dynasty published in 1931 and 1932, which listed Chinese former tributaries – essentially all neighbouring states except Japan, which had not paid tribute since the mid-Ming – with the implication that these were former possessions, with a different status from the rest of the world (Kawashima, 2009: 143–4). This was part of the emerging narrative of 'national humiliation' (*guochi*), which depicted the end of the Qing dynasty as a series of defeats and losses of not only parts of the Qing empire but also tributary states. On 'maps of national humiliation' published in 1910s to 1930s school textbooks, Korea, the Ryūkyū islands, and all of continental South-East Asia – along with Nepal and a big chunk of Central Asia – were depicted as 'lost territories' (*shidi*) that were, if not part of China's sovereign territory in a modern sense, at least part of its larger domain, where it held special rights (Huang Donglan, 2005: 27–37; Callahan, 2010: 99–105; Hayton, 2020: 201–2). This was also the time when the Chinese claims to islands in the South China Sea took shape, largely in reaction to activities by the imperial powers (Onodera, 2017: 144–5; Hayton, 2018; Hayton, 2020: 216–38).

Although this most virulent assertion of Chinese supremacy on its periphery did not become the official view of the Republican government, it remained an important part of the domestic discourse (Kawashima, 2009: 152–4).[2] This was also a sign of the spread of nationalist sentiments in China. The importance of nationalism as a driving force of modern Chinese history – its birth among Chinese intellectuals as a uniting force against the Qing, its invocation as a new national creed to unite the various ethnic groups of the crumbling empire and to replace the waning Confucian tradition, its spread in response to Western imperialism and to Japanese aggression, its central role in the founding of the two rival communist and nationalist parties, and its renewed explosion after the end of the Cold War as the CCP looked for a new ideology to complement communism – is well known and has been the topic of many studies.[3] The popularity of the 'maps of national humiliation' was also fuelled by nationalist resentment towards the imperial powers who had colonized all the 'lost territories' except the Kingdom of Siam. Yet the discourse lamenting the fact that China was no longer surrounded by deferential smaller neighbours and linking its humiliation with the loss of those 'dependencies' also laid the seed for an intolerance of any 'disrespectful' behaviour by those neighbours themselves, which would manifest itself time and again after the founding of the PRC.

Even though the shock of China's entrance into the modern international society of states was transformative in many respects, then, converting the Chinese elite to the idea of progress from chaos to order and forcing them to grapple with a steep loss of status and with the meaning of the legal principle of sovereign equality, it did not alter their conviction that international relations were inherently unequal and that China was naturally superior to its neighbours. Indeed, China understood modern international society not as a family of equal nation states but as 'a social Darwinian world, in which the status of a nation-state was determined by its economic and military strength' (Zhao Suisheng, 2015b: 981). In a world divided hierarchically between great powers and small states, China considered itself to be the only member of the first group in Asia, surrounded only by members of the second. In that sense, even if modern China did not think of itself as the centre of the world anymore and accepted the existence of other great powers, its self-perception as the centre of Asia did not weaken (Kawashima, 2004: 421).

---

[2] Maps of national humiliation were still published in the first years of the PRC (Kim, 1979: 42–4).

[3] Marukawa (2015) and Onodera (2017) are two excellent recent overviews of the topic, the first organized thematically and the second chronologically.

Moral superiority

In comparison with the order the virtuous Son of Heaven watched over, the Western-led international order may have seemed unjust and immoral in the eyes of the first generations of Chinese who encountered it, but that does not mean that they rejected out of hand the liberal values that were meant to underpin it. Most notably, the Chinese were among the most enthusiastic supporters of the liberal internationalist vision proposed by the American President Woodrow Wilson as the First World War was nearing its end. His endorsement of the principle of national self-determination implicitly condemned imperialism and raised high hopes among the Chinese for a more principled post-First World War order where their country would finally find justice (Kawashima, 2004: 251). Yet the failure of the Versailles Treaty to reflect Wilson's idealism quickly dashed those hopes, helping to launch the May Fourth Movement and to refocus Chinese intellectuals on the need to find a Chinese alternative to the dominant Western value system and the order it inspired, now considered irredeemably flawed and warlike (Yamagoshi, 2004; Onodera, 2017: 98–102).

Although the ensuing intellectual burgeoning spread in many directions, from a doubling down on liberalism to anarchism, it is today especially associated with the birth of the Chinese version of Marxism-Leninism, inspired by the Russian Revolution of 1917. Its vision for ordering the world as expressed by Li Dazhao, one of the founding fathers of the CCP, is revolutionary and utopian. It is revolutionary because it identifies China with a 'world proletariat' that needs to actively struggle against, and eventually overthrow, the capitalist imperial powers who dominate international society. It is also utopian because it then imagines a brotherly federation of free nations on all continents that would put an end to the exploitation of the weak by the strong and bring about world unity (Meisner, 1967: 144–5, 186). Such thinking was a patchwork of ideas either taken from Lenin and Trotsky or of Li's own creation. It was also in line, though, with the changes in the Chinese discourse on order outlined previously.

Li Dazhao's particular vision of order was anti-imperialist and equalitarian since it aimed for the abolition of the existing international hierarchy of power, allowing Asian and other non-Western people to have an equal role in realizing the ideal of a world united by faith in socialism. Yet this vision also opened the way for China to reclaim a position of superiority over both its neighbours and Western nations. Indeed, in Li's view, China, having been transformed under the pressure of the capitalist imperial powers while still maintaining its independence, was a 'proletarian nation' that 'stood in the vanguard' of the struggle against oppression (Meisner, 1967: 189). Even if all nations were to be equal in the transformed world that Chinese communists called for, this left the way open for a hierarchy based on each country's degree of progress in the struggle to realize the socialist utopia. China, as the leader of the revolution and the most virtuous nation according to the new standards of the proletariat, would naturally stand at the top.

This lingering hierarchical thinking nesting within an egalitarian rhetoric can also be found in the reconstruction of the image of imperial-era foreign relations that occurred in parallel with the development of Chinese Marxism-Leninism. As Motegi Toshio points out, the end of tributary-investiture relations with surrounding polities allowed the Chinese understanding of these relations to become detached from its past reality and idealized as a more just and moral order than the one prevailing in the Western international society (2009: 54). The most well-known illustration of this trend is Sun Yat-sen's 1924 speech in Kobe on pan-Asianism, in which, using the same language as Xunzi many centuries before him, he contrasted the 'hegemonic way' (*badao*), or rule through might practised by the West, and the 'kingly way' (*wangdao*), or rule through virtue, characteristic of 'Oriental civilization' and of China's imperial tradition.[4] In this idealized view, surrounding polities were seduced by Chinese rightful rule and willingly came to offer tribute to show their respect. This was in essence an expression of sincere belief in the narrative of transformation of the barbarians through the virtuous power of the Son of Heaven that pervades Chinese imperial histories. In a lecture in China a few months earlier on the 'principle of the nation' (*minzu zhuyi*), one of his famous 'three principles of the people', Sun also contrasted Western-style colonialism with the benevolent way in which China maintained its dominance in the past, which he argued protected surrounding polities and allowed them to maintain their independence for thousands of years.[5]

Those two speeches combined offer an ambiguous picture, where Sun condemns Western imperialism and supports universal equality in one breath and calls on his country to preserve the spirit of the kingly way the next. This seems to suggest that the kingly way is in fact compatible with equality, and implies a redefinition of the latter to conform with Chinese traditions. Equality means here mutual respect in the form of an equal dedication of big and small countries to their differentiated obligations in a hierarchical relation, namely, 'caring for the small state' and 'acknowledging the big state' respectively (Motegi, 2009: 54).[6] The idealized vision of the traditional ritual order could thus be reinterpreted to serve as a positive, gentler alternative

---

[4] Speech delivered in Kobe on 28 November 1924. Translated text available at https://en.wikisource.org/wiki/Sun_Yat-sen%27s_speech_on_Pan-Asianism.
[5] Speech delivered in Guangzhou on 2 March 1924. Text available (in Chinese) at https://zh.wikisource.org/wiki/三民主義/民族主義第六講.
[6] Equality also means in that sense simply non-interference of big countries in the affairs of smaller ones, a position endorsed today by scholars like David Kang (2003).

to the power politics and imperialism decried by Chinese leaders. Crucially, like the Marxism-Leninism of Li Dazhao examined earlier, it also opened the way for China to reassert a form of moral leadership internationally and in its neighbourhood in particular. Indeed, in the same speech on the 'principle of the nation', Sun Yat-sen also evoked the 'responsibility of all Chinese people' based on their 'inherent sense of peace and morality' to 'make the world one' and bring about the age of 'great harmony' (*Datong*, the same Confucian concept used by Kang Youwei).[7]

Yet Sun Yat-sen's invocation of China's traditional sense of morality did not imply a return to Confucianism, which had by then been rejected by him and other republican intellectuals to the benefit of nationalism and 'modern' thinking.[8] When later expanding on the ideas expressed in the speeches of 1924, Sun and his followers dropped the references to the imperial era. Instead, they repeatedly emphasized the potential for the 'three principles of the people' to save the whole of Asia and pledged Chinese support for the national liberation struggle against colonial powers (Kawashima, 2009: 151–2). Similar ideas were expressed by Sun's successor as leader of the Nationalist Party, Chiang Kai-shek. In his manifesto, *China's Destiny*, published during the Second World War, Chiang argued that China was seeking independence and strength 'motivated by a feeling of duty and responsibility' to fight imperialism rather than 'by greed for power or profits' (Chiang Kai-shek, 1947: 233–4). To justify his claim that China was not seeking to 'lead Asia', he also referred to an idealized past where, he claimed, his country only went to war with neighbours for self-defence and for the maintenance of peace and stability (Chiang Kai-shek, 1947: 233). If China did not seek to dominate Asia, though, its freedom and strength was necessary for the sake of the whole continent since without it 'the other nations of Asia [would] each fall under the iron heel of the enemy, and world peace cannot have a solid foundation' (Chiang Kai-shek, 1947: 234). The country was once again depicted as a benevolent protector of its neighbours.

We are not far here from Li Dazhao's vision of Chinese leadership as the vanguard 'proletarian nation', with national solidarity replacing class solidarity but China still given pride of place as an inspiration and guarantor of peace for the rest of the continent. This helps put references to China's 'inherent sense of morality' into perspective. Sun Yat-sen and Chiang Kai-shek after him were not advocating a return to pre-modern inter-state practices or

---

[7] In the sixth lecture on the 'principles of the nation' quoted previously.
[8] Joseph Levenson (1958: 105–8) has eloquently described how Chinese nationalists embraced nominal loyalty to Confucian traditions as a symbol of love of country while rejecting the actual content of those traditions. See also Mitter, 2004: 110–7 for an excellent discussion of the anti-Confucian activism of some participants in the May Fourth Movement and of their mitigated success in rooting the doctrine out of Chinese society.

a revival of state Confucianism. Rather, they sought to claim for modern China the mantle of the virtuous kingship of old to justify maintaining its role of overseer of Asia and to boost the argument that it offered a better kind of leadership to neighbours than the exploitative domination of the West.

Whereas Li Dazhao paved the way for Mao Zedong and other early CCP leaders to flesh out this discourse with the vocabulary of class struggle and socialist brotherhood, Sun Yat-sen proved more influential in the long term with his attempt to seize the mantle of Confucian morality (if not its actual content) to emphasize China's inherent virtues and justify its status of leader. A similar rhetoric is still used by Xi Jinping today. There were significant similarities in the way leading figures of the republican era depicted China's role in the more just international order they aspired to bring about. Namely, they all saw China as an example to follow in throwing off the yoke of imperialism and a benevolent overseer once liberation was achieved. They pledged to truly respect the legal right to equality of sovereign states – as opposed to the lip services paid by the West – in exchange for recognition of its superior status. This claim to superiority was consistently framed in moral terms by presenting China as the standard bearer for the righteous cause of the liberation of Asia from colonial domination and as a better alternative to the imperial great powers.

The shift one can observe from an absolutist vision of China's sense of its superior moral quality – the emperor was the most virtuous person in the world, full stop – to a relative one – China is more virtuous than Western great powers – is one of the most significant developments of the republican period. From then on, the vision of a better world that China advanced to legitimize its leadership aspirations would always take as its reference point the unjust and exploitative ways of the West and define itself in opposition to them.

Ritual

Just like the crumbling of China's traditional world view, the end of the ritual order described in the previous chapter did not come suddenly but in several steps during the 'era of negotiation'. Japanese scholars have helpfully described China's acceptance of Western diplomatic norms as a process in three stages. In the late Qing, having at first insisted that relations with all foreigners no matter their origins were 'barbarian affairs' (*yiwu*) to be dealt with under traditional ritual customs, the imperial court was forced by the defeat in the Second Opium War to accept to treat imperial powers differently, ceasing to use the term 'barbarian' and granting them permanent representations in the capital, hence entering a period of 'oceanic affairs' (*yangwu*) (Motegi, 1997: 38–9). What was initially a concession, hopefully temporary and limited in scope, to threatening Westerners became a permanent necessity after the shock of China's defeat against Japan in 1894–5 and the following acceleration of foreign (especially Russian) encroachment on Chinese territory. This made the imperial court acutely aware of the precariousness of its position and of the need to Westernize, marking the beginning of the period of 'foreign affairs' (*waiwu*) and of reforms aiming to transform the Chinese state and diplomatic apparatus wholesale, including in relations with smaller neighbours like Korea (Okamoto, 2009: 173, 175).

Eventually, then, China and all East Asian states still free from colonial rule had to adopt the Western style of relations between nation states, bringing the ritual order as it existed in one form or another during the whole imperial era to an end. This does not mean that rituals themselves lost all relevance to Chinese political life, of course. Faced with the challenge of forging a national identity that could unite the Chinese people behind the new republican state after the Xinhai Revolution, its leaders focused on public ceremonies (state funerals, national day celebrations, and so on), etiquette, decorum, and attire – in brief, traditional aspects of *li* that were at the core of their cultural upbringing – which they sought to reimagine to support their vision of a new citizenry for a modern state (Harrison, 2000; Zarrow, 2001). In relations with surrounding polities as well, traditional concepts were repurposed to support the building of a modern nation state. While trying to negotiate its relationship with Outer Mongolia, which had declared its independence after the Revolution, Beijing had accepted to recognize its autonomy while insisting on keeping suzerainty over it, a suzerainty expressed through a title granted by the Chinese president to his Mongolian counterpart and through adoption of the Chinese calendar (Motegi, 2009: 52–3). A traditional ritual form had been repurposed for the modern aim of affirming China's territorial sovereignty over Mongolia.

Rituals remained deeply relevant to a modernizing China beyond those callbacks to tradition also for the simple reason that ceremonies, etiquette, and decorum are integral to the Western style of politics and diplomacy as well, even if their importance is less openly acknowledged or proactively fostered than it is, or at least was, in the Middle Kingdom. As scholars like Edmund Leach (1965), Ferdinand Mount (1972), or David Kertzer (1988) have pointed out, despite the common view in the West that rituals are mostly irrelevant to a model of government emphasizing the rational and detached management of state affairs, they are in fact ubiquitous and constitutive of political life there as well, from the minute procedures of cabinet meetings and parliamentary debates to the customary public celebrations during national and religious holidays, and to the carefully staged performances of politicians during electoral debates.[9]

---

[9] See also the essays in the second half of Wilentz (1985).

Rituals thus still played a visible and important role in the constitution of state authority and national unity in the West. Chinese reformers seeking to build a modern nation state and induce citizens to identify with it thus had a rich repertoire of customs to adapt and take inspiration from (Zarrow, 2001: 176). They quickly instituted national days to celebrate momentous events in the fall of the Qing and the founding of the republic, most notably the 'Double Ten' (10 October) anniversary of an uprising in Wuchang, Hebei province that was taken to mark the beginning of the Xinhai Revolution. On this occasion, a series of rituals both taken from the West – putting up flags and decorations meant to represent the nation, military parades – and inspired by imperial traditions – sacrifices to the martyrs of the Revolution – were conducted (Zarrow, 2001: 159–60). Those customs, however, reflected different values and rationales than the ones we described in previous chapters. The primary purpose of the rituals of modern nation states is to symbolize the ties that bind rulers and ruled together in a single entity and to confirm the legitimacy of the political process in the eyes of the people (Zarrow, 2001: 156). They certainly confirm the special status of social elites who are given pride of place in national celebrations, for instance, but are not primarily meant to represent an overall social hierarchy on a day-to-day basis or to signify individuals' acceptance of it.[10]

Modern diplomacy, though, is a realm where ritual rules are both particularly developed and deliberately linked to questions of rank and status, as the elaborate ceremonies marking state visits or the minutiae of diplomatic protocol show today still (Wood and Serres, 1970: 17–22; Balzacq, 2020: 115). It is no surprise that Western diplomats of the late 19th century were impressed by the swiftness with which Chinese (and Japanese) representatives grasped and expertly applied those rules in their dealings with them (Paine, 2003: 356). The Chinese ritual tradition made officials keenly attuned to foreign customs in matters of etiquette and decorum, and easily able to adapt to them. There is obviously much more to establishing a Western-style diplomatic system than adherence to protocol and etiquette, and China faced the considerable challenge of building a new bureaucratic apparatus and training a new corps of diplomats charged with the unfamiliar mission of permanently representing their country in foreign capitals (Kawashima, 2004: Ch. 1 and Ch. 2; 2012: 462–5; Hakoda, 2009; Lin Xuezhong, 2009: 243–9). Yet beyond those pragmatic matters,

---

[10] After the foundation of the PRC, the CCP continued to make great use of rituals, now based on communist ideology, to bind Chinese society together and reinforce its ties to the party. This is how Simon Leys sees, for instance, the periodic episodes of 'class struggle' against designated 'traitors' fed to the masses in the Maoist period. They were a form of purifying ritual to release whatever anger might have accumulated towards the party (Leys, 1999: 393).

the moral character and capability to respect the rules of propriety (that is, the adherence to *li*) of the prospective envoys to Western capitals was also a topic of much concern (Kim, 1979: 39). The Chinese envoys and intellectuals who first witnessed Western diplomacy in action in Europe had indeed been quick to note that a common ethics underpinned it, which allowed relations to be conducted in accordance with *li* (Lin Xuezhong, 2009: 212–3; Suzuki, 2009: 77).

At the time Chinese envoys encountered it, this Western *li* was starting to symbolize diplomatic equality between states in some respects while still being fundamentally unequal in others. The Congress of Vienna of 1815 had agreed on a 'Regulation on the Precedence of Diplomatic Agents' which standardized the treatment of diplomatic envoys of similar ranks – standards that are still upheld today – but had been unable to settle the issue of precedence among various types of polities like kingdoms, empires, and republics (Nahlik, 1984). It took until the mid-20th century for the principle of diplomatic equality of all states to be fully established. In the meantime, Chinese statesmen had become increasingly aware of their country's lowered status in international society.

This was due to their traditional attunement to ritual minutiae, but also to the contrast Chinese diplomats could not help but observe between how Westerners treated each other and how they behaved towards other people. The common ethics and respect for propriety that Chinese envoys observed among Europeans prevailed only on the continent, among states that accepted each other as equals (at least among great powers). Those same states looked down on the people of Asia, no matter how much they respected Western rules of propriety. The Chinese thus found Western diplomats coming to their shores 'domineering and troublesome', keen to prevail over their counterparts even if not by force of arms (Suzuki, 2009: 77–8). As for Chinese envoys to Western capitals, they were treated according to local customs but as envoys of lower ranks rather than the full ambassadors of the great powers (Hsü, 1960: 180–91). It was only in the 1930s that China, now an ally in the war against Japan, was allowed to exchange ambassadors with major Western states (Kinoshita 2009: 188, 194–5). Diplomacy was thus bound with questions of hierarchy, just like the 'unequal treaties' forced by imperial powers on China. Kawashima Shin points out the importance of one diplomatic event, the second Hague peace conference of 1907, in crystalizing the Chinese consciousness of their diminished international position, and making the revision of the unequal treaties an overriding policy objective.[11]

---

[11] This next section on the two Hague conferences is based on Kawashima, 2004: 228–30 and Kawashima (2006).

The first conference in 1899 had been China's first encounter with international society as a whole, and an occasion to realize that it faced certain expectations if it hoped to maintain its standing. Chinese diplomats had argued for signing conventions regulating behaviour in times of conflict and promoting peaceful resolutions despite doubts about their efficacy in order to avoid isolation and ensure invitation to the next conference. Having a seat at the table was indeed seen as an important status symbol, to be secured by following the international consensus. Similar status concerns inspired insistent requests by Chinese diplomats already in Europe for Beijing to send a special ambassador to the second Hague conference in 1907, just like other countries, on the grounds that the status of representatives in the Hague reflected their country's status in the world and that a proper ambassador would restore Chinese honour. Those demands swayed the court despite its initial irresponsiveness. China also agreed to pay a share of the expenses for the conference corresponding to that of Western great powers despite the poor financial state of the Qing court. Both the cost bearing and the dispatch of a special ambassador were seen as ways to ensure China a high status by coming to the conference with 'state gifts' fitting its station (in their correspondence with Beijing, Chinese diplomats employed the ancient term of 'jade and silk' (*yubo*) used in traditional ritual exchanges between rulers). They expressed great satisfaction at the fruits this strategy seemed to bear when their country obtained the honorary chairmanship of a committee.

This small victory was, however, accompanied by a development that stunned Chinese representatives, centring on the mandate of judges nominated by different countries to the proposed international court of arbitration. An American proposal (subsequently rejected) divided the length of said mandates in different groups, with established great powers receiving permanent seats and other countries non-permanent ones of ten, four, two, or one years. The fact that Chinese mandates were to be of only four years due to its 'inappropriate' legal system left a deep impression on its diplomats, who described their country as reduced to a 'third-class' status. The fact that China was bearing costs equal to that of a great power was invoked in vain.

Chinese delegates at the Hague conference thus had faith that their adoption of Western diplomatic norms and their symbolic demonstrations of prestige would be enough to solidify their international status. That Western states evaluated their country according to different criteria came as a great shock. This misunderstanding illustrates well the fact that 'compliance with international standards' meant something different for the two sides. For imperial China, participation in the ritual order meant adhering to its 'standard of behaviour', which included conformity with ritual norms and demonstrations of deference to the Son of Heaven but no stipulation about a polity's internal organization. Chinese diplomats in the Hague had expected to follow the same logic by adhering to Western diplomatic behavioural norms, but the Western 'standard of civilization' was something more, and did include firm expectations about the structure and operation of the state domestically.

This realization pushed Chinese delegates returning from the Hague to stress to their superiors the need to accelerate domestic reforms and to recover full sovereignty by revising the unequal treaties in order not only to 'save the country', but to recover its international status as well – a concern that endured into the republican era. The unequal treaties and the constraints they imposed on China thus came to be seen as a badge of shame, a symbol of its inferior position in international society. It was through concrete diplomatic interactions with other states that the Chinese elite had come to this realization. The shock of being looked down upon in those interactions became a strong propellant of domestic reforms. The second Hague conference thus confirmed that the preservation of China's international status would remain an important driver of its modern foreign policy in an international society that was still animated by questions of ranking and hierarchy, even if they were expressed in more subtle ways than in the ritual order.

This is most clearly visible in China's diplomatic strategy in the League of Nations. Even as the discourse of Chinese moral leadership in Asia was emerging in intellectual circles, diplomats used this new forum to try and present themselves in a more concrete manner as the continent's leaders in international society. When it came to determining the membership of the League Council, the Chinese representatives advocated for an apportionment of the non-permanent seats by region with one seat reserved for non-Western states, a seat that they argued China should receive as the natural 'representative of Asia'. They were clear that only their country deserved that status, offering no hint of support to other Asian states' candidacy and refusing to recognize Japan's special status as one of the great powers while explicitly arguing that, as 'the most important nation in the Continent of Asia, [China] ought to receive due attention from the League' so that '[her] international position and the privileges to which she is entitled shall be fully recognized' (Zhu Zhaoshen, delegate to the sixth Assembly of the League of Nations in 1925 and 1926, quoted in Kaufman, 2014: 624).

The initial Chinese success in being elected to the Council was praised at home as a great mark of 'international honour' that gave it 'the same rank as the great powers' (Kawashima, 2006: 28; Kaufman, 2014: 623). Despite later setbacks due to instability within China itself, its diplomats made persistent efforts to secure a spot on the Council, invoking not only the 'representative of Asia' argument, but also China's population, place at the centre of Asia, and ancient civilization (Kawashima, 2006: 29). They also maintained a pledge to bear a similar portion of the running costs of the League as that of the established great powers despite the heavy strain this placed on fragile public finances (Kawashima, 2004: 330).

China's diplomacy in the League thus offers a clear picture of what the political elite of the republican era believed their country's international status should be in the modern international society. Namely, they expected it to be recognized as the 'natural' leader of their own region and an equal to the Western great powers globally. The League offered in their eyes the perfect platform to make that point since it had an 'internal ranking system' in the form of the distinction between Assembly and Council and the allocation of cost bearing for the organization, which 'could symbolically indicate which countries were most important' (Kaufman, 2014: 622). This demonstrates again the importance that Chinese statesmen placed on such formal status markers as they adapted to new diplomatic customs.[12] Those markers were not as central to the practice of modern diplomacy as they were to traditional Chinese guest ritual, but that did not make them meaningless in Chinese eyes – far from it. The problem was that China had few means to convince other states to grant it the symbolic recognition that it thought it deserved due to its weakness and domestic divisions. This was an important part of the 'national humiliation' that the leaders of the PRC would in later decades strive to wash away.

Conclusion

China's troubled modern transition and forced entrance into the Eurocentric international society of the early 20th century undoubtedly brought fundamental changes to its view of the world and of its own place in it. Order was not something to be maintained anymore but rather to be achieved through a process of evolution from a grim present to a brighter, even utopian future only reachable through struggle against hostile outside forces; China lost its place at the centre of its own world and had to grapple with the meaning of the legal principle of sovereign equality for otherwise hierarchical inter-state relations; Confucianism was rejected as the dominant ideology to the benefit of nationalism and Marxism-Leninism; China had to adopt Western norms of diplomacy. Yet all those changes did not mean an abandonment of the core principles of the traditional hierarchical order as

---

[12] Another example of insistence on proper status markers, in a purely Asian context this time, is the Republican government refusal to sign a treaty with Thailand as long as the Thai king insisted on calling himself *huangdi*, which in Chinese can only mean emperor and was the traditional title of the Son of Heaven. The refusal to endorse such a title for the counterpart of the Chinese president underlines the continuing importance of the correct use of names in Chinese diplomacy, or rather, since the issue was just as important for Thailand, for Asian diplomacy in general (Kawashima, 2004: 393–9).

highlighted in the previous chapters of this book, but rather an adaptation of those principles to new realities, shaped by victimization at the hands of the Western imperial great powers, later joined by Japan.

The impact China's experience in this period had on its world view and its aspirations later on cannot be overstated. The beginning of the 20th century saw both the birth of Chinese communism and of the narrative of national humiliation, of course, but also, more narrowly related to our study, laid the groundwork for China's vision of hierarchical order for the modern world. China would lead the struggle against the unjust Western domination of international society, eventually bringing about the establishment of a new order to replace the flawed existing one. In this new order, China, as overseer of Asia, would behave better than the other great powers and pledge true respect for the legal right to equality of sovereign states in exchange for recognition of its superior status. The country's imperial past was idealized and invoked to reinforce the argument that China was and remained uniquely virtuous.

China also quickly understood that behind the façade of equality that Western diplomatic rituals were meant to maintain, symbolic signifiers of ranking and relative position were still omnipresent in the structure of international forums and in informal and unwritten norms of behaviour through which diplomats made clear how highly or lowly they considered their counterparts. Chinese diplomats of the republican period and later under the PRC would consistently seek to use those features to their advantage, even if with limited success initially. Finally, the experience of foreign encroachment, territorial losses, and humiliation transformed the search for wealth and power to sustain China's desired international status into an enduring obsession. The next three chapters will show how those lessons animate its diplomacy towards Asia today.

5

The Pursuit of a Hierarchical Order in the People's Republic of China

The China ruled over by General Secretary of the CCP Xi Jinping since 2012 has come a long way from the divisions and weakness of the early 20th century. It is now recognized by all as an up-and-coming superpower capable of rivalling the US and putting its mark on international order. It seems eager to do so, especially in Asia, its immediate surrounding which it often calls its 'periphery' (*zhoubian*). In this chapter and the two following ones, we will examine how the traditional ideal of hierarchical order outlined earlier in this book, in the transformed shape it took during China's encounter with the modern society of nation states, continues to impact the country's foreign policy in Asia to this day. We will focus mainly on the contemporary period dominated by the figure of Xi Jinping, but will also trace back some of the features of China's vision for order today to their origins in earlier periods of the history of the People's Republic, namely the Maoist period (1949–1978) and the 30 years following the beginning of reform and opening under the leadership of Deng Xiaoping (1979–2008).

There is close to a consensus among analysts on this threefold division of the history of the PRC. This is certainly how Xi Jinping himself wishes to portray his country's trajectory. He presents himself as the most transformative Chinese leader since Deng Xiaoping at least, and promotes his own 'thought on socialism with Chinese characteristics for a new era' (*xin shidai Zhongguo tese shihui zhuyi sixiang*) accompanied by a new 'principal contradiction' to succeed that of the reform era, in conformity with the CCP's Marxist ideological framework.[1] Considering the CCP's determination to shape the

---

[1] That new contradiction is between 'unbalanced and inadequate development and the people's ever-growing needs for a better life', succeeding to 'proletariat versus bourgeoisie' in the Maoist era and 'the ever-growing material and cultural needs of the people versus backward social production' during reform and opening.

narrative of China's 'road to rejuvenation'[2] under its leadership, the official line advanced by the General Secretary and his team carries significant weight.

Many outside observers have in fact adopted similar demarcation lines between the era dominated by Mao Zedong, that launched by Deng Xiaoping and the current one (for example, Amako, 2014; Economy, 2018; Minzner, 2018). Although, as we have argued in the introduction to this book, the shift to a 'new situation' became manifest in 2009 already – the transition to 'reform and opening' similarly occurred over a number of years – this basic division between a Mao, Deng, and Xi period does reflect major shifts in China's guiding foreign policy strategy and we will adopt it here.

In many ways, the successive generations of PRC leaders remained consistent in their ambitions to order Asia on their terms, but the Xi Jinping period stands out for the determination with which those ambitions have been pursued. To examine in detail how Xi is building on traditional ideas to do so, we will examine in turn different elements of the ideal type of hierarchical order elaborated in Chapter 2. The first elements to be discussed are the two most fundamental ones, namely, the Chinese preoccupation with the establishment and maintenance of order and the belief that said order cannot be kept stable if it does not reflect the natural inequalities among people, or nations. This is the topic of this chapter, while the next one will focus on the matters of morality and ritual that are perhaps most characteristic of China's vision of order. Chapter 7 will finally discuss the PRC's use of the three traditional tools of rulership we identified earlier.

In the pages that follow, then, we will examine how Mao and his successors progressively reconciled themselves to an international order that, like the statesmen of the late imperial and republican period before them, they saw as unjust and deeply flawed. International relations were in their eyes an arena of power competition where the strong dominated and exploited the weak; yet they actively engaged in this competition even as they denounced it, and sought to climb the international hierarchy of power both to secure China from foreign threats and to increase the country's international status. Now that China's power and prominent role in international affairs is universally recognized, Xi Jinping still calls for major reforms to international order but also likes to present his country as its guardian and defender. How much he would actually like this order to change is a topic of much debate, but his determination to secure China's elevated status within it and to push smaller states to recognize their inferior position and behave accordingly is beyond doubt.

---

[2] *Fuxing zhi lu*, the name of the flagship permanent exhibition on the history of modern China at the National Museum in Beijing, which Xi Jinping made a point to visit as his first public act after taking office.

Ambivalent revolutionary and leader of the Third World

Mao Zedong remained a revolutionary at heart even after the founding of the PRC in 1949. He built on the modern Chinese understanding of international society examined in the previous chapter, seeing it as an arena of power competition rather than orderly inter-state relations where violence (either physical or structural through economic exploitation) would remain the norm as long as the capitalist countries imposed their domination on others (Kim, 1979: 65–6). In this sense, true international order did not exist in his eyes and a revolution to overthrow the existing hierarchy of power and privilege was necessary to achieve something more just and peaceful.

The Maoist era is accordingly often described as one of revolutionary diplomacy and this is certainly true at least in part, but in fact China's support for revolutionary movements abroad was only selective and varied in intensity over time. Already during Mao's lifetime, some scholars like Peter Van Ness pointed out that hostility or friendliness towards Beijing was much more predictive of Chinese support for revolution in a given state than its domestic situation (1970: Ch. 6). Similarly, Michael Leifer concluded from his examination of the PRC's activities in South-East Asia in the 1960s and early 1970s that it was in fact seeking to combat US influence in states aligned with the West while maintaining stable ties with more neutral or friendly ones, regardless of their domestic political model (1974: 82–7).[3] More recent works with better access to primary sources like archives and the memoirs of participants in the events of this period have emphasized variously China's revolutionary zeal (Garver, 2016: Ch. 8), its rivalry with the US for influence (Brazinsky, 2017), and its pragmatic search for security through the maintenance of a balance of power between the various political forces shaping its surroundings (Khan, 2018: 70 ff.). Those different motivations are not incompatible with one another, and it is in any case not our aim here to determine which of them best explains various policies of the Maoist era. Suffice to say that if China indeed at times supported revolutionary movements in its near abroad – most intensely in Vietnam, Laos, and Cambodia – this did not define its foreign policy wholesale.

The selectiveness of China's revolutionary fervour abroad thus left a gap in many cases between its diplomacy and Mao's calls to fight imperialism and reshape the world, a gap that was quickly filled by the Five Principles of Peaceful Coexistence. First enounced in their definitive form in the

---

[3] The period of the Cultural Revolution was an exception and led to serious disruptions even in relations with theretofore friendly countries like Myanmar and Cambodia (see Robinson, 1991: 241–4).

Sino–Indian Trade Agreement of 1954 on suggestion of Chinese Premier Zhou Enlai,[4] the Five Principles (mutual respect of territorial integrity and sovereignty, non-aggression; non-interference in internal affairs; equality and mutual benefit; peaceful coexistence) were embraced by the PRC as the guideline of its foreign policy towards states that were neither firmly aligned with the US nor part of the socialist camp. While the former were considered legitimate targets for revolutionary struggle and the latter brothers in this struggle, China was pledging to seek an equal and peaceful relation with all states outside of those two groups. In practice, then, while some national liberation movements in Asia (as well as Latin America and Africa) benefited from China's revolutionary assistance, especially in the early 1950s and in the mid-to-late 1960s, peaceful coexistence and diplomatic comity was advocated towards an ever-larger number of countries (Kim, 1979: 70–1).[5] In that sense, an embrace of international order and stability progressively took over China's initial revolutionary zeal (the early years of the Cultural Revolution being a significant bump along the way).

This evolution did not mean, though, that Mao and his colleagues had revised their view that international society was a locus of power competition organized as a hierarchy based on raw strength and exploitation of the weak by the strong. Their position in this environment was not advantageous. Theirs was, as Samuel Kim puts it, 'an underdog perspective from below, struggling to redefine the basic values and rules of the game in the international system' (1979: 92). Despite this precarious situation, the Chinese maintained their self-image as major players on the world stage and as the natural leaders of Asia. Taking on that role meant 'playing the game' of power competition, something that PRC leaders were clearly eager to do. Mao was in fact obsessed with surpassing the United Kingdom (UK) and eventually overcoming the US to become the world's foremost power, repeatedly making unrealistic plans to do so (Wang Fei-ling, 2017: 201). Even within the socialist camp, he bragged during the Great Leap Forward that an explosion in Chinese production of steel and grain would allow the country to create a land of plenty and enter communism before the Soviet Union (Lüthi, 2008: 90). He had more immediate ambitions as well, focused on Asia.

Mao had long embraced the idea that China was the natural overseer of the region. A textbook he co-authored in 1939 lamented that imperial powers had 'occupied many neighbouring countries formerly under [China's]

---

[4] On the origins of the Five Principles before that agreement, see Hsiung, 1972: 32–3; Brazinsky, 2017: 77–8.

[5] See Kim, 1979: 511–2 for a helpful chronological list of all the countries the PRC had entered diplomatic relations with by the time of Mao's death.

protection'.[6] His and his colleagues' perceptions of those countries in the early days of the PRC were fairly condescending. As Steven Levine writes, they viewed 'the countries of Asia – with the exception of modernized Japan – as either backward, subservient, or burdened with outmoded social and political systems in dire need of change. At best, Asia [was] the potential setting for a revolutionary transmutation in which China might play a catalytic role' (Levine, 1984: 111). Mao in fact did early on seek an understanding with Stalin to take prime responsibility for leading the revolutionary struggle in its neighbourhood, even if, as we noted previously, China's revolutionary activism turned out to be quite selective (Chen Jian, 2001: 120; see Shi and Chen, 1993 for a direct account of those discussions).

That Mao had to consult Stalin regarding leadership of the revolution in Asia was a result of the PRC's initial decision to 'lean to one side' by accepting the Soviet Union's assistance and acknowledging its top position in the world socialist movement. That attitude changed after the death of Stalin, however, opening a period of ambivalence about Soviet leadership.[7] On one hand, Chinese leaders voiced open doubts about the ideological stance of their allies, criticizing Secretary General Nikita Khrushchev's attempts to renege on the heritage of Stalin and his weakening resolve in the face of US imperialism. The CCP hence began to present itself as an alternative centre for the communist movement, the true guardian of the spirit of Marxism-Leninism, and the only one ready to support the world's anti-imperialist forces. On the other hand, though, Chinese leaders reaffirmed on multiple occasions that only the Soviet Union had the power to lead the socialist camp. As Mao himself put it in a speech during an important international congress convened in Moscow in November 1957, 'the socialist camp must have one head, and that head can only be the USSR' (quoted in Garver, 2016: 799).

This ambivalent attitude is revealing of the Chinese concern with order and hierarchy. To maintain the stability and the solidity of the communist movement, and to more effectively work to change an unjust international order, one state needed to lead the way while others followed. China quickly aspired to be that state – starting in 1956 at the latest (Lüthi, 2008: 62–3; Pantsov and Levine, 2012: 444) – but begrudgingly acknowledged its own weakness and thus continued to support the Soviet Union taking the role

---

[6] In 'The Chinese Revolution and the Chinese Communist Party', December 1939. Text available at www.marxists.org/reference/archive/mao/selected-works/volume-2/mswv2_23.htm#p1. An earlier version of the textbook actually talked more plainly of imperialists forcibly taking a large number of 'states tributary to China' (Schram, 1969: 375).

[7] The various events of these turbulent few years and the ups and downs of Sino–Soviet relations are well documented in Lüthi, 2008; Li and Xia, 2008; Pantsov and Levine, 2012: Ch. 29; Friedman, 2015: Ch. 1 and Ch. 2; Garver, 2016: Ch. 5.

instead despite its qualms. All the while it sought to gain power and to demonstrate its influence over the policies adopted by Moscow (Lüthi, 2008: 111–2; Garver, 2016: 122, 128).

The PRC's dissatisfaction with Soviet leadership only worsened, though, and the openness of its ambition to replace Moscow as the centre of the struggle against imperialism and colonialism grew accordingly. It made active efforts to create a subgroup within international society, composed of Asian and African states, where it could claim a dominant position and be recognized as leader in the fight against the predations of both the Soviet Union and the US (Suzuki, 2017: 230–5). This ambition reached its paroxysm during the Cultural Revolution, when Mao claimed the mantle of great helmsman of the communist movement and of true inheritor of the mission of world revolution and liberation of the non-Western world.

After that fever had subsided, China's leadership aspirations were redefined to become more inclusive. China's belated admission to the UN in 1971 was the occasion to forcefully state its ambition of leading the opposition from non-Western states against the 'imperialism and hegemonism' of the two superpowers that, in its telling, dominated international society through brute force. This was the role advocated by Deng Xiaoping in a prominent speech at the UN General Assembly in 1974, when he expounded on the 'three worlds theory' presented a few months earlier by Mao and posed as the spokesman for the aspirations of the oppressed 'Third World' (developing countries) to convince the 'Second World' (the industrialized nations) to support their cause and oppose the 'First World' (the two superpowers).[8] China even talked of its veto in the UN Security Council as the 'Third World veto' (Friedman, 2015: 198).

The PRC thus demonstrated a continued conviction that a leader was needed to advance the cause of justice in international society and that it should be the one to take on that mission. The limited means at its disposal did not temper its ambitions. The role of leader of the 'Third World' is in fact one that the Chinese statesmen of today continue to embrace, even if the term itself has fallen out of fashion. This is the most prominent legacy of the initial period of PRC history when it comes to order and hierarchy. China's revolutionary zeal under Mao's leadership, selective though it was, is now a thing of the past and his appetite for continuous disruption remains something of an aberration among modern Chinese leaders. In his understanding that the existing international order was a nefarious sort of hierarchy based on raw power and exploitation, however, and that the better order he sought to create would be a gentler sort of hierarchy where China

---

[8] Text of the speech at www.marxists.org/reference/archive/deng-xiaoping/1974/04/10.htm.

would regain a central place on the world stage, Mao was squarely within the Chinese mainstream. There is no 'socialist camp' in which China could claim leadership anymore, and the term 'imperialism' has largely disappeared from the Chinese vocabulary, but the idea that China is the natural leader of non-Western states, spearheading efforts to diminish the nefarious domination of the US and its Western allies, has endured.

Climbing the hierarchy of power and gaining followers

Deng Xiaoping built on and completed the stabilization of China's foreign relations that had started in the early 1970s, adopting an accommodative attitude towards the West and Japan and improving relations with other neighbours in order to guarantee a benign environment for growth and development at home. China committed to the maintenance of international order, with the clear understanding that adhering to its standards was an expedient means to obtain the wealth and power necessary to again be fully in control of its own destiny (Zhang Yongjin, 1998: 106). This did not mean it had abandoned its chosen role as leader of the Third World in the quest for international justice. In his work report at the sixth National People's Congress in June 1983, Premier Zhao Ziyang spoke of a 'sacred duty' (*shensheng yiwu*) to support the struggle of Third World countries to defend their rights and advocated for the establishment of a 'New International Economic Order' (*guoji jingji xin zhixu*) more to the advantage of non-Western states.[9] Reform and opening had thus led to a moderation of language but not to a rethink of China's leadership claims. In fact, to boost these claims, the CCP launched a revision of the official history of the Second World War, aiming to depict China as a key actor in the defeat of Japan and the founding of the post-war order – and rehabilitating the record of the then-ruling Nationalist Party in the process (Mitter, 2020: 215 ff.).

China's rulers were, however, more realistic than in previous decades about the mismatch between their country's weakness and its ambitions, hence the focus on economic development at home. In a 1984 speech to a Party commission, for instance, Deng expressed his hope that, once its economy had quadrupled in size, 'China will be truly powerful, exerting a much greater influence in the world. That's why we have to work hard' (Deng Xiaoping, 1994: 70). The successive shocks of the Tiananmen incident and

---

[9] Zhao Ziyang, '1983年政府工作报告' [1983 Government Work Report], 6 June 1983. Text available at www.gov.cn/test/2006-02/16/content_200823.htm. The 'New International Economic Order' was originally a set of proposals for a more equitable international economic system advanced by developing countries in the UN in the 1970s, and endorsed by China.

the fall of the Soviet Union gave the CCP even more pause and led to the decision to 'keep a low profile' for the time being. In December 1990, as China was internationally isolated following Tiananmen and as the Soviet Union was falling apart following the fall of the Berlin Wall, Deng asserted in a talk with members of the CCP Central Committee that China 'absolutely cannot [become the leader of the Third World] – this is one of our basic state policies. We can't afford to do it and besides, we aren't strong enough' (Deng Xiaoping, 1994: 350). Even if Deng went on to pledge that China would 'never' seek leadership, the way he framed his rejection in terms of insufficient means and power suggested that this stance could be reconsidered if and when the country had successfully developed. Perhaps in preparation for that day, China renewed its cooperation with the G77, the largest group of developing countries at the UN, but made sure to stay apart (and above) the rest of its members by not formally joining it and insisting on issuing joint statements and holding meetings as 'the G77 and China'.[10]

Deng was not alone in linking the adoption of a modest stance on the international stage with an evaluation of the prevailing balance of power. Speaking in 1998 to assembled Chinese ambassadors in Beijing, General Secretary Jiang Zemin followed his exhortation to 'keep a low profile' and to focus on development with the remark that 'China's national conditions and the international balance of power determine that this is what we must do'.[11] By then, the scale of China's 'economic miracle' was starting to become apparent, as was the understanding that development was first and foremost the means for China to recover its rightful place among the world's great powers. In a book published in 1997, a group of well-connected scholars argued that 'a rising China will never be a nation that is satisfied with only food and shelter' and that it should enjoy 'a position as an irreplaceable major world power'.[12]

In accordance with the spirit of 'seeking truth from fact' (*shishi qiushi*, Deng's favourite idiom), Chinese policy makers and scholars in fact sought to measure the pace and trajectory of their country's rise and of the accompanying changes in the international pyramid of power. A desire to accurately assess the prevailing 'international structure' (*guoji geju*) is another prominent feature of the reform and opening period. The concept of 'international structure', omnipresent in Chinese writings about world affairs,

---

[10] Ministry of Foreign Affairs, '七十七国集团' [Group of 77], www.fmprc.gov.cn/web/wjb_673085/zzjg_673183/gjjjs_674249/gjzzyhygk_674253/qsqg_674549/gk_674551/.

[11] In Jiang Zemin, 'Speech to the Ninth Ambassadors Meeting' (江澤民：在第九次駐外使節会議上講話), 28 August 1998 (Jiang Zemin, 2006: 202).

[12] Wen Jieming et al (eds), *Chatting with the General Secretary* (翁杰明等編：於總書記談心), 70 and 233, quoted in Wang Fei-ling, 1999: 24.

'refers to [their] understanding of the international power configuration' and reflects a preoccupation with China's position relative to other major powers, especially those at the top of the international pyramid (Zhu Liqun, 2010: 18; see also Zhou Fangyin, 2017).

Chinese scholars started to argue in the early 1980s already that, now that their country was focusing squarely on the task of acquiring wealth and power, ways needed to be found to rationally evaluate its progress (Pillsbury, 2000: 210–1). This eventually evolved in the concept, widely used and researched from the 1990s onwards, of 'comprehensive national power' (*zonghe guoli*). This concept was meant to reflect calculations of a given country's strengths and weaknesses through a range of qualitative and quantitative indicators and to allow comparison between states to 'scientifically' determine the shape of the prevailing international power structure (Pillsbury, 2000: 203–5; see also Chan, 1999: 30–3; Zheng Yongnian, 1999: 114–22; Yan Xuetong, 2006; Chuwattananurak, 2016: 2–7). The obsession with 'comprehensive national power' confirmed the widely shared understanding that China was pursuing modernization in order to climb the ranks of a hierarchy dominated by the West (see, for instance, Huang Shuofeng, 1992: 299–304). This also implied that China's neighbours outside of Japan did not really factor in Chinese power calculations, and its superiority was assumed as a given. Discussions of China's response to potential regional wars were focused on how to respond to a US or Russian intervention, while neighbouring forces themselves were not considered a challenge worth much thought (Pillsbury, 2000: 280).

The thorough study of comprehensive national power was but one sign of China's obsession with its 'international status' (*guoji diwei*). As Deng Yong writes:

> Chinese officials and analysts alike have, since the mid-1990s, evoked 'international status' ... as if it were the most desirable value, the one that leads to power, security, and respect. Judging by the frequency of the term's use in official Chinese discourse and scholarly analyses, the PRC may very well be the most status-conscious country in the world. (2008: 8)

Indeed, the term 'international status' was used several times by Jiang Zemin and his successor Hu Jintao in their five-yearly work reports to the National Party Congress (in 1997 and 2002, and 2007 and 2012 respectively), as well as by Xi Jinping in 2017.[13] Reflecting this heightened awareness, a group

---

[13] Jiang Zemin, '高举邓小平理论伟大旗帜 把建设有中国特色社会主义事业全面推向二十一世纪' [Hold High the Great Banner of Deng Xiaoping Theory for the All-Round Advancement of the Cause of Building Socialism with Chinese Characteristics

of scholars at the Shanghai Academy of Social Sciences has, since 2003, published an annual 'report on China's international status'.

Chinese efforts to raise its international status after the end of the Cold War were at first largely targeted at Asia. Following the 1997 Asian financial crisis, China engaged in a veritable charm offensive towards its neighbours. This included notably forging a 'partnership of good neighbourliness and mutual trust' with the Association of South-East Asian Nations (ASEAN), supporting the creation of an ASEAN+3 mechanism with South Korea and Japan and of a multilateral currency swap arrangement (the so-called Chiang Mai initiative), proposing and concluding a China–ASEAN free trade agreement, and acceding to the Treaty of Amity and Cooperation, one of the founding texts of ASEAN. China even signed on to a declaration pledging self-restraint and cooperation in the South China Sea, where territorial disputes had remained a recurring source of tensions. In other parts of its neighbourhood, it also recruited Central Asian states and Russia to formally establish the Shanghai Cooperation Organization (SCO) after several years of less institutionalized dialogue and proposed and convened six party talks on North Korea's nuclear programme.[14]

Many have highlighted the various strategic objectives behind this engagement policy, such as combating the perception of China as a threat in the region, forestalling any attempt from the US to recruit neighbours for a return to Cold War style containment, guaranteeing a peaceful environment for China's rise, responding to the growing interdependence of regional states within a globalizing economy, or boosting domestic economic growth,

---

to the 21st Century], 12 September 1997, www.gov.cn/test/2007-08/29/content_730 614.htm; Jiang Zemin, '全面建设小康社会 开创中国特色社会主义事业新局面' [Build a Well-off Society in an All-Round Way and Open a New Phase in the Project of Socialism with Chinese Characteristics], 8 November 2002, www.fmprc.gov.cn/ce/cech/chn/xwss/t115277.htm; Hu Jintao, '高举中国特色社会主义伟大旗帜 为夺取全面建设小康社会新胜利而奋斗' [Hold High the Great Banner of Socialism with Chinese Characteristics and Strive for New Victories in Building a Moderately Prosperous Society in All Respects], 15 October 2007, www.gov.cn/ldhd/2007-10/24/content_785431.htm; Hu Jintao, '坚定不移沿着中国特色社会主义道路前进 为全面建成小康社会而奋斗' [Firmly March on the Path of Socialism with Chinese Characteristics and Strive for a Moderately Prosperous Society in All Respects], 19 November 2012, http://cpc.people.com.cn/n/2012/1118/c64094-19612151.html; Xi Jinping, '哈决胜全面建成小康社会 夺取新时代中国特色社会主义伟大胜' [Secure a Decisive Victory in Building a Moderately Prosperous Society in All Respects and Strive for the Great Success of Socialism with Chinese Characteristics for a New Era], 18 October 2017, www.gov.cn/zhuanti/2017-10/27/content_5234876.htm.

[14] For a fuller account of China's more active posture in Asia in the early 2000s, see Shambaugh, 2004/05: 72–89. The reasons behind this turn towards an active posture have much to do with some positive diplomatic interactions with neighbours in the 1990s, and will be discussed in the next chapter.

especially in underdeveloped western and south-western provinces (for example, Takahara, 2004: 23–4; Shambaugh, 2004/05: 71; Foot 2005: 144–52; Goldstein, 2005: 119–28; Zhang Yunling and Tang Shiping, 2005: 52–4; Deng, 2008: 234–8; Goh, 2013b: 57). As several Chinese scholars pointed out, though, a proactive regional diplomacy was also a means for the PRC to demonstrate it could be a responsible great power by fostering regional stability and cohesion, with the aim to obtain the support of its neighbours in its quest to raise its status on the global stage (Men Honghua, 2001: 187; Pang Zhongying, 2001: 33, 35; Xiao Huarong, 2003: 48–49; Wang Yizhou, 2007: 113, 235). Hu Jintao himself on two occasions urged the building of 'peripheral geostrategic support' (*zhoubian diyuan zhanlue yituo*), thus explicitly evoking the need to unite the 'periphery' behind China in its quest for international influence.[15]

As China's assessment of its international status became more confident and positive due, on one hand, to the rapid economic development that attracted the attention and admiration of the world in the 2000s and, on the other, to the success of its efforts to engage Asia, its leaders and intellectuals became more serious about advancing a Chinese vision of international order. Most notably, Hu Jintao proposed in 2005 the concept of 'harmonious world' (*hexie shijie*).[16] In many respects, he was building on ideas advanced by previous generations of leaders – including the advocacy for a 'new international political and economic order' – and going all the way back to the Five Principles of Peaceful Coexistence. Yet the 'harmonious world' was still notable in its global scope and its emphasis on dialogue and mutual learning among different civilizations, implying the Chinese one was not only equal to that of the West, but had something to teach others, too.

In retrospect, some Chinese scholars described the articulation of this more ambitious vision as the moment where the PRC acted to 'take the initiative' and to assume great power responsibility by spreading Chinese peaceful cultural values (Sun and Luan, 2013: 25). To go along with the official sloganeering, prominent voices in the academic world made growing efforts to flesh out a Chinese vision of world order based on its own traditions (Lynch, 2009: 95–101; Callahan, 2011: 2–3; Nordin, 2016: 35–53). By the late 2000s, then, the Chinese discourse about international order had become more ambitious to reflect the country's growing power. This was in line with

---

[15] The formulation was included in a speech at a Central Diplomatic Work Conference in August 2006 (Hu Jintao, 2016: 510) and at the 11th Conference of Chinese Diplomatic Envoys in July 2009 (summary available at www.china-embassy.or.jp/chn//zgxw/t574 326.htm).

[16] The concept was outlined in a White Paper on 'China's peaceful development road' published in December 2005, available at www.china.org.cn/english/2005/Dec/152 669.htm.

the logic of the reform and opening era. Whereas the Maoist era saw an unrealistic claim to be the vanguard of a worldwide revolt against an unjust world regardless of China's weakness, the post-1978 period emphasized the rational assessment of China's international position as the basis for decisions about how assertively it should advocate for reforms of international order. Seen from that perspective, Xi Jinping's move away from 'keeping a low profile' and his open ambitions for an even stronger China do not seem like such a break with the past.

Recovering China's 'rightful place' in the Xi Jinping period

Signs that China would be shifting towards a more assertive international posture were evident before Xi Jinping became General Secretary in September 2012, then. We may recall from the introduction of this book that 2009 marks a turning point of sort with the declaration of a 'new situation', where China is better placed to compete with the West than it used to be. Xi's accession to power undoubtedly confirmed and accelerated the shift away from 'keeping a low profile', though, as he replaced that posture with one of 'striving for achievements' (*fenfa youwei*) (Yan Xuetong, 2014). While the speed and intensity of this shift may have taken some party elders by surprise, it should be assumed that they knew what kind of leader Xi aspired to be before endorsing him. As Andrew Nathan and Andrew Scobell note, their choice 'signalled the intention to give China a more assertive international voice' from the start (Nathan and Scobell, 2012: 61).

This intention, as just noted, is born of the experience of China's rise and of the resulting power shift. China now has both the material capabilities to proactively reshape its environment – after more than 30 years of rapid economic growth, China's Gross Domestic Product and military expenditures are the world's second largest and its technological base is increasingly sophisticated – and the confidence to do so. The aforementioned declaration of the 'new situation' in 2009 already emphasized a favourable change in the international balance of power. The perception that the current period is one of great opportunities due to China's growing power and Western decline only solidified over the following years. Eight years later at the 19th Party Congress in October 2017, Xi Jinping proudly declared that the Chinese nation 'has stood up, grown rich, and is becoming strong' and used the terms 'strong country' (*qiangguo*) 19 times.[17] At a Diplomatic Work

---

[17] Xi Jinping, 'Secure a decisive victory in building a moderately prosperous society in all Respects and strive for the great success of socialism with Chinese characteristics for a new era', 18 October 2017, www.xinhuanet.com/english/special/2017-11/03/c_136725 942.htm.

Conference eight months later, he further noted that China was in its best period of development in modern times while the world was in its biggest period of change in a hundred years, and that those two trends were fuelling each other.[18] Power dynamics being central to China's understanding of the modern international society, this assessment provides the basis for a more assertive foreign policy (Yamaguchi, 2016: 66, 71).

In China's view, then, now that it is nearing the top of the global hierarchy of power, it can unabashedly conduct a 'major country diplomacy with Chinese characteristics' (*Zhongguo tese daguo waijiao*) that sees the country 'moving closer to centre stage and making greater contributions to mankind'.[19] China still describes itself as one of several 'poles' in a multipolar international system. For instance, a White Paper on China's stance towards 'Asia-Pacific security cooperation' lists five 'major countries' in the region, namely, India, Japan, and Russia, as well as the US and China itself.[20] In practice and in China's domestic discourse, though, one defining feature of the 'major country diplomacy with Chinese characteristics' in Xi Jinping's new era seems to be a growing focus on the US as the only other acknowledged great power.[21] Some Chinese scholars have also talked of a switch from 'one super[power], several strong [powers]' (*yichao duoqiang*) – the post-Cold War structure dominated by the US with several major players below it – to a bipolar international structure of 'two super[powers], several strong [powers]' (*liangchao duoqiang*) (Yan Xuetong, 2011b; 2015b; Jin Canrong, 2017b). With the US, China is therefore seeking an equal relationship, as seen in its advocacy of a 'new type of great power relationship' featuring 'mutual

---

[18] '习近平：努力开创中国特色大国外交新局面' [Xi Jinping: Striving to open a new phase in great power diplomacy with Chinese characteristics], *Xinhua Online*, 23 June 2018.

[19] Xi Jinping, 'Secure a decisive victory in building a moderately prosperous society'.

[20] China's State Council Information Office, 'China's policies on Asia-Pacific security cooperation', January 2017, www.xinhuanet.com/english/china/2017-01/11/c_135973 695.htm.

[21] Interview with a senior professor at Peking University, Beijing, 13 March 2018. See also Zeng and Breslin, 2016; Zeng Jinghan, 2017. Russia also has a special place in official talks of great power relations because, although the balance of power between it and China is increasingly unequal in the latter's favour, their cordial relationship has long been used by Beijing as a model for others, dating back to the mid-1990s. It is still doing so now, presenting the relationship as the model for the equal 'new type of great power relationship' that it seeks with the US. Dai Bingguo, a former high-ranking diplomat, explicitly said so at a commemorative event in 2016 (see 張光政 [Zhang Guangzheng] '中俄关系是新型大国关系的典范' [Sino–Russian relations are the model for the new type of great power relations], *People's Daily Online*, 8 June 2016). China has accordingly sought to avoid open frictions and has accommodated Russia's interests in their bilateral relation (Charap, Drannan, and Noël, 2017). It, however, has no qualms in exploiting its superior capabilities to increase its economic and political imprint in Central Asia at Russia's expense (Wilson, 2021).

respect' (Li Cheng and Lucy Xu, 2014). There is, furthermore, growing confidence in the country that the favourable trends identified by Xi Jinping are set to extend into the next decades, allowing China to eventually surpass a declining America and reach the top of the international pyramid of power (Doshi, 2021: 271–2).

Regardless of the consequences this would have for China's relation with the US, the country is already open about its ambition to assume leadership in international society. Xi said as much in a speech in 2017, enjoining China to 'lead' (*yindao*) in creating a more just international order and in preserving international security and stability.[22] Xi's understanding of international order shows much continuity with his predecessors, but now emphasizes China's status as a 'responsible great power' ready to take up custodial duties and propose reforms. His stated goal is to reinforce existing organizations and mechanisms – mostly by increasing the voice of developing countries and diminishing those of developed ones to arrive at a more 'just' and sustainable repartition of power and global resources – and not to replace or destroy them. The new structures China has endorsed or created – the Asia Infrastructure Investment Bank and the New Development Bank associated with the Brazil, Russia, India, China, and South Africa (BRICS) grouping – are similarly depicted as supplements to existing organizations rather than competitors, aiming to contribute to the needed rebalancing of influence away from the West (Cheng, 2018: 116). In fact, Xi and other senior officials have repeatedly described China as a 'protector of international order' (*guoji zhixu de weihuzhe*). This was even before the start of the presidency of Donald Trump, whose disregard for international norms and aggressive posture towards the rest of international society allowed China to draw an even sharper distinction between the 'hegemonism' of the US and its own proclaimed determination to support international order.[23]

Considering China's supportive attitude towards the UN – with the notable exception of any initiative focusing on the promotion of democracy and human rights[24] – the International Monetary Fund, the World Trade

---

[22] '习近平首提 '两个引导' 有深意' [The 'two leaderships' put forward by President Xi Jinping have deep meaning], *Studying China*, 21 February 2017.

[23] This argument was made by Xi in a speech at the World Economic Forum in Davos in January 2017 and repeated many times by other Chinese leaders and by state media. Trump's loss after four years did nothing to change this message. For the original, see 'Full Text of Xi Jinping keynote at the World Economic Forum', *CGTN*, 17 January 2017.

[24] China does not reject engagement on these issues within the UN framework, but works hard to control the agenda of organs dedicated to them, most prominently the Human Rights Council, and to redefine the meaning of 'democracy' and 'human rights' in a way that includes its 'democratic dictatorship' and 'developmental rights' while de-emphasizing liberal meanings (Foot, 2017; Worden, 2020).

Organization, and other organs in which international order is embodied – it is evident that the experience of the reform and opening period has convinced China that, even though it had no say in shaping the existing order, it could advocate its vision of international justice from within and aim for evolution rather than for radical change. As Zhao Suisheng (2018) puts it, the reforms that it pursues are meant to raise its own position further and gain greater influence on global governance issues rather than altering the fundamental rules of the game.

Those fundamental rules anyway already include the principle that large countries should have a disproportionate say in the management of international affairs, a principle that China unsurprisingly fully endorses. The PRC does consistently say it opposes exclusive 'clubs' and 'cliques' such as the G7 or the 'quad' between Japan, the US, India, and Australia, but only, it seems, when it is not itself a member. In fact, through the embrace of its rights as one of the five permanent members of the UN Security Council and through its active promotion of other groupings such as the G20 and the BRICS, both created after the 2008 financial crisis, China continues to demonstrate that it prefers ' "essentially hierarchical and exclusionary" and "power-centred" forums for global governance ... in negotiating for change' (Zhang Yongjin 2016: 815). There is, however, no indication that China seeks to replace such mechanisms with ones that would affirm its domination. Even scholars seeking to imagine a new 'Chinese order' (*zhonghua zhixu*) combining Chinese traditions and modern norms end up endorsing the idea that, even if China reaches a hegemonic position, it would continue to work as part of a concert of great powers to give central directions to international society (Jiang Junbo, 2015: 39).

At the global level, then, China characterizes its objective as obtaining an equal say with Western great powers, and the US in particular, in managing international order. Within Asia, however, its aim is more clearly to consolidate a position of undisputed superiority over surrounding states. This aspiration becomes clear, according to Gilbert Rozman (2012), by observing the evolution of China's academic discourse on cooperation in Asia over the first decade of the 20th century. Whereas Chinese commentators at the turn of the century saw China's growing role in the region as part of the global process of multipolarization and acknowledged the important position of ASEAN, Japan, and even potentially of the US (if it were to abandon any 'hegemonic' design), ten years later, the focus was much more on a project of community construction within Asia, led by China and to which the US presence was only an obstacle. For Rozman, this signifies the reaffirmation of a Sinocentric view of the region.

It is easy to conclude from certain remarks made by Xi Jinping that he indeed holds this view. We could mention his call for 'the people of Asia to run the affairs of Asia, solve the problems of Asia and uphold the security of Asia'[25] or his remark to the American then Secretary of State John Kerry that 'the broad Pacific Ocean is vast enough to embrace both China and the United States'[26] – implying that the US should give China more space on its side (Zhao Suisheng, 2015a: 382). Most meaningful is perhaps his assertion that China's strategic objective in its 'peripheral diplomacy' – a term that in itself reflects a sense of centrality[27] – is first and foremost to 'abide by and serve the "Two Centuries" objective to realize [the] great rejuvenation of Chinese nation'.[28] The 'great rejuvenation of the Chinese nation' (*Zhonghua minzu weida fuxing*), which Xi calls his 'Chinese dream' (*Zhongguo meng*), is his favourite slogan, although one with a long history before his arrival to power.

In Wang Zheng's words, the idea of rejuvenation, evoked in one form or another by every modern leader (except Mao, more interested in revolutionary change) and by late Qing reformers before them, expresses the Chinese people's 'determination to restore themselves to their former position and glory' after the humiliations they were subjected to in the 19th and 20th centuries (2012: 237; see also Yan Xuetong, 2001: 33–4; Wang Zheng, 2013: 9). By embracing the great rejuvenation as his main objective, then, Xi has sought to unite the Chinese people behind the Party to accomplish the task of recovering the status and respect that their country enjoyed at the height of its imperial splendour. This is also a callback to ideas that date from the rise of Chinese nationalism in the early 20th century (evoked in the last chapter), such as the mobilization of citizens around the drive to build a strong nation state capable of defending itself against hostile foreign forces, the invocation of an idealized imperial past to extol the inherent moral virtue of the Chinese nation and to justify the central position it claims in Asia, or the yearning to wash away the stain of the 'century of humiliation' by obtaining the renewed deference of other states. To capture this spirit, Renmin University professor Jin Canrong (2017a) has described

---

[25] Xi Jinping, 'New Asian security concept for new progress in security cooperation', 21 May 2014, www.cica-china.org/eng/zxghd/yxdscfh/t1170132.htm.

[26] David Brunnstrom, 'Despite tension, Xi says U.S.–China relations are stable', *Bloomberg*, 17 May 2015.

[27] Xi Jinping is not the first Chinese leader to use that term. Premier Li Peng was in fact already doing so in 1988, see Li Peng, '1988年政府工作报告' [1988 Government Work Report], 25 March 1988, www.gov.cn/test/2006-02/16/content_200865.htm.

[28] Speech at a 'Peripheral Diplomacy Work Conference' on 25 October 2013, www.cciced.net/ccicedn/NEWSCENTER/LatestEnvironmentalandDevelopmentNews/201310/t20131030_82626.html. The 'Two Centuries' goals refer to the CCP's aim to create a 'moderately well-off society' by the hundredth anniversary of the Party in 2021 and to become a 'strong, prosperous, democratic, civilized, harmonious, beautiful and modern socialist country' by the time of the centenary of the PRC in 2049.

the defining mission of the Xi era as 'obtaining dignity' (*huode zunyan*) by 'winning more respect' (*yingde gengduo zunzhong*) in international society.

If the purpose of 'peripheral diplomacy' is to serve the 'great rejuvenation', then, it must in some way demonstrate that China has returned to a central position and that it is again receiving due deference from its neighbours. Striving for the re-establishment of a hierarchical order means for China first to increase the amount of attention and energy it grants to Asia as compared with other areas of its diplomacy. In the 2000s, the periphery was already described as 'of primary importance' (*shouyao*) but relations with other great powers were even more crucial, being 'key' (*guanjian*).[29] In the current diplomatic parlance, though, relations with great powers and with the periphery have become equally the 'main focus' (*zhongdian*).[30] Tsinghua University professor Yan Xuetong (2015a) has argued that, since the support of China's neighbours is necessary to complete this rise and achieve the 'great rejuvenation', relations with them are in fact now more important even than relations with the US superpower.

Even before Xi Jinping came to power, the CCP had determined that, to obtain this support, China needed to play a custodial role in the region. In his report to the 18th Party Congress in November 2012, Hu Jintao for the first time called for using China's economic development to 'bring better benefits to peripheral states'.[31] As two Chinese scholars put it, this emphasis on sharing the fruits of Chinese growth signalled a shift from 'managing the periphery' (*jingguan zhoubian*) to 'stabilizing and harmonizing the periphery' (*wending zhoubian, hexie zhoubian*) to fulfil the country's responsibility as a great power (Li and Li, 2015: 50). Even if all those terms suggest a relation of superior/overseer to inferiors/overseen, the latter two are more proactive and reflect well China's determination to reshape regional order in a way that enhances its role and status.

Even as China claims the role of great power responsible for the well-being of Asia, though, it is now also clearer in spelling out its expectation

---

[29] Hu Jintao stated that 'great powers are key, the periphery is of primary importance' (*daguo shi guanjian, zhoubian shi shouyao*) in his speech at the Central Diplomatic Work Conference of August 2006 (Hu Jinato, 2016: 508). Chen Xiangyang (2009) traces the slogan to an earlier speech by Hu at the tenth Conference of Chinese Diplomatic Envoys in August 2004, although it is not included in published summaries or abstracts (one summary can be found at www.npc.gov.cn/zgrdw/npc/wbgwyz/hyhd/2004-08/30/content_332176.htm).

[30] This is according to top-ranking diplomat Yan Jiechi, see Yan Jiechi, '深入学习贯彻党的十九大精神,奋力开拓新时代中国特色大国外交新局面' [Deeply study and carry out the spirit of the 19th Party Congress, strive to open a new phase in great power diplomacy with Chinese characteristics for a new era], *Seek Truth*, 30 November 2017.

[31] Hu Jintao, '坚定不移沿着中国特色社会主义道路前进 为全面建成小康社会而奋斗'.

that neighbours know their place as small states. The aforementioned 2017 White Paper on security cooperation in the Asia-Pacific makes a distinction between major countries and 'small and medium-sized countries [who] need not and should not take sides among big countries' – or, in other words, should not align with the US against China.[32] This was only a repeat of remarks made two years earlier by Vice Foreign Minister Liu Zhenmin at the Xiangshan Forum (China's response to the Shangri-La Dialogue on Asia-Pacific security).[33] Foreign Minister Wang Yi also spelled out expectations for China's smaller neighbours during his annual press conference in March 2014, when he emphasized that China 'will never accept unreasonable demands from smaller countries'.[34]

All those comments demonstrate an understanding that China, as the foremost Asian great power, and its neighbours have clearly distinct roles to play in the region, and that the maintenance of order requires both to stick to their natural position, dictated by their size. Yet Chinese leaders do not justify their vision of a hierarchical order only in terms of differences in national power – that is, after all, the Western way of thinking they condemn – but rather in terms of the moral virtues that both large and small states should adopt in recognition that their different size creates different obligations. Indeed, one of the most distinct features of China's diplomatic discourse is its moralism – a feature also inherited from the imperial past. It is to this moralism that we turn our attention first in the next chapter.

Conclusion

The Western-led order Chinese statesmen encountered in the late 19th century was in their eyes just as hierarchical as the traditional Sinocentric one but brutish and unjust, and sustained only by raw power politics. They thus had a responsibility to bring about something better. There was indeed never any doubt in Chinese minds that their country was a great power that should be treated as equal by Western ones and should be accepted as a leader by other states. This was particularly true of the nations of Asia, which China still considered its natural followers in the modern world. The leaders of the PRC have inherited this understanding and adopted various strategies to recover the country's 'rightful place' at the centre of a more just order.

---

[32] 'China's policies on Asia-Pacific security cooperation'.
[33] Liu Zhenmin, 'Uphold win-win cooperation and promote peace and stability in the Asia-Pacific', 17 October 2015, www.fmprc.gov.cn/mfa_eng/wjdt_665385/zyjh_665391/201510/t20151017_678395.html.
[34] 'Foreign Minister Wang Yi meets the press', 8 March 2014, http://sl.china-embassy.org/eng/zgyw/t1135385.htm.

Under Mao, China sought, albeit only half-heartedly, to upend the existing order and hierarchy of power through revolutionary change, trying to overcome its weakness with fervent belief in a 'sinified' Marxist-Leninist doctrine, which would hopefully allow it to quickly catch up with developed countries. All the while, it promoted a utopian vision of socialist world harmony, even if it made only selective efforts to realize this vision. It saw other Asian states as followers either in the pursuit of world revolution or at least in opposing the 'hegemonism' of the two Cold War superpowers. The idea of revolutionary change was abandoned over the course of the 1970s and, with the launch of reform and opening, China focused instead on development at home, with the aim to climb the international hierarchy of power within the framework of existing institutions – while still advocating reforms to create a new and more just order. It also focused on establishing itself as one of the poles in a multipolar system and on obtaining support from other Asian states in that endeavour, while still keeping a relatively low profile. This changed as its power grew, culminating with Xi Jinping's proclamation that the time to take leadership and achieve the 'great rejuvenation of the Chinese nation' had come. By then, China had managed to rise within the existing order and had taken on the mantle of a responsible great power. The CCP's explicit goal was now to preserve international order and to push for the reforms necessary to ensure its durability by giving a bigger voice to underrepresented developing countries – China first among them, of course. In Asia, China's ambitions to take leadership have been clearer as it seeks to limit the role of the US – the sole peer competitor it countenances – and to claim a custodian role in exchange for the deference of its neighbours. Its argument is that, unlike Western great powers, it deserves this exalted position because it offers a morally superior type of leadership. It is to this claim that we turn our attention next.

6

Moral Discourse and Ritual in Contemporary Chinese Diplomacy

From its early days, the PRC has taken as its banner the fight for 'international justice'. This fight was first about recovering China's own 'rightful place' in international society after the abuses suffered at the hand of imperial powers during the 'century of humiliation', but it did not stop there. Indeed, Chinese leaders have consistently presented themselves as advocates of the rights and aspirations of all non-Western states for a more just world (Mitter, 2003: 218 ff.). Under Mao, this meant condemning imperialism and offering rhetorical support for national liberation movements. In the reform and opening period and especially after the end of the Cold War, Mao's successors have defined international justice as absolute respect for sovereignty in the face of Western interventionism and criticism of non-democratic domestic governance regimes, as well as a fairer repartition of economic resources. This is still the message promoted by Xi Jinping today.

The advocacy of 'international justice' is just one aspect of the moralism that characterizes Chinese leaders' rhetoric on the international stage. As Chih-Yu Shih notes, a moralizing discourse has remained a central pillar of Chinese political culture, with the consequence that 'the Chinese seem obliged to envision international politics as fashioned of some sort of moral hierarchy' (1993: 2–3). The PRC claims the top spot in this moral hierarchy by favourably comparing itself to the West. Having concluded early on that these Western powers were morally corrupt and that their domination over international society was illegitimate, modern Chinese statesmen have consistently advocated a 'better' way to conduct international relations that would justify their country's eventual return at the top of the international hierarchy as a more virtuous leader for the nations of the world. Examining this discourse of moral leadership as articulated by the CCP is the first task of this chapter.

Its second task is to consider how this discourse translates into diplomatic practice. We may recall from Chapter 2 that ritual, or behaviour according to the rules of propriety, is intimately linked with moral cultivation in the traditional Chinese conception of order. Concretely, this meant that the superior virtues of the Chinese emperor were demonstrated by his capacity to establish the 'code of proper behaviour' that regulated relations with neighbouring polities and to have them recognize his primacy through their diplomatic interactions. Acceptance of this code was in turn how other polities displayed their own moral qualities. In other words, ritualized diplomacy was the concrete embodiment of the moral hierarchy over which the Chinese court presided. As long as ritual propriety was upheld, the negotiation of individual foreign relations could be quite flexible. This link between moralizing discourse and diplomatic practice has survived the transition to modernity. PRC leaders have not only pledged to create a 'better' mode of international relations, but have also sought to translate it into a modern 'code of proper conduct'. Other states have been judged by their willingness to adhere to this code. This chapter discusses both the Chinese claim to be a morally superior leader to Western states and its efforts to give reality to said claim through its diplomatic initiatives.

The PRC takes its first steps on the international stage

The PRC started its life diplomatically isolated and without representation in international organizations. This did not prevent it from quickly claiming to offer a more virtuous form of leadership than other great powers and trying to demonstrate through its diplomacy that this claim was being accepted by other states. These early experiences already reveal at least three ways in which imperial traditions were inherited by China's communist leaders.

The first is the consistency of its discourse of moral leadership but also its adaptability to changing circumstances. The heart of the PRC's message has long been the Five Principles of Peaceful Coexistence first enounced in the early 1950s and still regularly invoked today.[1] These principles are in a sense very banal, being only reformulations of tenets found in many fundamental texts of international law such as the Charter of the UN and endorsed by all states on the planet. Successive PRC leaders have nevertheless kept referring to them as a point of contrast with the domineering attitude and reliance on brute power they have consistently criticized the West for. From the very start, the core of China's claim to moral superiority is

---

[1] As already noted in the previous chapter, these principles are mutual respect of territorial integrity and sovereignty, non-aggression, non-interference in internal affairs, equality and mutual benefit, and peaceful coexistence.

that, unlike Western great powers who only profess to respect the basic principles of international relations issued from their own traditions while constantly violating them in practice through colonialism and other forms of exploitation, the leaders of the CCP are committed to building a just international order based on the Five Principles and defending the rights of developing countries against predation.

This discourse was initially complemented by other elements that reflected the context of the early Cold War, where China had joined the communist side and where movements of national liberation around the world were fighting to bring an end to Western colonialism. As discussed in the previous chapter, the CCP quickly began to contest the Soviet Union's central position in the socialist camp. Its criticism of Moscow's leadership became increasingly open as it claimed to be the true upholder of the spirit of brotherly solidarity among communist parties and a more dedicated opponent to Western imperialism (Chen Jian, 2001: 148; Lüthi, 2008: 182–3). It also presented itself as the vanguard of the movement for national liberation in Asia in particular, claiming to have provided the interpretation of communist doctrine most appropriate for the region and offered a model for others to follow (Fitzgerald, 1964: 48–9). One of the PRC's founding fathers, Liu Shaoqi, for instance, told representatives of neighbouring countries that 'the way taken by the Chinese people ... is the way that should be taken by the peoples of many colonial and semi-colonial countries in their fight for national independence and people's democracy'.[2] When its prospect for being recognized as head of the socialist camp dimmed due to the excesses of the Cultural Revolution, however, the discourse of Chinese 'vanguardism' was swiftly put aside and the PRC refocused on advocating a better type of international relations writ large. That aspect of China's claim to moral leadership was then further refined, adapted, and strengthened by successive generations of leaders.

A second revealing feature of early PRC foreign policy is its renewed determination to use every diplomatic means available to raise its status on the international stage. By the 1950s, the norms of protocol through which diplomatic encounters were meant to represent the sovereign equality of states had become well established. As we noted in Chapter 1, these give states much less space to demonstrate their superiority over their peers through formal interactions. Superiority in status can, however, still be asserted at the margins of official state ceremonies, through the language adopted in joint documents, in the informal interactions between state representatives, and in certain aspects of protocol in multilateral settings. This is part of what Hans

---

[2] Speech to a meeting of the World Federation of Trade Unions in Beijing, November 1949, reproduced in d'Encausse and Schram 1969: 271).

Morgenthau calls the 'policy of prestige' among contending great powers (1948: 51–4). China has proven an adept and eager practitioner. Within the constraining boundaries of modern diplomatic norms, it has always actively sought ways to boost its prestige.

Even in its initial efforts to expand the number of countries with which it had diplomatic relations, the PRC did not forget to try to boost its status, seeking endorsement of the Five Principles by including them in as many bilateral treaties and agreements as it could (Lee, 1967: 248). India and Myanmar played a useful role as early boosters of this strategy by enthusiastically endorsing said principles as the basis of an Asian path to a more peaceful world (Brazinsky, 2017: 78–81). Mao also repeatedly sought to invite the leaders of various non-Western states and national liberation movements to Beijing so as to 'showcase himself as the leader of the People's Movement around the world' (Amako, 2014: 11).

At the multilateral level as well, China used two occasions in the 1950s, a peace conference on East Asian conflicts in Geneva 1954 and the famous Bandung conference of 1955, to present itself as a reasonable major country ready to promote peaceful coexistence with its neighbours and to defend the interests of Asian countries against the destructive influence of the US (Zhang Shu Guang, 2007). The Chinese performance at Bandung, in particular, came to be celebrated for years and decades to come as the proof of the country's ability to seduce others and to take leadership on the world stage (Finnane, 2010). In the decade that followed, the PRC sought – with very mixed results – to use international conferences among non-Western states as means to contest the Soviet Union's position of leader of the socialist movement (Friedman, 2015: 97–8, 117, 145, 155).

It was, however, in relations with North Korea and Vietnam, its two closest neighbours who most benefited from its assistance, that Chinese leaders worked the hardest to establish a superior-to-inferior relationship. This particular focus on demonstrating the PRC's superiority in its immediate surroundings is the third way in which its early decades are instructive. With regard to North Korea, Shen Zhihua (2016: 259–60) has noted how Mao's hierarchical view of his relation with Kim Il Sung helps explain the mix of extraordinary forbearance (in tolerating destabilizing political purges within North Korea or in agreeing to resolve a territorial dispute to its advantage) and constant displeasure with Kim's lack of deference to Beijing's wishes (in the conduct of the Korean War or in his push for a '*Juche*' (self-reliance) line aiming for autonomy from China). As Shen concludes, Mao's view of his own role as a traditional benevolent suzerain deserving of respect was a constant factor in the contentious history of China–DPRK relations.

The records of Chinese leaders' discussions with Vietnamese interlocutors in Beijing (collected in Westad et al, 1998) reveal an understanding of the relation between the two sides equally reminiscent of imperial traditions.

Namely, they saw themselves as teachers welcoming Vietnamese supplicants and offering assistance to a former tributary (Westad et al, 1998: 18). In their interactions with guests from Vietnam (and Laos and Cambodia, which were also recipients of support), they frequently stressed the importance of the Chinese revolutionary experience and of the CCP's interpretation of Marxism-Leninism as guides to the liberation of Indochina. Mao and his colleagues appear didactic and authoritative and seem to be giving instructions while their guests, respectful and deferential, offer praise and talk of 'reporting' to the CCP (Westad et al, 1998: 66–75, 90).

These kinds of exchanges show how the traditional logic of Chinese ritual can endure in modern diplomatic exchanges, where the manner of interactions between it and its close neighbours reflects their superior-to-inferior relations. As Chen Jian notes, despite repeated pledges to treat South-East Asian revolutionaries as equals, Chinese leaders' demeanours show that 'they believed that they had occupied a position from which to dictate the values and codes of behaviour that would dominate their relations with their neighbours' and that they expected due deference to reflect 'the Vietnamese recognition of China's morally superior position' (2001: 237). Showing deference also meant avoiding actions that would displease Beijing, especially getting too friendly with the two superpowers.[3] The 'codes of behaviour' that the PRC sought to impose on its smaller neighbours thus included both an expectation of respectful demeanour and abidance by Beijing's red lines. While this imperious attitude went into partial eclipse during the reform and opening period, it has come back to the fore under Xi Jinping.

From 'Five Principles' to 'community with a shared future for mankind'

As noted earlier, China started to abandon the advocacy of national liberation and focus on the more general claim to offer a better model of international relations already in the 1970s. Most notable was Deng Xiaoping's speech at the UN General Assembly of 1974, where he decried at length how the Soviet Union and the US were acting in a domineering and exploitative way while pledging that China would oppose oppression in all its forms and advocate for the rights of developing countries to absolute respect for sovereignty, greater participation in international decision making, and equitable economic relations based on the Five Principles.[4] This discourse

---

[3] See, for instance, an April 1966 conversation regarding Vietnam's relation with the Soviet Union (Westad et al, 1998: 92, 94).

[4] Text of the speech at www.marxists.org/reference/archive/deng-xiaoping/1974/04/10.htm.

was the basis on which Deng's successor built in the following decades. Jiang Zemin presided over a first update, proposing a 'new security concept' (*xin anquan guan*) to reflect its assessment of a world transformed by the end of the Cold War.[5] Except for a new emphasis on economic security achieved through mutual cooperation and joint prosperity in acknowledgement of the progress of globalization and economic interdependence, Jiang largely stuck to familiar language, stressing the importance of the Five Principles for the maintenance of international peace and criticizing Western 'hegemonism' and 'power politics', now branded as 'Cold War mentality'. By rejecting the antagonism and division into camps of the previous decades, then Foreign Minister Qian Qichen said in December 1997 that China would lead the way in building a 'new type of inter-state relations' (*xin xing guojia guanxi*).[6] Hu Jintao brought his own contribution with his concept of 'harmonious world' presented in 2005.[7] He was again mostly reiterating well-known talking points while adding an emphasis on sharing the fruits of economic development, christening the now omnipresent slogan 'win-win cooperation' (*hezuo gongying*) and expressing support for multilateralism and the UN. The latter point was meant to favourably contrast China's attitude with the unilateral policies of the US under George W. Bush.

Having succeeded Hu at the head of the CCP, Xi Jinping had to propose his own concept, even if it was to reiterate by now familiar ideas. In fact, he has offered two, namely, the 'new type of international relations' (*xin xing guoji guanxi*) and the 'community of human destiny' (*renlei mingyun gongtongti*, or 'community with a shared future for mankind' in most official translations). Foreign Minister Wang Yi has described the core principles of the 'new type of international relations' in familiar terms (mutual respect, fairness and justice, win-win cooperation), once again drawing a contrast with Western 'hegemonism' and power politics.[8] As for the 'community with a shared future for mankind', Wang sees it emerging from the awareness that 'all countries and peoples live on the same planet, and thus have their

---

[5] The 'new security concept' was first proposed in 1996 but presented in its definitive form in a speech in Geneva in March 1999 (available at www.fmprc.gov.cn/ce/ceun/eng/zghlhg/cj/unga/t29298.htm). On the elaboration and first mentions of the 'concept' in the years beforehand, see Takagi, 2003: 69–73.

[6] Ma Shizhen and Zheng Yuanyuan, '多极化进程加快 中国外交成果丰硕' [The process of multipolarization accelerates, China's diplomatic achievements are plentiful], *People's Daily*, 18 September 1997. This is very close to the 'new type of international relations' promoted by Xi Jinping and examined later.

[7] The 2005 White Paper outlining the concept can be found at www.china.org.cn/english/2005/Dec/152669.htm.

[8] For instance, in a speech at the Symposium on International Developments and China's Diplomacy in 2017, www.fmprc.gov.cn/mfa_eng/wjdt_665385/zyjh_665391/201712/t20171210_678651.html.

future closely intertwined like passengers on the same boat'.⁹ In his most detailed explanation of the 'community' concept to date, during a speech at the General Assembly of the UN in September 2015, Xi Jinping evoked

> partnerships in which countries treat each other as equals, engage in mutual consultation and show mutual understanding ... a security architecture featuring fairness, justice, joint contribution and shared benefits ... open, innovative and inclusive development that benefits all ... inter-civilization exchanges to promote harmony, inclusiveness and respect for differences ... an ecosystem that puts mother nature and green development first.

He also repeated common Chinese talking points promoting more just, equal, and mutually beneficial international relations while throwing in a few allusions to UN priorities like sustainable development into the mix.¹⁰

Xi's addition to the Chinese cannon of slogans thus fits the established pattern whereby previously proposed concepts are 'refined' and elaborated on without going further than enunciations of general principles that few states would object to (Rolland, 2020: 37–8). Their main purpose is still to favourably contrast a virtuous China advocating equality and justice in world affairs with Western powers stuck in the past and guilty of exploiting their economically dominant position to dictate to other states how to run their own affairs. Nevertheless, the talk of 'community with a shared future for mankind' now attracts significantly more attention because under Xi, a more powerful and self-confident China has been far more proactive in translating its discourse of leadership into action to create Sinocentric patterns of diplomacy (and to challenge liberal aspects of the global governance regime, though this is beyond the remit of this book). Before examining those actions, we should, however, point out two more ways in which the Chinese claim to moral superiority has been adapted to changing circumstances, namely a multiplication of allusions to traditional virtues and the elaboration of a message directed at Asia specifically.

Returning to 'traditional virtues'

With the launch of reform and opening in China, and even more so with the end of the Cold War, the idea that China could use communist ideology to strengthen its claim to virtuous leadership became fully discredited. It took several more years for an alternative to emerge. The first hints of a return

---

⁹ *Ibid*.
¹⁰ Text of the speech at www.mfa.gov.cn/ce/ceie/eng/ztlt/2d2/t1321126.htm.

to the argument, already advanced by Sun Yat-sen at the beginning of the 20th century, that China's moral superiority was grounded in its uniquely peaceful and harmonious traditional culture appeared in the early 2000s. At a speech in the US in 2002, Jiang Zemin had said that 'the Chinese nation has inherited from ancient times a fine tradition of honesty, harmony and good faith' and had extolled the virtue of seeking 'harmony without sameness' (*he er bu tong*) – a saying from the Analects – to allow for the peaceful coexistence of countries with different beliefs.[11] Hu Jintao doubled down on such rhetoric, not least by repeatedly evoking the traditional concept of 'harmony' (*hexie*). Yet this was nothing compared with the deluge of similar references coming from Xi Jinping and his team.

This starts with a reformulation of Sun Yat-sen's distinction between the 'way of the hegemon' (*badao*) practised by the West – the term was, for instance, used by Yang Jiechi, China's highest-ranking diplomat, in a 2017 article[12] – and China's 'way of the king' (*wangdao*). If Xi Jinping himself has not (yet) used the latter term in a speech,[13] he has nevertheless been particularly keen to extol China's traditional virtues. In a major address to a 2014 Central Conference on Work relating to Foreign Affairs, he evoked the 'need to stick to a correct view of righteousness and interest and to strike a balance between righteousness and interests, the need to emphasize good faith, to attach importance to friendship, to champion justice and to cultivate morality'.[14] Among those terms, 'justice' is the most typical of contemporary Chinese diplomatic rhetoric, being frequently associated with 'fairness' (in the expression *gongping zhengyi*) to describe the advocacy of a more equitable world order that gives greater voice to developing countries while respecting existing principles of international law and upholding the central role of the UN in international affairs.[15] Other terms evoked by Xi Jinping are more explicit callbacks to Chinese traditions. Most significant is the 'correct view

---

[11] 'Speech by President Jiang Zemin at George Bush Presidential Library', 24 October 2002, www.fmprc.gov.cn/ce/ceno/eng/dtxw/t110222.htm.

[12] Yang Jiechi, "推动构建人类命运共同体（认真学习宣传贯彻党的十九大精神）" [Promoting the construction of a community of destiny for mankind (earnestly studying, disseminating and implementing the spirit of the 19th Party Congress)], *People's Daily Online*, 11 November 2017.

[13] Some Chinese scholars have not been so shy. See, for instance, Yan Xuetong, 2008: 159–60; Tang and Chen, 2015; Zhang Rongming, 2015; Jin Fenglin, 2018.

[14] '习近平出席中央外事工作会议并发表重要讲话' [Xi Jinping chairs the Central Conference on Foreign Affairs Work and gives an important speech], *Xinhua Online*, 29 November 2014. English summary of the speech available at www.fmprc.gov.cn/mfa_eng/zxxx_662805/t1215680.shtml.

[15] See, for instance, Wang Yi, '以习近平新时代中国特色社会主义思想引领中国外交开辟新境界' [Leading Chinese diplomacy to open new frontiers with Xi Jinping's thought on socialism with Chinese characteristics for a new era], *People's Daily*, 19 December 2017.

of righteousness and interests' (*zhengque yi li guan*) mentioned several times in Xi Jinping's address.

This concept, introduced by Xi in 2013 and used frequently since, is, according to Yan Xuetong, 'as theoretically significant [as] the Chinese dream' (2014: 18). It is meant to epitomize the CCP's commitment to propagate Chinese virtues just as much as it pursues the national interest. In an article discussing the concept's significance, Wang Yi describes it as a reflection of Chinese morality and sense of responsibility, and of the 'important essence of China's excellent traditional culture'.[16] Quoting Confucian classics, he invokes moral and behavioural norms inherited from Chinese history that supposedly privilege righteousness over the pursuit of interest. He goes on to depict the PRC as the inheritor of this tradition ever since its founding, evoking Chinese aid to developing countries and various other achievements. The Foreign Minister therefore argues that the CCP has always behaved according to Chinese virtues and is already striking the right balance between justice and interests. In fact, Xi Jinping himself speaks of 'sticking to' (*jianchi*) that balance. At an event commemorating the birth of Confucius, Xi made the point even more clearly, stating that 'the Chinese communists have always been faithful inheritors and upholders of the country's fine cultural traditions'.[17]

This reveals the true meaning of contemporary Chinese leaders' callbacks to tradition. Namely, they are no signs of a fundamental rethink of China's foreign policy strategy to replace existing international practices with pre-modern ones, but rather attempts to mobilize an idealized vision of its past to bolster the country's long-standing claim to moral superiority. The same can be said of recent Chinese attempts to invoke the country's resistance to Japanese aggression during the Second World War, with the aim of picturing it as a defender of world peace and as one of the progenitors of the post–Cold War international order. This, the CCP hopes, will 'add moral weight' to China's growing international presence and strengthen its claim to leadership (Mitter, 2020: 214). The references to a traditional sense of righteousness are meant to reinforce the same point: China, uniquely among the world's great powers, is diligently following the 'way of the king' and thus reigns supreme in the moral realm.

---

[16] Wang Yi, '坚持正确义利观 积极发挥负责任大国作用——深刻领会习近平同志关于外交工作的重要讲话精神' [Sticking to the correct view of righteousness and interests, actively displaying the actions of a responsible great power: deeply understanding the spirit of comrade Xi Jinping's important speech on diplomatic work], *People's Daily*, 10 September 2013.

[17] 'Xi Jinping's Speech in Commemoration of the 2,565th Anniversary of Confucius' Birth', 24 September 2014, available at http://library.chinausfocus.com/article-1534.html.

China: the 'friendly neighbour'

Since the end of the Cold War, Chinese leaders have also complemented their general advocacy of a new type of international relations with a claim to virtuous leadership directed at Asia in particular. As early as 1992, Premier Li Peng talked of a policy of 'good-neighborly friendship' (*mulin youhao*).[18] The expression then became a regular part of Jiang Zemin and Hu Jintao's report to the five-yearly Party Congress, accompanied each time by stronger commitments to pursue regional cooperation.[19] To elaborate on these pronouncements, State Council member Tang Jiaxuan pledged in September 2003 that China would never 'abuse or disrupt its neighbourhood' but instead strive to create a 'safe and wealthy neighbourhood'.[20] Premier Wen Jiabao gave a more detailed exposition of those principles in a speech at an ASEAN meeting one month later, when he presented China's more active role in the region as a gift to other states, linking the concept of 'rich neighbourhood' to shared development and the deepening of regional economic integration and that of 'safe neighbourhood' to the peaceful resolution of differences and to the 'proactive' maintenance of regional peace and stability.[21]

Perhaps most significant was his explanation of the meaning of China's 'good neighbourhood' stance, the basis of its whole regional policy, which he said reflected the Chinese people's innate 'amity, benevolence and goodness' (*qin ren shan*) towards neighbours and love of harmony, inherited from past generations. Xi Jinping has embraced this language with gusto, evoking Confucian values when describing China's 'peripheral diplomacy'. At the first ever central work conference on the topic in October 2013, he expanded on the 'good neighbourhood' policy by calling on China's diplomacy to 'prominently embody the ideas of amity, sincerity, generosity

---

[18] Li Peng, '1992年政府工作报告' [1992 government work report], 20 March 1992, www.gov.cn/test/2006-02/16/content_200922.htm.
[19] Jiang Zemin, '加快改革开放和现代化建设步伐 夺取有中国特色社会主义事业的更大胜利' [Step up the pace of reform and opening and of modernization, seize an even greater victory in the undertaking of socialism with Chinese characteristics], 12 October 1992, www.gov.cn/test/2008-07/04/content_1035850.htm. For other reports, see note 12 in Chapter 5.
[20] '大湄公河次区域经济合作部长级会议召开 国务委员唐家璇出席开幕式并讲话' [The ministerial conference for economic cooperation in the Greater Mekong Subregion convenes, State Council member Tang Jiaxuan attends the open ceremony and gives a speech], 19 September 2003, www.mfa.gov.cn/ce/como//chn/xwdt/wjyw/t25964.htm.
[21] '温家宝总理出席东盟商业与投资峰会并发表演讲' [Premier Wen Jiabao gives a speech to the ASEAN trade and investment summit], 8 October 2003, http://lu.china-embassy.org/chn/xwdt/t26502.htm.

and inclusiveness' (*qin, cheng, hui, rong*).²² Those are all concepts with a rich history in Chinese literature and political thought, but judged by his injunctions after invoking them, it seems that Xi is mostly interested in using them to frame China's more proactive pursuit of existing policies. The PRC had long called for solidarity among developing nations on the international stage, but Xi talks of 'keeping watch and defending one another' (*shouwang xiangzhu*), an idiom from Mencius. China has also long used the language of friendship among nations, especially in Asia, but Xi calls for making neighbouring states 'more friendly, more intimate, more approving, more supportive' and for 'treating peripheral states earnestly and sincerely'. China's oft-stated support for shared and 'win-win' development is also strengthened with talk of 'advocating inclusive thinking' and 'insisting on the principle of mutual benefits' in economic cooperation with the periphery.

Xi's message is, therefore, that the long-standing advocacy of solidarity, friendship, and common development is a sincere reflection of China's unique moral qualities, which should make its leadership welcome by neighbours. In exchange, China expects them to embrace virtues of their own. As Xi says, if China acts in accordance with the ideals it advocates (or 'practices what it preaches' *shenti lixing*), this should make them 'the shared ideals and code of conduct' (*gongtong linian he xingwei zhunze*) for the whole region. If China practises benevolence by treating smaller states with friendship and respecting their sovereignty, then, the latter should exercise wisdom by refraining from provoking China or aligning with Western powers against it.²³ Since, as we have highlighted previously, the PRC has in the CCP's telling always behaved according to the highest moral standards, this puts the onus on other states to reciprocate. It is also revealing that Xi Jinping talks of Confucian virtues becoming a 'code of conduct' for the region. Taking leadership in the region increasingly means dictating how others should behave as well to demonstrate China's central position. This trend in fact started in the 1990s, initially in a gentle and careful manner.

First steps in regional diplomacy

The general aim of Chinese diplomacy in the period of reform and opening was to create space for China's rise by privileging stability in its foreign relations, keeping a low profile and integrating more closely into international society so as to receive broad international acceptance and prevent excessive

---

22 '习近平：让命运共同体意识在周边国家落地生根' [Xi Jinping: Let awareness of the community of shared destiny take root in peripheral countries], 25 October 2013, www.xinhuanet.com//politics/2013-10/25/c_117878944.htm.

23 Interview with a senior professor at Fudan University, Shanghai, 16 March 2018.

criticism from abroad (Deng Yong, 2011). If maintaining stable relations with international society writ large was China's overall purpose, its position in its own region remained 'of primary importance' (*shouyao*), as Hu Jintao put it in the early 2000s (Hu Jintao, 2016: 508). After the end of the Cold War, China quickly established diplomatic ties with the new states of Central Asia and normalized relations with the last East Asian states that were or had become estranged during the Cold War (South Korea, Vietnam, Cambodia, Indonesia). The 1990s saw a steep increase in the number of bilateral visits between high-ranking officials of China and its neighbours. Jiang Zemin himself went on several official and state visits, on which occasions joint declarations were often released to mark the occasion and to obtain endorsement by other states of Chinese favourite diplomatic slogans like the Five Principles and 'good-neighbourly friendship'. It should be noted that Jiang never went on such visits without first receiving his counterparts in Beijing and being formally invited. Coming to pay respects in the Chinese capital was thus the price to pay to receive a reciprocal gesture from the Secretary General, which put him in a position of superiority over his guests who had to make the first step. With the accumulation of high-level visits, this reinforced the image of China as a centre of activity in Asia to which others were attracted.

Two diplomatic experiences of the 1990s were crucial in accelerating China's engagement with its neighbourhood. The first was its initial steps in ASEAN-centred institutions like the ASEAN Regional Forum (ARF), which it joined on invitation from South-East Asian states. It discovered then that the norms promoted by ASEAN – expressed in the 1967 Treaty of Amity and Cooperation (TAC) – were quite similar to its own Five Principles and that its southern neighbours shared its preferences for a style of diplomacy focused on establishing a stable framework to advance cooperation without requiring many concrete commitments of participant states (Foot, 1998: 428; Lanteigne, 2005: 104; Ba, 2006: 169). This opened the way for China's conversion to this form of multilateralism – or what one Chinese analyst called 'flexible multilateralism' (*linghuo de duobianzhuyi*) (Pang Zhongying, 2001). The second experience was the Asian financial crisis of 1997. China then played a stabilizing role by not devaluating the renminbi, attracting plaudits from abroad and leading to self-congratulatory statements praising its own 'responsible' attitude (Johnston, 2008: 135). This convinced China that its neighbours would be supportive of its attempts to display leadership. The greater confidence gained from previous engagement with ASEAN combined with the demonstrated boost to China's status received during the crisis made it a turning point towards a more proactive regional posture (Deng Yong, 2008: 233).

This more proactive posture included a further intensification of bilateral visits with all states in the region and frequent participation in a variety of regional forums and summits (Shambaugh, 2004/05: 78–9; Ku, 2006: 121–7). These all served to maintain stable relations between China and its neighbours even as its rise was altering the geopolitics of the region, and allowed it to concretely demonstrate its ability to play the role of regional leader – and to be recognized and accepted as such. One particularly noteworthy initiative in that regard was the 'Six Party Talks' proposed in 2003 by China to deal with the North Korean nuclear programme. Even if progress on solving the issue proved glacially slow, the talks were hailed in China as a triumph for its diplomacy, demonstrating its capacity to assume leadership by convening all stakeholders (including major powers like the US, Russia, and Japan) around one table (Shirk, 2007: 125–6).

Overall, then, even if bilateral and multilateral diplomatic interactions placed Chinese leaders on equal footing with their counterparts, the sheer number of visits they gave and received, and their omnipresence in regional meetings – an increasing number of which were organized in China itself – helped them to demonstrate a prominence that no other state in the region or outside (including the US) could match. Rather than individual diplomatic moves, it was the sheer volume of multilateral and bilateral exchanges that China was engaged in that cumulatively demonstrated its growing centrality in the region.

China also sought to enhance its role in existing multilateral structures or to shape their evolution in a way that underlined its rising status as its power grew. The SCO, formed by China, Russia, and three Central Asian states, is widely recognized as a 'Chinese project' whose activities and agenda expanded to accompany its rise, and as an example of China successfully shaping an institution to boost its international status (Galyamova, 2010: 319). Beijing was not so successful in East Asia, though. Its attempt to transition from the ASEAN+3 framework (which includes ten ASEAN countries, China, Japan, and South Korea) into an East Asia Summit (EAS) with the same membership but less centred on ASEAN, where it could more easily take the initiative, was thwarted by a coalition of neighbours, who preferred a larger gathering including a broader range of states and eventually prevailed in enlarging the new structure's membership (Kim, 2010). China's attitude became much less enthusiastic as a result and Beijing started to advocate making ASEAN+3 the most important regional forum instead. As the 2000s came to a close, China still participated diligently in a range of ASEAN-led institutions including the EAS but it had also created a range of alternative Sinocentric forums. This trend only strengthened under Xi Jinping.

Establishing China's central position

Xi's administration has indeed doubled down on the regional engagement of the late 1990s and 2000s, while making renewed efforts to centre Asia's diplomatic life on China itself. The heart of this strategy is the BRI, Xi Jinping's flagship project to link China with markets and energy reserves in Eurasia (and increasingly around the globe) through maritime and overland infrastructure building. The Secretary General argues that no initiative better reflects China's determination to be a new, non-exploitative type of great power. In his speech to the first Belt and Road Forum (BARF) held in May 2017, Xi pledged that 'China will enhance friendship and cooperation with all countries involved in the Belt and Road Initiative on the basis of the Five Principles of Peaceful Co-existence' and that 'in pursuing the Belt and Road Initiative, we will not resort to outdated geopolitical manoeuvring. What we hope to achieve is a new model of win-win cooperation'.[24]

The BRI is a very ambitious project with multiple economic and security aims such as stabilizing China's periphery through economic development, gaining footholds in key locations around Eurasia, Africa, and beyond, securing access to energy and raw materials, opening markets for Chinese companies, and exporting capital and excess production capacities (for example, Johnson, 2016: 19–20; Cai, 2017: 3–14; Miller, 2017: 30–4; Rolland, 2017: 93–120). These objectives should, however, not eclipse the symbolic value of the BRI as an overarching framework through which Chinese leaders can demonstrate that they are indeed the overseers of a friendly and cooperative pattern of inter-state relations. Attracting others to participate in this pattern is the most direct way to receive international acceptance of their claim to virtuous leadership. In other words, the BRI – and multiple other diplomatic initiatives like the establishment of the AIIB or the revitalization of the pre-existing Conference on Interaction and Confidence-Building Measures in Asia (CICA) – are not only means to achieve China's economic and security objectives, but also have value in and of themselves as tools to consolidate the country's status as a great power at the centre of regional and increasingly even global order.

The same can be said of Xi Jinping's most recent proposals, a 'Global Development Initiative' (GDI) and a 'Global Security Initiative' (GSI), announced in 2021 and 2022 respectively. In typical fashion, official descriptions of the content of both initiatives have remained quite vague,[25]

---

[24] 'President Xi's speech at opening of Belt and Road forum', *Xinhua*, 14 May 2014.
[25] The GDI is described as 'people-centred' and supportive of economic development in the Global South. It also pledges to offer Chinese assistance and financing to the UN for its Sustainable Development Goals (see 'Chair's statement of the high-level dialogue on global development', 24 June 2022, www.fmprc.gov.cn/eng/zxxx_662805/202206/t20220624_10709812.html). As for the GSI, Foreign Minister Wang Yi uses typical Chinese talking points denouncing the West's 'Cold War mentality', 'hegemonism', and 'power politics' to present the initiative as a better, more cooperative, and sustainable security architecture (Wang Yi, '落实全球安全倡议, 守护世界和平安宁' [Implement the Global Security Initiatives, safeguard world peace and tranquillity], *People's Daily*, 24

but this has not prevented Chinese diplomats from pushing as many countries as possible to express support in joint statements after both bilateral and multilateral meetings and from publicly celebrating this 'broad support' afterwards.[26] A group of 'friends of GDI' was even launched at the UN, and its first 'high-level virtual meeting', hosted by the Chinese Foreign Minister, took place in May 2022. Regardless of their more concrete objectives – boosting China's role in development assistance for the GDI and opposing the strengthening of the US alliances and partnerships network across Eurasia for the GSI – the two initiatives then seem, like others before them, to have been at least partly designed as new means to clearly demonstrate China's leadership of international society and the allegiance it receives from others.

The BRI nevertheless remains the most significant and concrete attempt yet to give shape to China's vision of a Sinocentric order. It serves as the focal point of several pre-existing trends. In a way, it is simply a consolidation of the various dialogue mechanism that China has been establishing with groups of countries within Asia and further abroad over the last 20 years (Aoyama, 2016: 8). Those various mechanisms are part of what one Chinese scholar calls 'diplomatic efforts to advance the formation of an international network structure on a global scale', starting on China's periphery and extending outwards to other regions (Su Hao, 2009: 47). Each initiative typically includes regular meetings at the leader or foreign minister level – in Asia, China now has such mechanisms with ASEAN, with the five Mekong region countries in South-East Asia, with Central Asia, and with all South Asian countries except India and Bhutan; beyond Asia, there are regular summits with Pacific island nations and African, Arab, Central and Latin American, and Central and East European states – along with several sectorial and functional cooperation mechanisms.

Such frameworks reflect Chinese preferences in the practice of multilateral diplomacy, namely, flexible rules of engagement that seek to maintain a continuous process of dialogue rather than reach binding collective commitments, the progressive institutionalization of secondary forums focused on various issue areas, and the frequent release of joint statements that pledge cooperation and friendship and evoke the principles associated with the 'new type of international relations'.[27] In this shape,

---

April 2022). This is yet another reformulation of China's claim to offer a morally superior type of international relations than the Western one, and more pointedly a not-so-subtle demand that Western states abandon their alliance system and give China (and its close partner Russia) a greater say in the making of the global security architecture.

[26] See, for instance, 'Wang Yi: the Global Development Initiative enjoys broad support from the international community', 25 April 2022, www.fmprc.gov.cn/mfa_eng/zxxx_662805/202204/t20220425_10673499.html.

[27] On the underlying logic of China's multilateral engagement strategy, see also Qin Yaqing, 2011: 138–9; Kavalski, 2013: 261–3.

Chinese-style multilateral diplomacy fulfils well, in a contemporary form, the two functions of ritual evoked in Chapter 3. They are first asymmetric in nature. Formulas like the 10+1 often used to characterize its dialogue with ASEAN states effectively symbolize the disparity in power and status between the two sides and the way in which a dominant China, as the initiator, welcomes a group of smaller states to develop friendly relations. Every summit is also the occasion for a Chinese leader to reiterate pledges of virtuous leadership and have them endorsed in joint declarations celebrating the positive state of relations between the two sides based on the principles, such as mutual respect and mutual benefits, long advocated by the PRC. These mechanisms furthermore afford Chinese bureaucrats a significant degree of control over the agenda, process, and pace of engagement (Jakóbowski, 2018: 663). They have used this control to establish a variety of secondary forums and preparatory meetings that enmesh partners in an ever-growing web of regular interactions centred on China. This creates a pattern whereby the country's leading role in promoting 'win-win cooperation' among states is constantly demonstrated and endorsed by other participants in those forums. Secondly, China's 'forum diplomacy' is a flexible framework in which it can negotiate individual relationships according to changing needs and international circumstances. Those forums are designed to keep proceedings informal and focused on general principles of engagement. When it comes to discussing the actual implementation of the broad agreements reached at the multilateral level, partners are 'funnelled' towards bilateral negotiations where China's hand is stronger (Jakóbowski, 2018: 661–2).

The BRI serves to accentuate those features. It is first even more asymmetric, gathering any country willing to participate under China's banner (the first BARF in May 2017 in Beijing attracted 29 heads of state and representatives from more than 130 countries; for the second forum in May 2019, those numbers were 37 and 150 respectively). Furthermore, whereas the various regional forums are held alternatively in China and abroad, BRI-related events typically take place in China, reinforcing its ability to conduct 'host diplomacy' (*zhuchang waijiao*). The expression was used in March 2014 by Foreign Minister Wang Yi to express his expectation that China's hosting of two major international summits that year – CICA and the Asia-Pacific Economic Cooperation (APEC) summit – would be the occasion to 'display hosting superiority' and to 'put forward Chinese positions'.[28]

---

[28] '两大会议聚焦安全经济 是今年中国外交重头戏' [Two big meetings focused on security and economics are the highlight of Chinese diplomacy this year], *Xinhua Online*, 8 March 2014.

The occasions for China to welcome foreign heads of state and other high-level visitors for international forums have indeed progressively multiplied since the turn of the century to reach a very high frequency. 2017, for instance, saw China hosting not only the first BARF but also a summit of the BRICS, a special working group meeting of CICA, a plenary session of Interpol, a meeting of the foreign ministers of the Lacang–Mekong cooperation mechanism, another BRI-related forum on security cooperation and a 'CCP in Dialogue with World Political Parties High-Level Meeting'. This is on top of yearly or biyearly events like the Boao economic forum (a security forum, Xiangshan, was not held in 2017), the Davos summer meeting, a world Internet conference, and several regional expos attracting traders and dignitaries from across Eurasia. Numerous bilateral diplomatic visits – including from the heads of state of ten Asian countries – complete a very busy diplomatic schedule.[29]

One Chinese commentator celebrates this growth in 'host diplomacy' as an important way to raise China's status and influence by establishing itself as an independent overseer of regional and global governance, by demonstrating its leadership abilities in front of the whole world and by shaping the international agenda with its ideas about the 'new type of international relations' (Ling Shengli, 2017: 26). Another argues that 'host diplomacy' is the concrete manifestation of Xi Jinping's ideas about international relations (Jia Wenshan, 2017). A third notes that this growth has gone hand in hand with the world's growing appreciation for China's proposals and ability to be an example to others (Chen Dongxiao, 2014: 10–1). If representatives from around Asia and beyond frequently gather in Beijing on the CCP's invitation, it is indeed because China's rapid development is an appealing success story that has greatly raised its international profile. Yet its busy diplomatic calendar in turn also serves to consolidate its status as a centre of international affairs.

---

[29] It should also be noted that, before the COVID-19 pandemic, Xi Jinping had been exceptionally well travelled and had visited all of China's neighbours (Japan should have been the last one to welcome him before the pandemic disrupted those plans), in several cases as the first Chinese head of state to do so. In 2017 alone, he was in Kazakhstan, Russia, Vietnam, and Laos. As was the case for Jiang Zemin and Hu Jintao, his official and state visits abroad were typically the occasions to release joint declarations endorsing China's diplomatic slogans, or to establish partnerships or upgrade existing ones. Partnerships are a crucial part of Chinese diplomacy and will be discussed in the next chapter. During the pandemic, Xi Jinping halted foreign trips altogether, but his two top foreign policy officials (Yang Jiechi and Wang Yi) maintained a heavy travel schedule. Xi also avoided meeting visiting foreign dignitaries, but made virtual speeches to countless international meetings, many of them still held in China with some foreign visitors despite the country's strict border controls. Even a global pandemic was not enough to meaningfully diminish China's enthusiasm for 'host diplomacy'.

For that purpose, Chinese leaders have mastered the use of their role as hosts to put themselves forward. In the rules of protocol of contemporary diplomacy meant to represent the sovereign equality of states, hosting duties are indeed an exception since hosts are necessarily the focus of attention and have a special role in proceedings, welcoming all their guests, making prominent speeches, and generally serving as masters of ceremony. They are also in charge of how international meetings are staged. Chinese leaders take full advantage of this role by choosing grand venues aiming to represent the size and might of their country, welcoming guests one after the other in grand settings and giving multiple addresses in front of assembled statesmen standing (or rather sitting) to attention. They also typically offer lavish gifts to their guests that are meant to display China's superiority and 'cultural greatness' (Ceulemans, 2021: 136–7).

Taking the first BARF as an example, Xi Jinping welcomed visiting dignitaries in a sumptuous room in the Great Hall of the People (the main event took place in the still quite imposing National Convention Centre), and gave addresses to the welcoming banquet, to a leader's round table, and at the opening ceremony, where the leaders of Russia and Turkey – the two largest powers present after China – and the General Secretary of the UN were also invited to give speeches praising the BRI, while other leaders were relegated to the plenary session that Xi did not attend. In this way, prominent international forums held in Beijing are not only the occasion for Xi and his colleagues to enact the role of international leader, but also to signify how they rank their foreign partners.

The BRI, being most distinctively China's own initiative rather than a common project with other states and being directed entirely from Beijing, thus is a particularly effective framework to obtain all the benefits of 'host diplomacy'. It has raised the profile of other events like the Eurasia, South-East Asia, and South Asia expos as well, hence serving as an amplifier of the country's various initiatives and further boosting China's status.[30] The BRI also accentuates the degree of control Chinese bureaucrats can exert on the process of diplomatic engagement. If the BARF and other dialogues convened by China to discuss the initiative are nominally multilateral, the BRI is in fact more of a hub and spokes structure whereby all interested countries negotiate projects bilaterally with Beijing. Furthermore, outside of its focus on infrastructure building and connectivity, the principles guiding it are rather vague and it lacks any kind of founding document, leaving even more flexibility for Beijing to shape various BRI partnerships to its convenience. The joint communiqué of the leaders round table at the first

---

[30] China has also established a yearly International Import Expo connected to the BRI, the first of which took place in November 2018.

BARF evoked the five 'pillars' of the initiative – policy consultation, trade promotion, infrastructure connectivity, financial integration, and people-to-people exchanges – but otherwise only affirmed participants' commitment to cooperation and coordination in all concerned fields (along with their support for international peace, stability, and the creation of a 'community with a shared future for mankind').[31]

The Memorandums of Understanding (MoUs) on the BRI that China has signed with more than 130 countries do not contain much more information. Most of them have not been released to the public, but if the preliminary Memorandum of Arrangement concluded with New Zealand and the MoU concluded with Latvia are any guide, they include an endorsement of China's plans to build the BRI in 'the Silk Road spirit' of 'peace and cooperation, openness and inclusiveness, mutual learning and mutual benefit' along with reiterated pledges to cooperate in the previously-mentioned fields and mentions of various pre-existing bilateral and multilateral projects.[32]

The purpose of the MoUs thus seems to be merely to open the way for cooperation on more specific projects by officially making the signing party a member of the BRI. They are more than anything symbols of other states' endorsement of China's vision and status as a virtuous great power. The CCP seems keen to emphasize the point. An official 'list of deliverables' of the BARF included a long list of various MoUs and other agreements concluded with individual participating countries (and international organizations).[33] On the occasion of the signing of an MoU with Nepal, Xinhua quoted the country's Deputy Premier Minister as declaring: 'Nepal has just become a member of the China-proposed Belt and Road Initiative, thanks to the Chinese leadership for introducing such a wide concept that seeks to enhance mutually beneficial cooperation between China and various countries and regions around the world.'[34]

In fact, as China's flagship initiative, the BRI offers an immediately recognizable formula to symbolize other states' endorsement of China's enlightened leadership in multilateral as well as bilateral settings. Chinese leaders have pushed for, and obtained, inclusion of approving references to or straightforward praises for the BRI in joint declarations issued during various

---

[31] 'Joint communiqué of leaders roundtable of Belt and Road forum', 15 May 2017, www.xinhuanet.com/english/2017-05/15/c_136286378.htm.

[32] Text of the MoU with New Zealand available at https://eng.yidaiyilu.gov.cn/wcm.files/upload/CMSydylyw/201703/201703310337058.pdf, that with Latvia at http://tap.mk.gov.lv/doc/2016_11/AM_MoU_EN_20161024.2386.docx.

[33] 'List of deliverables of Belt and Road forum', 15 May 2017, www.xinhuanet.com/english/2017-05/15/c_136286376.htm.

[34] 'Nepal, China sign bilateral cooperation agreement under Belt and Road Initiative', *Xinhua*, 12 May 2017.

summits and international forums.³⁵ The initiative has thus already proven of great value in strengthening China's rhetorical imprint on international diplomacy, demonstrating that its partners increasingly accept that it is the one defining the terms of engagement and the agenda for cooperation. China's neighbours are also asked on a regular basis to endorse other prominent ideas like the 'community with a shared future for mankind'.³⁶

Defining 'improper behaviour'

Through various initiatives culminating in the BRI, then, China has managed to create a sustainable diplomatic pattern that reinforces its central position on the international stage and gives reality to the narrative whereby Beijing proposes a morally superior 'new type of international relations' that is gratefully accepted by others. Participation in this pattern of relationships is the 'correct' behaviour that neighbours are expected to engage in to show their support. Today's China is, however, also quite clear on what it considers 'improper' behaviour. Namely, any action that disrupts relational harmony and crosses China's red lines is considered out of bounds. As noted earlier in this chapter, in the Mao era, these red lines mostly concerned relations with rival great powers. That is still the case today, as pursuing security cooperation with the US without taking into account Chinese concerns can quickly attract Beijing's ire, but a whole range of other actions are now also deemed unacceptable. Chinese leaders have made sure to clarify what those entail, notably by promoting the concept of 'core interests' (*hexin liyi*). Its origins can be traced back to the mid-2000s,

---

[35] A few examples will suffice: The Sanya declaration of the first Lancang–Mekong cooperation leaders' meeting in March 2016 (www.fmprc.gov.cn/mfa_eng/wjdt_665385/2649_665393/201603/t20160323_679441.html), the Astana declaration of the SCO June 2017 summit (http://eng.sectsco.org/load/297146/), and the joint communiqué of the fourth round of political consultations between Chinese and African foreign ministers in September 2017 (www.fmprc.gov.cn/mfa_eng/wjdt_665385/2649_665393/201709/t20170922_679505.html). Of particular note is a 'Beijing declaration' that the CCP had endorsed by the representatives of around 300 foreign political parties, some of them high-ranking government figures, during the aforementioned 'CCP in dialogue with world political parties high-level meeting' of December 2017. The document, prepared largely by the Party's propaganda department, effusively praised not only the BRI but also CCP leadership in bringing about a 'community with a shared future for mankind' and building a beautiful world. See '中国共产党与世界政党高层对话会 北京倡议' [High-level dialogue of the Chinese Communist Party and world political parties, Beijing declaration], 3 December 2017, www.xinhuanet.com/world/2017-12/03/c_1122050731.htm.

[36] See, for instance, 'Wang Yi meets with Prime Minister Thongloun Sisoulith of Laos', 31 March 2018, www.chinaembassy.org.sg/eng//jrzg/t1547617.htm; 'Xi calls for building of China–Cambodia community of shared future', *Xinhua*, 21 January 2019.

when it started to spread through China's diplomatic discourse, signalling a more hard-line attitude towards security and sovereignty issues (Swaine, 2010: 3–4; Maeda, 2012: 3–4; Heath, 2014: 110-1). In their definitive form enounced in a 2011 White Paper, the 'core interests' encompass 'state sovereignty, national security, territorial integrity and national reunification, China's political system established by the Constitution and overall social stability, and the basic safeguards for ensuring sustainable economic and social development'.[37]

Xi Jinping has here again doubled down on such language, frequently pledging to safeguard China's 'core interests' and warning anyone who would undermine them that they 'simply cannot be sacrificed'.[38] By emphasizing their non-negotiable nature, he stresses that China will never tolerate either criticism of its domestic affairs or any behaviour that could harm its security and sovereignty claims over Taiwan and disputed waters in the East and South China Sea. Protecting 'core interests' is further described as a crucial part of the 'great rejuvenation of the Chinese nation', which implies washing away the stain of the 'century of humiliation' inflicted by imperial powers, restoring the inviolability of China's borders, and guaranteeing its absolute right to govern itself as it wishes. Any state that impedes those goals is in this narrative disrespecting a great nation. This effectively makes restraint from 'provocative' actions and critical statements a litmus test of the deference China demands from smaller states.

In Chinese leaders' telling, such demands are only fair since they themselves have steadily pledged to avoid confrontation. The 'community with a shared future for mankind', like its predecessors in the long line of Chinese diplomatic slogans, does not try to deny that all relations between states entail some differences and disagreements on issues big and small, but advocates putting those aside and focusing on areas where cooperation is possible, in the hope that years of positive interactions can eventually build enough trust for conflicts to be resolved without acrimony. This view has been expressed in different ways. Zhou Enlai popularized the expression 'seeking common ground while reserving differences' (*qiu tong cun yi*), a version of which he used at the Geneva and Bandung conferences of the early 1950s to urge participants to put ideological differences and more concrete gripes aside and focus on what they agree on (Liu Tuyao and Cheng Ruishan, 2007). Deng Xiaoping advocated 'shelving [territorial] disputes and pursuing joint

---

[37] White Paper on 'China's peaceful development', available at http://english.gov.cn/archive/white_paper/2014/09/09/content_281474986284646.htm.

[38] In his speech at the November 2014 Central Conference on Work Relating to Foreign Affairs already quoted earlier.

development' in relations with Asian neighbours.[39] Today Foreign Minister Wang Yi describes the 'new type of international relations' as one that 'avoids conflict and confrontation' (*bimian chongtu duikang*) to focus on exchanges and cooperation.[40] Xi Jinping himself has called for creating partnerships in the Asia-Pacific both with those who share China's aspirations and outlook and with those ready to 'seek common ground while reserving differences'.[41]

None of these formulas implies that China will compromise on issues in conflict. They are rather a promise not to actively create tensions around them. This is, of course, a much easier attitude to maintain far from Chinese shores than close to them. In Africa, Latin America, or the Middle East, its only concern is to maintain stable diplomatic relations, secure economic access, and obtain support for its policy towards Tibet, Xinjiang, Hong Kong, and Taiwan – something that most states are happy to provide (Nathan and Scobell, 2012: 30). Disputes are more likely on China's borders, where sovereignty issues have bedevilled relations with several neighbours. In those relations where conflicts do arise, China's rhetorical pledge to put differences aside puts the onus on other states to show equal restraint. Here again, it is claiming the moral high ground and setting out expectations for reciprocal treatment. All tensions that do occur are in its telling the result of a failure of other states to fulfil their own obligation to avoid conflicts.[42]

China's red lines have thus been set out in stark terms, and neighbours are expected to internalize them and behave consequently. Bilahari Kausikan, a former Singaporean diplomat, has vividly described how Chinese officials consistently hammer home their expectation that smaller neighbours show proper deference to reciprocate Beijing's benevolence and generosity, and internalize this mode of 'correct thinking' so that it naturally leads to 'correct behaviour' (2016). William Callahan has compared demands for acknowledgement of Chinese sovereignty over much of the South China Sea in particular with demands for tribute in pre-modern East Asia (2004: 58, 98–9). The analogy is valid if tribute and recognition of sovereignty claims are considered a form of symbolic acknowledgement of Chinese superiority. The South China Sea is indeed the most prominent apple of discord between

---

[39] Ministry of Foreign Affairs, 'Set aside dispute and pursue joint development', www.fmprc.gov.cn/mfa_eng/ziliao_665539/3602_665543/3604_665547/200011/t20001117_697808.html.

[40] 王毅 [Wang Yi], '构建以合作共赢为核心的新型国际关系' [Constructing a new type of international with win-win cooperation at the core], *Study Times*, 20 June 2016.

[41] In a speech at the opening ceremony of the APEC CEO Summit in November 2014, http://politics.people.com.cn/n/2014/1109/c1001-25999767.html.

[42] For an example of the history of the South China Sea disputes framed as a series of provocative actions by other claimants testing China's consistent restraint and constructive behaviour, see Fu and Wu (2016).

China and its southern neighbours. Today, any attempt by smaller neighbours to exploit economic resources in disputed areas without Chinese permission is seen as an intolerable infringement on its 'maritime rights and interests', just as is any rhetorical or legal challenge to Chinese sovereignty claims (Kotani, 2013: 32–8; Kardon, 2015: 7–19).

Yet Chinese demands for concrete demonstrations of deference are broader than this single issue, since it is at the end of the day up to China to determine what constitutes an intolerable 'provocation', and since it has become increasingly intolerant of any challenge or criticism whatsoever. A constant theme in Chinese writings on territorial disputes in recent years is that other claimants are 'in collusion' with the US in provoking maritime tensions and are playing into Washington's hands as it seeks to contain a rising rival (Li Mingjiang, 2012: 3). Such criticism echoes the admonition of Chinese leaders that small states in East Asia should show the wisdom not to align with any great power against another. Chinese officials have also made clear in private settings that they view smaller neighbours' challenges of China's sovereignty claims or criticism of its actions in the South China Sea and elsewhere as signs of a failure to show proper deference to Chinese greatness.[43]

The PRC's embrace of the language of 'inviolable core interests', absolute sovereignty, and absolute security has thus hardened its attitude and reduced the space for negotiation around contentious issues. When any action taken by a neighbour for the sake of national security becomes a sinful offence to 'core interests' because it potentially has an impact on China's own security, the onus is entirely on the other side to amend its behaviour, even if this means undermining what it also considers a crucial national interest. A notable example is the decision by South Korea to install an American-built missile defence system in response to the threat from the North in January 2016. Foreign Minister Wang Yi declared flatly that the deployment 'goes far beyond the defence need of the Korean Peninsula' and would 'jeopardize China's legitimate rights and interest'.[44] South Korea's behaviour was particularly condemnable because it was seen as a potent symbol of the country's alignment with the US against China. A Foreign Ministry spokesperson put it in plain terms: 'By getting on board with the

---

[43] The most famous instance of such private remarks is then Foreign Minister Yang Jiechi's irritated response to criticism from his Singaporean counterpart at the 2010 ASEAN summit, when he snapped back that 'China is a big country and other countries are small countries, and that's just a fact'. This reaction was triggered by the spectacle of several South-East Asian states following the US' lead in criticizing China's behaviour in the South China Sea. See Callahan, 2016: 231; Hayden, 2016 for other examples.

[44] Ministry of Foreign Affairs, 'Wang Yi talks about US's plan to deploy THAAD missile defense system in ROK', www.mfa.gov.cn/ce/ceus//eng/zgyw/t1340525.htm.

U.S., the ROK has involved itself in tipping the scale of regional strategic balance'.[45] This offence was enough to put South Korea in the doghouse for more than a year, with China virtually breaking up official contacts and using economic means to put pressure on South Korea to reconsider (Swaine, 2017: 2). Beijing only relented after South Korea had 'made amends' by offering assurances (dubbed the '3 no's') that it would not deploy any additional anti-ballistic missile systems, participate in a US regional missile defence network, or participate in a trilateral military alliance with the US and Japan.[46]

This hard-line attitude is the sharp edge of China's vision of modern hierarchical relations in Asia, where its willingness to treat others benevolently finds its limits and where showing respect and deference means refraining from asserting one's interests and needs if they conflict with those of Beijing. From China's point of view, its use of coercive means in retaliation to others' 'offences' is always justified since it is only 'punishing' those who breach the rules of propriety that should ensure cordial relations among Asian states. Obviously, its neighbours do not share that view. In any case, there are here too clear elements of continuity with the way it used its power in the imperial past. It is to this topic that we turn our attention in the next chapter.

---

[45] Ministry of Foreign Affairs, 'Foreign Ministry spokesperson Lu Kang's regular press conference', 11 July 2016, www.mfa.gov.cn/ce/ceus//eng/fyrth/t1379216.htm.

[46] Park Byong-Su, 'South Korea's 'three no's' announcement key to restoring relations with China', *The Hankyoreh*, 2 November 2017.

7

Traditional Tools of Rulership in the Modern World

To wrap up the argument of this book, this chapter looks at the way in which the three traditional 'tools of rulership' identified in Chapter 2 – namely, language, awesomeness, and profits – are being employed by the PRC to achieve the vision of a hierarchical international order. Needless to say, those tools have uses other than the ones that will be highlighted here. Yet the orientation towards maintenance of order and of China's central position is an important one that has deep historical roots and has remained visible throughout the history of the PRC. As noted in Chapter 4, before 1949, a weak and divided China beset by foreign invasion and internal strife was in no position to devote resources to support its position in international society. In its early years, the PRC was still relatively weak but did seek to make use of the power that naturally comes from having founded a unified government ruling over the world's largest country to sustain its status claim on the world stage. In these early endeavours, it was already clear that traditional ways of thinking about the use of power had endured through the transformations of the early 20th century. This remained true throughout the following decades, and has become more apparent than ever under Xi Jinping. The following pages will discuss in turn how each of the three 'tools of rulership' continue to be used in ways reminiscent of China's imperial past, starting with language. Here, two aspects deserve particular attention. First, PRC leaders have dedicated much attention to their country's overall ability to have its voice heard internationally and control how its foreign relations are depicted. Second is a more specific use of 'names' in one of the central pillars of PRC foreign policy since the 1990s, namely, a network of partnerships that is the closest thing China has to a modern ranks and titles system.

Increasing discourse power

The PRC was initially a poor and technologically backward country, so the resource the CCP could use most liberally was its ability to speak to its citizens and to the rest of international society. Despite his hostility towards Confucius, Mao in fact saw much value in his doctrine of the 'rectification of names' as long as it was adapted to fit revolutionary purposes. In a letter to fellow communist leader Zhang Wentian, he argued that for names to be rectified, they needed to be guided by a good understanding of reality acquired through practice, since 'if the facts are unclear, then the names will not be correct'.[1] If this principle was respected and names were made to conform with circumstances – or at least the Marxist understanding of them – they could serve as crucial tools in the revolutionary struggle. We can see in the belief in the power of correct 'names' one root of the CCP's mighty 'propaganda' (*xuanchuan*) apparatus – a word that in Chinese simply means 'to disseminate' or 'to proclaim'. What the Party seeks to disseminate is the correct way to characterize the various problems and issues China faces so that it can guide the people towards the 'right' solution. Anyone either inside or outside China that promotes ideas hostile to the Chinese state needs to be countered rhetorically as well. Indeed, Mao 'referred to China's ideological war with the Soviet Union as a struggle over "proper names"' (Sorace, 2017: 8).

Christian Sorace aptly characterizes the PRC as a 'discursive state' for which propaganda and the promotion of correct language is a fundamental tool to shape the behaviour of its citizens (2017: 6). Discussing the control over 'formulations' (*tifa*) that is central to the PRC's propaganda system, Perry Link emphasizes their power to 'cut off alternative ways of thinking and limit the conceptual horizons of the people who adopt them' (2013: 275). Although the CCP's ability to promote its discourse towards the rest of international society is far more limited than in the domestic spheres – in Mao's time, it essentially amounted to state media and to leaders' declarations, along with the hosting of underground radio stations for certain Asian revolutionary movements – a keen attention to the realm of language and rhetoric was from the start an important feature of its foreign policy. As its rivalry with the Soviet Union grew, the PRC sought to invite students and revolutionary activists from across the developing world to 'educate' them and convince them that the Chinese interpretation of Marxism-Leninism was the correct one and that it was the true leader of world revolution (Friedman, 2015: 49, 53). The CCP also gave significant rhetorical support through state medias to revolutionary movements around the world – a

---

[1] 'To Zhang Wentian', 20 February 1939. Reproduced in Schram 2005: 33.

support much more widespread than grants of financial or military assistance (Van Ness, 1970: 204–8).

After the abandonment of the Maoist line, the objective of the CCP's international discourse strategy switched to depicting China as a cooperative and peace-loving country. This message was propagated through foreign language news outlets, through a new system of government spokesperson, and in the public speeches of leaders (Wang Hongying, 2003: 51–2; Ni Chen, 2011: 74–80). These efforts had at first a defensive purpose, aiming to 'explain China to the world' so as to correct the negative image spread by the Western press and fuelled by concerns about China's growing strength (Aoyama, 2014: 16). Chinese leaders clearly already believed that combating Western criticism and seizing ground in the realm of international speech was essential to the country's rise.

This belief seems to have only strengthened over the years, and was eventually encapsulated in the idea of a fight for 'discourse power' (*huayuquan*). The expression started to appear in Chinese academic writings in the early 2000s and had become mainstream by the end of the decade (Takagi, 2011: 4–5; Wang Hung-jen, 2015: 176–7). Its importance has only grown since and Xi Jinping has used it many times. As Takagi Seiichirō notes, 'discourse power' is related to two other concepts also frequently referenced by Chinese leaders and scholars, 'soft power' and 'public diplomacy', but it implies a greater focus on competition between states in which 'discourse' is an area of struggle (2011: 8).[2] Discourse power thus refers to the marshalling of the resources of the state in a way that is effective enough to overcome the opposition of rivals (that is, Western powers) and to propagate one's message to the outside world in a convincing way. In a sense, then, rivalry with the West is seen as a new battle over 'names' like the one against the Soviet Union in the 1960s, focused this time not on questions of Marxist ideology but on the best way to describe China itself so as to make it a more appealing international leader. One commentary in the Party's leading theoretical journal *Qiushi* describes discourse power as the ability to define the 'criteria for right and wrong, true and false, good and evil, beautiful and ugly' (Zhang Guozo, 2009). Mastering this is seen as crucial to ensure that China successfully grows into a respected great power since, as a prominent scholar argues, no country can successfully rise without having its own discourse (Zhang Weiwei, quoted in Wen Jian, 2016: 36).

---

[2] Soft power is, simply put, the power 'that arises from the attractiveness of a country's culture, political ideals, and policies' (Nye, 2004: x). Public diplomacy is the effort to improve a country's image among ordinary citizens around the world through information campaigns and outreach efforts in order to gain soft power.

Concretely, waging this campaign means improving the quality of Chinese external propaganda by making sure it resonates with different publics, increasing the visibility of Chinese media abroad and encouraging Chinese leaders and diplomats to take any opportunity they get to directly address the international community through speeches, newspaper editorials, and interviews (Zhao Kejin, 2016: 556–9). Those efforts were already underway before Xi came to power, but he has repeatedly insisted on their importance since then.[3]

The purpose of strengthening China's discourse power, according to Xi, is to 'shape China's national image' (*guojia xingxiang*) in four directions, that of a harmonious and culturally rich 'civilized major country', that of a stable, prosperous, and unified 'Eastern major country', that of a 'responsible major country' ready to promote international peace and development and contribute to mankind's well-being, and that of a 'socialist major country' full of hope and vitality.[4] The way China is to be described to the outside world is thus laid out quite clearly, in the hope that other states will more easily acknowledge its status as a leading great power if they are exposed to this positive discourse. Xi has also urged the creation and use of 'Chinese social sciences theories' to interpret Chinese behaviour so as to further raise its discourse power (Rolland, 2020: 28–9).

Creating a network of partnerships

Belief in the power of controlling the language used to describe China and its relations with the word also expresses itself in a much more precise and pointed way, namely, in China's 'partnership diplomacy'. Its origins can be traced to the early 1990s, when the first partnerships were concluded with major powers and important countries in other regions of the world, starting with Brazil in 1993 and Russia in 1994. Those early agreements did not have a broader strategic significance for China, however, and were simply understood as symbols to celebrate a healthy and well-developed relationship (Masuda, 2000: 87–8). In the years prior, Beijing had observed

---

[3] See, for instance, a heavily publicized speech at a Party conference on news and public opinion work in February 2016, where Xi called to 'optimize the strategic arrangement' of the CCP's international propaganda to tell China's story well and make its overseas media more influential ('哈坚持正确方向创新方法手段 提高新闻舆论传播力引导力' [Adhere to the correct direction, innovative methods and means, improve the guiding force of news and public opinion], *People's Daily*, 20 February 2016).

[4] In a speech in December 2013 to the 12th collective study session of the 18th Central Committee Politburo. See '习近平: 建设社会主义文化强国 着力提高国家文化软实力' [Xi Jinping: Build a socialist cultured strong country and striving to improve the soft power of national culture], *Xinhua Online*, 31 December 2013.

the increasing use of partnerships by Western states but was not yet sure what this new trend meant for the nature of the international order after the end of the Cold War – beyond a conviction that those states were simply continuing their power-political struggle with new tools (Sun Baoshan, 1999: 90; Ebihara, 2000: 25; Ning Sao, 2000: 4).

Eventually, though, China came to see partnerships as useful means to achieve its strategic objectives, that is, first and foremost, to maintain a favourable environment for its economic development by building friendly, formally equal ties with all the major powers (Masuda, 2000: 100; Goldstein, 2001: 846–8; 2005: 130–5; Cheng and Zhang, 2002: 255–7). Starting in 1997, China thus concluded a flurry of agreements to build partnerships with major countries like France, the UK, the US, Japan, and India.[5] China was here belatedly taking part in a global trend with many participants but quickly stood out for its enthusiasm and for the care it took in elaborating a network of agreements. Indeed, partnerships were identified as a core part of the 'new type of inter-state relations' that China aimed to build (Sun Baoshan, 1999: 89; Ebihara, 2000: 27).

They were appealing tools for several reasons, first among them their flexibility. Partnerships are general agreements at the leadership level to pursue cooperation and strengthen bilateral dialogue in different fields, not a list of concrete commitments enshrined in treaties. Their symbolic nature – they are meant to signify both sides' determination to ensure long-term stability in their relationship and leave aside issues in conflict – and their function as frameworks to maintain a steady process of mutual engagement and cooperation without any specific goal in mind were equally valuable to Chinese leaders (Strüver, 2017: 36–7).

All partnerships were not equal, though, and not all partners were given equal status. Seen as a network rather than as a series of discrete agreements, China's promotion of partnerships reveals its leaders' enduring belief in the power of names to serve as a guide for 'proper' inter-state interactions. Each agreement came from the start with a combination of various qualifiers such as 'strategic', 'comprehensive', 'constructive', and 'cooperative'. Various partnerships were thus hierarchically organized in different layers according to which qualifiers were attached to them, although in those early days the overall logic of the Chinese classification system had not yet been fully rationalized. Different analysts depicted different pyramidal structures. Joseph Cheng and Zhang Wankun, for instance, saw five to six levels of partnerships, with strategic ones with the US – the global hegemon – and Russia – its most important partner among the great powers – at the top, followed by comprehensive ones with other great powers and major regional powers

---

[5] A list of the first batch of partnerships can be found in Cheng and Zhang, 2002: 237.

with which China had relatively conflict-free ties, partnerships with regional organizations, and other types of partnerships with important neighbours with which China had major issues in dispute (Japan and India) or other lesser states in the developing world (2002: 244–5). Su Hao saw instead four layers of partnerships with major great powers, regional powers, and organizations, other states, and long-standing friends in the Global South (2000: 11–2). Still, all agreed that Chinese diplomats carefully chose the name of each partnership and the language used to describe them, denoting different expectations and valuation for different relations (Su Hao, 2000: 11; Cheng and Zhang, 2002: 244).

Partnerships thus offered something that Chinese leaders highly valued, namely, a flexible, adaptable, but stable framework within which to deal with a changing international situation, allowing for the 'categorizing' (*dingwei*) of various partners and characterization of their relation with the PRC, seen as essential for the subsequent development of healthy ties.[6] We noted in Chapter 3 that Chinese statesmen of the imperial era seemed to possess an 'urge to classify' the polities they were dealing with. The attribution of the 'correct' status to foreign rulers was considered a prerequisite for conducting relations with them. The PRC's enthusiastic embrace of partnerships and the use it makes of them suggests that its leaders have inherited this urge from their distant predecessors.

Although great powers were initially the most prominent targets of Chinese efforts, its neighbourhood was not left out. Not only India and Japan but also Pakistan and South Korea were part of the first wave of partnerships concluded. ASEAN also became a partner in 1997. Partnerships were already seen then as an important tool for establishing a Chinese lead regional order.[7] The use of partnerships would only expand during the 2000s, adding new counterparts and upgrading existing ones to reflect deepening relations. Their number truly exploded after 2008, even as the use of various qualifiers was rationalized to produce a more coherent pyramid of partners based on clearer, though still flexible, criteria. They have become a characteristic feature of 'major country diplomacy with Chinese characteristics' under Xi Jinping, who in 2014 called for the establishment of a 'global network of partnerships'.[8] In a speech in December 2017, Foreign Minister Wang Yi

---

[6] The Chinese media have repeatedly used the phrase 'China has always used "partnerships" to categorize bilateral relations'. See, for instance, '中国有哪些伙伴关系' [What partnerships does China have], *Qilu Evening News*, 31 March 2014.

[7] Jiang Zemin praised the 1997 partnership with ASEAN for contributing to 'the establishment of a fair and rational international order' and to 'the promotion of the lofty cause of the peace and development of Asia and the world'. See Jiang Zemin, '建立面向二十一世纪的睦邻互信伙伴关系' [Building a partnership facing the 21st century based on good neighbourliness and mutual trust], *People's Daily*, 17 December 1997.

[8] At the 2014 Central Conference on Work Relating to Foreign Affairs.

described China's network of partnerships as an important manifestation of its commitment to a 'new type of international relations'.[9] The PRC now has such relations with more than 80 countries and several international organizations. The majority of them has been concluded or upgraded since 2010, with a noticeable acceleration after Xi took power. Two scholars at the Central Party School call this period the 'perfecting stage' (*wanshan qi*) of China's partnership strategy (Men and Liu, 2015: 72).

Partnerships are thus a key feature of contemporary Chinese diplomacy. The joint declarations through which they are typically announced include both formulaic elements – references to typical Chinese diplomatic terms like mutual benefits, mutual respect, respect for sovereignty, equality, multipolarity, and a more just international order; promises to strengthen high-level exchanges and deepen cooperation in economic, technical, educational, and cultural fields; declarations of support for various international organizations (either global or regional) – and elements more specific to each relationship depending on the size, geographical location of the partner, and its common history with China.[10] Several also directly resonate with Chinese security concerns by expressing support for Chinese sovereignty over Taiwan or pledges not to enter an alliance with a third country that could be harmful to the other. Most recent ones also include pledges of support for the BRI.[11]

These partnerships help sustain the Sinocentric pattern of diplomacy described in the previous chapter in several ways. First, they serve as prominent 'deliverables' to advertise state visits by Chinese leaders abroad or by counterparts to Beijing (Feng and Huang, 2014: 14). Secondly, they grant a significant degree of control to Beijing over the 'scope, content and pace of engagement' in its foreign relations (Medeiros, 2009: 86). Thirdly, they endorse the Chinese diplomatic rhetoric about a better type of international relation and contribute to the propagation of its 'major country' image (Sun Jingxin and Lin Janwei, 2015: 37). Yet partnerships are much more than simple 'marketing tools' boosting China's profile. What they offer is a way to organize almost all China's foreign relations in one coherent structure, indicating each country's rank and status with relative clarity.

Granted, the extent to which the design of said structure of partnerships has been deliberately planned over the long term should not be overestimated.

---

[9] Speech at a Symposium on International Developments and China's Diplomacy, www.fmprc.gov.cn/mfa_eng/wjdt_665385/zyjh_665391/201712/t20171210_678651.html.

[10] Based on the reading of several declarations on the formation or upgrade of partnerships with countries in East Asia, Central Asia, Africa, and Europe issued over the last decade and a half. Several of them will be referenced later.

[11] In fact, there is quite a lot of overlap between partner countries and participants in said initiative (Chen Xiaochen, 2016).

Several Chinese scholars who have analysed it advocate a more rational approach to determining what each level of partnership entails and what the criteria are for choosing one type of partnership over another in any given relationship (Men and Liu, 2015: 94). Case in point, 'comprehensive strategic cooperative partnerships' (*quanmian zhanlüe hezuo huoban guanxi*) seemed until recently to be reserved for China's close neighbours in South-East Asia, but in 2016, partnerships with the Republic of Congo, with Senegal, and with the African Union were upgraded to the same level. Zimbabwe and Namibia were added to the list two years later. One Chinese scholar suggests as motivation for the expansion of this type of partnership to African states that Xi sees relations with them as a model to demonstrate how his 'new type of international relations' can be realized (Zhang Ying, 2018: 35–6).

In any case, this suggests that the design of the overall structure of China's partnerships network is still a work in progress open to modifications to fit the country's immediate diplomatic priorities. Nevertheless, compared with the early 2000s, the various kinds of partnerships have now been organized and rationalized into a relatively clear structure, even if much ambiguity remains concerning the criteria for particular countries' placements. This structure gives pride of place to Asia where most of the high-ranking countries are located. Table 7.1 summarizes the different ranks of China's partnerships on the continent.

Outside of a few one-in-a-kind agreements, all partnerships are either 'cooperative', 'strategic', 'comprehensive', or a combination of the three. 'Friendly' (*youhao*) and 'omnidirectional' (*quanfangqyi*) also make several appearances. These different combinations create a ranking order between partners, or a 'layering' (*cengcixing*) system as several articles quoted in this section put it. All of China's Asian neighbours are part of it in one way or another, except for Japan and North Korea. The partnership with Russia, which uses a different word for 'cooperative' (*xiezuo*) that denotes closer coordination, and the 'all-weather' (*quantianhou*) one with Pakistan stand out, reflecting the importance that Beijing attaches to relations with those two particular states. The former is today the model for the 'new type of great power relations' and the latter is the flagship member of the BRI.

'Comprehensive strategic cooperative partnerships', containing the whole range of typical qualifiers, stand one rank lower. The aforementioned African exceptions aside, they are reserved for the five countries of the Mekong region (Myanmar, Thailand, Laos, Cambodia, and Vietnam), a mark of their importance in Chinese foreign policy. Other countries in China's 'periphery' (Bangladesh, South Korea, Afghanistan, and Sri Lanka) are classified as 'strategic cooperative partners', one echelon below. India was in the same category until 2014, when on the occasion of a state visit to New Dehli by Xi Jinping to mark a 'year of friendship', the two countries agreed to establish a special 'development partnership' (*fazhan huoban guanxi*). Going

Table 7.1: China's partnerships in Asia (as of 2021)

Rank	Type of partnership	Countries
1	Comprehensive strategic coordination partnership for a new era/All-weather strategic cooperative partnership	Russia/Pakistan
2	Comprehensive strategic cooperative partnership	Myanmar, Thailand, Cambodia, Laos, Vietnam
3	Strategic cooperative partnership/Development partnership	South Korea, Bangladesh, Afghanistan, Sri Lanka, Turkey/India
4	Comprehensive strategic partnership	Kazakhstan, Uzbekistan, Tajikistan, Kyrgyzstan, Indonesia, Malaysia, Mongolia, ASEAN
5	Strategic partnership	Turkmenistan
6	Omnidirectional cooperative partnership/Comprehensive cooperative partnership/Comprehensive friendly cooperative partnership	Singapore/Nepal, East Timor/Maldives
7	(Comprehensive) strategic cooperative relationship	Philippines, Brunei

further down the ladder we find 'comprehensive strategic partnerships' followed by simple 'strategic partnerships', in which categories are ASEAN as well as other neighbouring states like the five Central Asian countries (Kazakhstan, Uzbekistan, Tajikistan, Kyrgyzstan, and Turkmenistan), Indonesia, Malaysia, and Mongolia – along with Iran and many states of all sizes on other continents. Finally, some neighbours are 'omnidirectional friendly cooperative partners' (the Maldives), 'comprehensive cooperative partners' (Nepal and East Timore), 'omnidirectional cooperative partners' (Singapore), or even not partners but part of a 'comprehensive strategic cooperation relationship' (the Philippines), or, at the lowest echelon, simply a 'strategic cooperation relationship' (Brunei).

Looking at the whole network in Asia, then, a hierarchical structure does exist with Russia and Pakistan sitting on top, followed by continental South-East Asian states and other neighbours arranged in a varied patchwork below them, where the relative ranking of each state becomes increasingly ambiguous the further one goes down the ranking order. Ambiguity is a key word here, since there is no official policy document clarifying what distinguishes one type of partnership from the other. Outside of the Mekong region, only three neighbouring states qualify for a 'cooperative' partnership, which Liu and Fang argue signifies an emphasis on mutually beneficial economic ties and policy coordination (2016: 76). Yet China promotes economic 'win-win cooperation' in all its foreign relations and one can doubt there is more policy cooperation with Myanmar, say, or South Korea, than with Malaysia or Kazakhstan.

Take the example of Myanmar, who became a partner in 2011, and Kazakhstan,[12] whose partnership was upgraded the same year. The declarations announcing these agreements contain fairly similar language about increasing cooperation between all branches of government, setting up regular meetings at the very top (between foreign ministries in the first case, prime ministers in the second), and strengthening mutually beneficial economic and technical cooperation.[13] The Chinese Foreign Ministry web page about relations with the two countries describes roughly similar levels of governmental interactions and trade figures.[14]

The appendage or not of the terms 'comprehensive', which is meant to refer to the breadth of the areas of cooperation between two partners and the depth of their relationship in each area, and of the term 'strategic', which underlines cooperation in defence and security issues and the connection of the partnership with international or regional geopolitics is somewhat easier to understand (Liu Bowei and Fang Changping, 2016: 76). More areas of cooperation are indeed generally evoked in 'comprehensive' partnerships than in non-comprehensive ones,[15] and 'strategic' partnerships contain more references to defence, security, and regional cooperation than non-strategic ones.[16] There are ambiguities here too, however.

Take the examples of Afghanistan, Sri Lanka, and Bangladesh, all upgraded from 'comprehensive' to 'strategic' cooperation partners between 2012 and 2016. The announcements to that effect did include slightly more emphasis on defence cooperation in the case of Sri Lanka and on coordination in international and regional affairs in the two other cases, but those were

---

[12] The partnership with Kazakhstan was affixed the term 'permanent' (*yongjiu*) at a summit in Beijing in September 2019, likely to acknowledge the country's special importance as the largest in Central Asia and the most active BRI participant.

[13] The declaration on the partnership with Myanmar is available at www.gov.cn/jrzg/2011-05/27/content_1872426.htm and the one with Kazakhstan at www.gov.cn/ldhd/2011-06/14/content_1883456.htm.

[14] www.fmprc.gov.cn/web/gjhdq_676201/gj_676203/yz_676205/1206_676788/sbgx_676792/ and www.fmprc.gov.cn/web/gjhdq_676201/gj_676203/yz_676205/1206_676500/sbgx_676504/ respectively.

[15] Compare, for instance, the 2011 declaration of a 'comprehensive' partnership with Kazakhstan referenced earlier with the non-comprehensive partnership announced with Turkmenistan two years later (www.gov.cn/ldhd/2013-09/04/content_2480874.htm).

[16] Compare, for instance, the announcement of a 'strategic' partnership with Thailand in 2008 (www.gov.cn/jrzg/2012-04/19/content_2117598.htm) with the non-strategic one with Nepal the next year (www.gov.cn/jrzg/2009-12/30/content_1500381.htm).

part of a broader increase in pledges to cooperate in all areas (political, economic, cultural, technical) that typically accompany the switch from non-comprehensive to comprehensive partnerships.[17] The change in qualifiers this time was thus not really a reflection of the evolving content of the agreements with these three countries, but rather a consequence of previous developments in their relationship with China. They were already comprehensive cooperation partners, and China was apparently reluctant to make them full 'comprehensive strategic cooperative partners' – perhaps to maintain a distinction with the Mekong region states, or to leave space for further upgrades down the line – leaving a switch to 'strategic' as the logical choice.

This reveals the contingent nature of the development of each partner relationship. China has developed its network on a case-by-case basis, depending on past developments in each relationship, on its evaluation of their current state at any given time, and simply on factors like the diplomatic agenda of its leaders. For instance, the only country in Central Asia that is not yet a 'comprehensive' strategic partner is Turkmenistan, but there is little difference between the depths of its bilateral interactions with China and those of neighbouring Tajikistan or Kyrgyzstan, say, according to the Chinese Foreign Ministry's website.[18] Turkmenistan stands out, certainly, for its 'permanent neutral' status and for not being part of the Shanghai Cooperation Organisation, but this would in theory be a reason to avoid a strategic partnership, meant to include more of a focus on international and security issues, rather than a comprehensive one. A better explanation may simply be the vagaries of China's diplomatic agenda. Tajikistan and Kyrgyzstan's 'comprehensive strategic partnerships' were announced during state visits to Beijing, and a future visit by the Turkmen President may yield a similar upgrade. One could also mention the additional prefixes, such as 'closer' (*gengjia jinmi*) in the case of India or Bangladesh, 'generational friendship' (*shidai youhao*) in the case of Nepal and Sri Lanka, or 'keeping

---

[17] For the joint declarations with Afghanistan announcing a 'comprehensive' partnership in 2006 and the upgrade to 'strategic' in 2012, see www.gov.cn/gongbao/content/2006/content_352476.htm and www.mfa.gov.cn/ce/celt//chn/xwdt/t939513.htm respectively. For the joint declarations with Sri Lanka (2005 and 2013), see www.gov.cn/gongbao/content/2005/content_64190.htm and www.chinatoday.com.cn/ctchinese/news/article/2013-05/30/content_545631.htm. For Bangladesh (2005 and 2016), see www.fmprc.gov.cn/chn//pds/ziliao/1179/t190790.htm and www.mfa.gov.cn/web/ziliao_674904/1179_674909/201610/t20161015_7947721.shtml. All those switches confirm that 'strategic' is considered a higher ranking than 'comprehensive'.

[18] See www.fmprc.gov.cn/web/gjhdq_676201/gj_676203/yz_676205/1206_676980/sbgx_676984/, www.fmprc.gov.cn/web/gjhdq_676201/gj_676203/yz_676205/1206_676908/sbgx_676912/, and www.fmprc.gov.cn/web/gjhdq_676201/gj_676203/yz_676205/1206_676548/sbgx_676552/ respectively.

with the times' (*yushi jujin*) in the case of Singapore, that are sometimes added to different partnerships, giving them yet more unique flavours that do not seem to obey any overarching logic.

The ambiguities and particularities of Chinese partnerships are thus a feature rather than a bug, and an integral part of China's network-building effort. Keeping the rules of engagement loose grants China a high degree of flexibility in how it deals with any given partner, allowing it to adapt to how their relationship evolves. By not setting strict criteria as to what qualifies a country for a certain type of partnership, China also enhances its control over the precise shape of the ranking order in which its partners are placed, as policy makers in Beijing are the only ones capable of determining where any relationship should be slotted. What matters is that it is slotted somewhere, or, in other words, that the status of each partner and the nature of its relationship with China is properly defined and included into an overall structure, even if some categories have been created for one state only.

That is not to say that each state's relative ranking is meaningless. The link between intensity of interactions and the characterization of partnerships may not be very solid, but partners are still arranged according to more diffuse criteria such as their strategic importance as well as their 'degree of intimacy and distance' to China (*qinshu yuanjin*) (Liu and Fang, 2016: 76). The first criterion, strategic importance, is not sufficient to explain the ordering of partnerships. For instance, China is putting similar emphasis on the two components of the BRI, the 'Silk Road Economic Belt' running through Central Asia and the '21st Maritime Silk Road' running through South-East Asia. It has also underlined its concern about separatist and terrorist threats in Xinjiang. Yet all Central Asian states are still ranked lower in partnership terms than continental South-East Asian states. We could also mention Indonesia, the largest state in South-East Asia and one in a position to control the southern end of the South China Sea. As such, it would be expected to hold a high strategic significance but it is only, so to say, a 'comprehensive strategic partner'.

Regarding the second criterion, we should first note that proximity to China is not to be understood in a geographical sense, but in terms of relational closeness in a similar fashion to intimacy (although geographical distance still plays a role since most high-ranking partners are neighbours of China). In that guise, it is, of course, rather vague as it could refer not only to how 'comprehensive' and 'cooperative' bilateral interactions actually are, but also to degrees of cultural closeness, to the length of a country's history of diplomatic engagement with the PRC, to how often the two sides take common positions on international issues, or to the prevalence of issues in conflict in the relationship. Even if one were to simply associate intimacy with friendly relations generally speaking, the correlation between degree of friendliness and partnership characterization is far from absolute. China has indeed developed uniquely close ties to Russia and Pakistan since the end of the Cold War (or even before in Pakistan's case), but below them, not all states of the Mekong region are on equally cordial terms with their northern neighbours (the territorial dispute with Vietnam in the South China Sea comes to mind), while Nepal, the only South Asian state outside of the special cases of India and Pakistan that is not yet a 'strategic cooperative partner', has in fact a much longer history of friendship towards China than, say, Bangladesh. This is to say nothing of the absence of partnership with North Korea, supposedly China's only real ally (Feng Zhongping and Huang Jing, 2014: 8).

Nevertheless, intimacy, tempered with strategic and geographical considerations, is still the closest thing to an overarching organizing principle for China's hierarchy of partnerships. It is first emphasized by China itself in the announcements of new or upgraded partnerships. They typically start with praise for the friendship between the two sides and the steady pace at which bilateral cooperation is developing, statements that tend to be more effusive for higher-ranking agreements and to mention cultural affinity, shared values (those of the Five Principles or the 'new type of international relations'), common struggles of the past, common views of international issues, and anything that can underline the closeness of the two sides. Secondly, the fact that intimacy is a rather vague concept that can be understood in different ways relates to the flexible nature of the rules surrounding partnerships, which are meant to leave China's as the sole interpreter of their meaning.

Simply put, it is up to Beijing to decide how intimate, or friendly, any potential partner country is and, if it is 'deserving' of a partnership, what rank is most appropriate for it. Finally, this criterion of intimacy is another expression of the moral virtues that Chinese leaders say should guide relations with smaller neighbouring states.[19] Understood this way, the granting of a partnership or the upgrade of an existing one is an acknowledgement that the other side is fulfilling his side of the bargain by adopting what China considers a friendly enough policy towards it. As Feng Zhongping and Huang Jing put it, a 'solid record of cooperation' built with any given state 'can be widely seen as a blessing for further upgrading the partnership, or a good omen for initiating [one]' (2014: 9). In other words, partnerships serve as indicators of the degree to which China sees various neighbouring relations as stable and productive, as well as milestones towards further development in those ties. Taken as a whole, they place China at the centre of a network of

---

[19] As we may recall, Xi Jinping has repeatedly evoked intimacy (*qin*) as one of the principles that should guide China's peripheral diplomacy. See, for instance, his speech at the Peripheral Diplomacy Work Conference in October 2013.

relationships organized according to its own criteria and guiding its partners towards acceptance of its leading role in the region.

Demonstrating China's awesomeness

If partnerships serve as milestones on the road to ever-closer ties between China and its neighbours, the People's Liberation Army (PLA) – and the Chinese coastguard in the maritime sphere – are there to warn off states that show signs of deviating from that road. After decades of rapid economic growth and correspondingly large increases to military budgets, the PLA has become a formidable force. Yet even before China managed to build a 'strong army', it did not hesitate to employ force as a tool of statecraft, relying on the sheer number of its soldiers rather than technological sophistication. Already in the early days of the PRC, its leaders talked of the use of military force in terms of 'awesomeness' and 'punishment' reminiscent of the imperial era.

The PLA had in fact spent much of its first 30 years of existence engaged in fighting with its rival in the Chinese civil war, with Japan and after the communist victory with the US on the Korean Peninsula, all for the sake of taking control of China and defending it against foreign threats. Mao was keenly aware of the prestige these successful campaigns had brought the CCP. This was one of the reasons he invoked when he confidently proclaimed that the East (communist) winds would prevail over the Western (capitalist) ones in a famous speech in Moscow in November 1957.[20] This prestige did not prevent China from being challenged by India in disputed territories in the Himalaya. After months of tensions and what it described as repeated Indian incursions, China decided to launch a major offensive based on familiar reasoning. India was deliberately trying to 'attack China's prestige in the third world' and was showing through its assertive behaviour that it did not 'respect the power of New China'. It therefore needed to be taught a lesson that would 'cause the aggressors to receive their proper punishment'.[21] Once that punishment was administered through an overwhelming victory on the battlefield, China suspended its offensive and sued for peace.

A similar 'punitive' logic dictated the war on Vietnam 17 years later, shortly after the death of Mao. In that case, the tensions over Vietnam's lack of deference, touched on in the previous chapter, eventually culminated in

---

[20] 'Speech at a meeting of the representatives of sixty-four communist and workers' parties', 18 November 1957. Text available at https://digitalarchive.wilsoncenter.org/document/121559.

[21] All three quotes are from Garver, 2006: 113, 110, and 114 respectively. The first and the third quotes are in fact themselves taken from Xu Yan's *True History of the Sino-Indian Border Self-Defensive War* (徐焰：中印边界争端和冲突的历史真相), written on the basis of unique access to primary sources.

a border war in early 1979, following Vietnam's invasion of Cambodia and, Beijing claimed, repeated border incursions. The Chinese response to such 'provocations' was, according to Deng Xiaoping, to 'teach Vietnam a lesson and give her some punishment, reduce her arrogance, and then withdraw troops' (Shi Hua, 1979: 55; see also Shih Chih-Yu, 1990: 119–20; Zhang Xiaoming, 2015: 65). The echoes of the 'punitive expeditions' of yore are clear. The fact that such utterances came from Deng Xiaoping right at the time that he was consolidating his authority and launching his country towards 'reform and opening up' also suggests, unsurprisingly, that such views did not suddenly disappear with the death of Mao. If China remained ready to use force thereafter to awe and 'punish' neighbours with whom it had maritime territorial disputes, though, the war of 1979 remains to this day the last large-scale military conflict in which it has been engaged.

In the following decades, even as the PRC focused on self-strengthening, it largely refrained from boasting about its growing power on the international stage. This started to change in the late 2000s, however. Take military parades, an obvious and widely used means to display a country's military might (Morgenthau, 1948: 54). There were three between 1979 and 2009. The first one of 1984 and the second of 1999 had a clear domestic focus – aiming to legitimize the reform and opening course taken by Deng Xiaoping and to reassure the army of its continuing importance despite the focus on economic development for the former, and seeking to consolidate the authority of Jiang Zemin for the latter – with few references to security issues (Taiwan excepted) or to the outside world.[22] The parade of 2009, held a few days after the announcement of the 'new situation' evoked at the very beginning of this book, was a more conscious effort to 'comprehensively display ... the overall might of the nation', as an outline issued by the PLA eight months beforehand put it (quoted in Ye and Barmé, 2009). The parade featured lots of new and sophisticated weaponry and this time was advertised to the world with extensive official media coverage in several foreign languages. In his speech, Hu Jintao enjoined the PLA to 'safeguard national sovereignty, security and territorial integrity', a formula absent from Jiang Zemin's speech in 1999.[23] This was in line with the progressive spread of a tougher rhetoric on security and sovereignty issues in the years prior.

Xi Jinping has been even less shy about showing off the fruits of China's military build-up. He used the 60th anniversary of the end of the Second

---

[22] See a summary of the character of both in Ye and Barmé, 2009. See also Christopher S. Wren, 'China displays its big missiles on anniversary', *The New York Times*, 2 October 1984; Seth Faison, 'A half-century in China: the celebration; a day of joy and jubilation, all very carefully staged', *The New York Times*, 1 October 1999.

[23] '首都举行盛大阅兵仪式和群众游行' [Grand military parade and march of the masses held in the capital], *People's Daily*, 2 October 2009.

World War in 2015 to organize a parade with great fanfare. On that occasion, more advanced weaponry was prominently displayed in front of the international media and of several heads of state who had responded to the invitation to attend the event. An even bigger parade was held in 2019 for the 70th anniversary of the founding of the PRC. These were not the only occasions for Xi to attract attention to the military power China had acquired, since he also took part in several large-scale and well-publicized inspections of troops in China's border regions – in Hong Kong in June 2017 (although this show of force was directed more at parts of the city's population than at the outside world), in Inner Mongolia in August 2017, and in the South China Sea itself in April 2018 – each time stressing the need to build a strong army and a strong navy.[24]

'Establishing awesomeness' in the near seas

The last of these troops inspections, in the South China Sea, fits within a pattern of assertion of military power in China's near seas and in the skies above them. While this maritime expansion has greatly picked up pace since 2009, it started much before that. In the East China Sea, the Japanese government started to note the growing presence of Chinese scientific research vessels and navy ships in waters claimed by both countries as part of their Exclusive Economic Zone in the late 1990s. These moves were most likely intended to demonstrate China's growing military strength and ability to defend its maritime interests, and more immediately to warn Japan off for its willingness to develop its alliance with the US and to foster closer ties with Taiwan (NIDS, 2000: 104–6).

In the South China Sea, the expansion of the PRC's maritime presence had begun in the 1970s already. Its most dramatic move was the takeover, after a military clash, of the Paracel islands in 1974 in response to what China called 'provocations' from South Vietnam (Lo Chi-Kin, 1989: 58). Even if the Chinese government never gave an official justification for the seizure two decades later of Mischief Reef, a rock in the Spratly Islands previously controlled by the Philippines, many observers suspect that this was once again a 'punitive action' taken in retaliation for Manila's willingness to grant the right to conduct hydrocarbon exploration to an American company (San Pablo-Baviera, 2002: 257). More broadly, the expansion of military patrols

---

[24] Minnie Chan, Stuard Law, and Naomi Ng, 'Hong Kong's PLA garrison stages biggest military parade in 20 years as Xi Jinping inspects troops', *South China Morning Post*, 30 June 2017; Michael Martina and Ben Blanchard, 'China's Xi calls for building elite forces during massive military parade', *Reuters*, 30 July 2017; 'Chinese president calls for establishment of world-class naval force', *CGTN*, 12 April 2018.

throughout the area was intended notably to 'display our military power' and thus impress upon other claimants to disputed islands in the region the risks of provoking their giant neighbour.[25] This kind of activity truly picked up after 2006, when the Chinese government approved the conduct of 'regular rights protection patrols' (*dingqi weiquan xunhang*) in the East China Sea, a system that was later expanded to all sea areas to which China laid claim and has been steadily strengthened since (Wu, 2014).

Even if those are the responsibility of Chinese coastguard agencies, the presence of PLA navy vessels in China's near seas has also grown increasingly visible over the past decade. In the South China Sea, it has been complemented by an ambitious programme of artificial islands building on virtually all the features China occupies in the Spratly Islands, where outposts capable of monitoring the region and of supporting military operations have been established. The objectives pursued by China with this growing show of force include making the surrounding waters less hospitable to the US naval presence, seen as the greatest threat to its security (potentially in conjunction with its major regional allies Japan and Australia), preparing for a contingency around Taiwan, and asserting its sovereignty over disputed land features and its 'rights and interests' in waters in the East and South China Sea.[26] To accomplish all this, Chinese analysts talk of the necessity to 'establish [China's] awesomeness' (*liwei*) in the eyes of its neighbours and the US to make sure they think twice before infringing on the country's 'core interests'.

For instance, one article prominently featured in the *People's Liberation Army Daily* in a special edition to celebrate the 40 years of reform and opening talks proudly of the rapid development in military technologies having 'strengthened the army's awesomeness and propagated national prestige'.[27] Another article in a research journal managed by the same *PLA Daily* urges Chinese soldiers to be 'capable of fighting to stop war, fighting to establish awesomeness'.[28] This resonates with Xi Jinping's

---

[25] From the memoir of Admiral Liu Huaqing, commander of the PLA Navy from 1982 to 1988, quoted in Fravel, 2008: 293.

[26] These are the major concerns listed in the section on China's national security situation (along with terrorism, separatism, and 'anti-China' forces abroad) in a 2015 defence White Paper. Ministry of Defense, 'China's military strategy', May 2015, http://eng.mod.gov.cn/publications/node_48467.htm.

[27] Zhang Jiaguo, '人民战争思想的历史性飞跃' [The historic leap of the thinking on people's war], *People's Army Daily*, 12 December 2018.

[28] Xin Shihong, '强军备战，决不给觊觎者任何机会' [Strong army and preparation for war, never give any occasion to those who covet], *National Defense Reference*, 7 September 2015.

repeated injunction to military personnel that they should be 'prepared for fighting wars'.[29] Since China sees itself as virtuous and inherently peaceful, any such war would from Beijing's point of view be a defensive response to others' aggression. As the aforementioned 2015 defence White Paper puts it, China's posture is that 'We will not attack unless we are attacked, but we will surely counterattack if attacked'. Such a counterattack would thus aim to be so resolute and impressive that no other state would dare provoke China again.

This concerns not only powerful potential 'aggressors' such as the US, but also small neighbours who have, in China's telling, for too long taken advantage of its weakness to encroach on its rightful territory. As Xi Jinping put it in a speech at a work meeting on border and ocean defence, in modern history, 'there was a time when China was poor and weak and in a situation of being taken advantage of, suffering several hundred encroachments large and small on land and sea by foreign enemies'.[30] Now that China is strong, then, such intrusions are not to be tolerated anymore, even coming from smaller states who were themselves victims of imperial predation. When incidents occur and Chinese rights are again trampled, as it sees it, commentators are quick to point to a failure to establish its awesomeness as the reason for the misbehaviour of its neighbours.[31] In order to remedy this, three naval officers suggest, China should 'make clear its bottom line' (*liangming dixian*) and 'display its power' (*zhanshi shili*) to deter others from causing incidents.[32]

Establishing deterrence means not being afraid to get into fight when 'provoked'. Sun Shuxian, a senior coastguard officer, said in July 2012 shortly after the end of the confrontation between China and the Philippines at

---

[29] For instance, during an inspection to the Southern Theatre Command charged with overseeing the South China Sea and Taiwan. See Kristin Huang, '"Prepare for war", Xi Jinping tells military region that monitors South China Sea, Taiwan', *South China Morning Post*, 26 October 2018.

[30] Li Ganshe, '习近平接见第五次全国边海防工作会议代表 李克强张高丽参加' [Xi Jinping meets the delegates attending the Fifth National Border and Coast Defense Work Meeting, Li Keqiang and Zhang Gaoli also attend], *People's Daily*, 28 June 2014.

[31] See, for instance, this response to the Philippine coastguard's attempt to arrest Chinese fishermen in Scarborough shoal in April 2012 and that to another arrest this time by North Korea one month later: '专家：中国在南海必须要立威 别让菲越头脑发热' [Experts: China must establish its awesomeness in the South China Sea, must not let the Philippines's head get to hot], *Global Times*, 15 April 2012; '媒体称中国应通过解救遭朝鲜扣押渔船立威' [Media call for China to establish its awesomeness by rescuing the fishing boat detained by North Korea], *Global Times*, 18 May 2012.

[32] Lt. Comm. Jin Jing and Commanders Xu Hui and Wang Ning, quoted in Martinson and Yamamoto (2017).

Scarborough shoal, which ended with China seizing control of the shoal from the Philippines, that

> although we do not advocate provocations, we are not afraid of provocations and we cannot accept provocations. We cannot simply respond with statements that [these actions] are illegal and invalid, we must make provocateurs pay a price. By killing one to scare a hundred, we can avoid a worsening of the situation.[33]

In practice, Chinese vessels have indeed got into an increasing number of confrontations with neighbouring states in the East and South China Sea since 2010 (Iida, 2015: 176–81).

These kinds of remarks reveal the weight of traditional modes of thinking on the calculus made by China in such situations of crisis. It is 'punishing' neighbours that have strayed from the proper path of 'seeking common ground while reserving differences' and caused disruption to the 'harmonious' pattern of inter-Asian relations that Beijing promotes. It argues that this punishment is not dealt out of vindictiveness but for the higher purpose of establishing China's awesomeness to ensure that offenders will amend their behaviour and refrain from further exactions. This is typically how any use of force against other states in the South China Sea is framed, a policy that You Ji (2013) describes as one of 'reactive assertiveness' – although he seems to ignore the fact that the expanding presence of Chinese military, coastguard, and fishing vessels in the area is at the origin of much of the increase in frictions. In any case, China's attitude towards South-East Asian states provides the best evidence that it still sees itself as a benevolent overseer having to impose discipline with an iron fist on wayward smaller states.

Bestowing, and withdrawing, economic benefits

The lure of profits is another tool China has used both as a stick to complement the use of force in 'punishing' offenders and as a carrot to incentivize neighbouring states to accept China's vision of hierarchical order. We discussed in the previous chapter China's harsh reaction against South Korea after its decision to deploy an American missile defence system on its territory. The response included severe restrictions on the travels of Chinese tourists to the country, limitations on imports of Korean cultural products, and the targeting of Lotte, the company that owned the ground on which the American missile defence system was to be set up.

---

[33] '孙书贤：日本若敢越红线 中方不惜一战' [Sun Shuxian: If Japan dares to cross the red line, China will not hesitate to fight], *Phoenix TV*, 13 July 2012.

These sanctions were not set out in official promulgations or codified into laws. Rather, economic costs were imposed 'through informal measures such as selective implementation of domestic regulations, including stepped-up customs inspections or sanitary checks, and uses extra-legal measures such as employing state media to encourage popular boycotts and having government officials directly put informal pressure on specific companies' (Harrell, Rosenberg, and Saravalle, 2018: 2). The Chinese National Tourist Administration published a travel notice warning citizens to 'carefully choose their travel destination' and highlighting purported dangers faced by Chinese travellers in South Korea.[34] In parallel, tour operators virtually stopped offering trips to the peninsula.[35] Meanwhile, Chinese state media encouraged a consumer boycott on certain prominent South Korean products (cars, cosmetics), while popular Korean TV dramas and artists became inaccessible to the Chinese public.[36] Many Lotte stores were forced to close by local authorities on the basis of safety violations.[37] In all cases, the hand of the central government remained hidden, but taken together, those restrictions unmistakably took the appearance of an organized campaign aiming to send a message. Namely, committing an 'offence' against China would have serious consequences for lucrative economic ties.

This was not an isolated case either, as China has imposed trade restrictions on several Asian states since 2010 in retaliation to behaviour deemed provocative, such as Japan's arrest of a fishing boat captain guilty of ramming a coastguard vessel in 2010, the Philippines' actions during the Scarborough shoal incident of 2012, and a visit by the Dalai Lama to Mongolia in 2016. In all those cases, the restrictions were never officially announced, were narrowly targeted to sectors where dependence on China was high – namely, rare earths exports to Japan, tourism to the Philippines, and mineral resources from Mongolia – and were not comprehensive or systematic (Harrell, Rosenberg, and Saravalle, 2018: 42–3, 47; Lai, 2018: 177–9). The punitive intention behind them was nevertheless made clear. After the Dalai Lama's visit to Mongolia, for instance, Foreign Minister Wang Yi told his counterpart on the phone that the incident had negatively affected ties between the two countries and that he '[hoped] that Mongolia has taken this lesson to heart'.[38]

---

[34] Chinese National Tourist Administration, '赴韩国旅游提示' [Notice on travel to South Korea], 3 March 2017, www.mct.gov.cn/zxbs/cxts/201703/t20170303_832101.htm.

[35] 'South Korea tourist numbers plummet by two-thirds after China boycott', *South China Morning Post*, 23 May 2017.

[36] Mengqi Sun, 'China protests South Korea's antimissile system – with consumer boycotts', *The Christian Science Monitor*, 4 March 2017.

[37] Song Jung-a, 'South Korea retailers a casualty of political stand-off', *Financial Times*, 11 September 2017.

[38] Christian Shepherd, 'China says hopes Mongolia learned lesson after Dalai Lama visit', *Reuters*, 24 January 2017.

The Chinese use of economic sanctions is therefore similar to its use of military force, in the sense that it is meant to be retaliatory and to establish China's power to inflict pain on any state that engages in behaviour that it says damages its 'core interests' (Reilly, 2012: 123).

Yet there is another less punitive side to China's use of economic levers to obtain compliance from neighbours. In the last decade, several prominent PRC scholars have noted approvingly how their country has started to make greater use of the wealth and resources generated by its rapid economic development to win support for its leading role from other Asian states.[39] Some, like China Institute of International Studies vice-president and occasional diplomat Ruan Zongze, have called to 'make China's economic strength congeal into diplomatic power', notably by better integrating foreign aid giving and diplomacy.[40] After the announcement of the BRI, Renmin University professor Shi Yinhong (2015) noted that China was increasingly focusing on what he called 'strategic economy' (*zhanlüe jingji*), or the strategic use of economic resources to achieve China's foreign policy objectives, even drawing a parallel with the *heqin* policy of the Han dynasty more than two thousand years ago. Song Guoyou of Fudan University for his part noted that the BRI marked the 'mutual embrace of economy and diplomacy' (2015: 23).

Chinese leaders have indeed become more open in their intentions to use economic benefits to attract support from other states. We may recall from Chapter 5 that Hu Jintao had spoken in his report to the 18th Party Congress in November 2012 of 'bringing better benefits to peripheral states'. The same expression was then used several times by Xi Jinping, for instance, at the Peripheral Diplomacy Work Conference of 2013, at the Boao Forum for Asia the same year, and at the first BARF in 2017.[41] On the occasion of a trip to Mongolia, he was more explicit, indicating that this meant 'China is willing to provide neighbouring countries including Mongolia with opportunities and space for common development. All countries are welcomed to board the train of China's development. In cooperation with

---

[39] Although it is not openly acknowledged, on top of official trade, investments, and assistance, this includes Chinese patronage of local elites in certain partner states through various unofficial and corrupt means, Cambodia being a case in point (Horton, 2020: 9).

[40] Ruan Zongze, '让中国经济实力凝成外交力量' [Make China's economic strength congeal into diplomatic power], *Global Times*, 22 October 2012.

[41] On the Peripheral Diplomacy Work Conference of 2013, see note 22 in Chapter 6. The two other references are '习近平在博鳌亚洲论坛2013年会上的主旨演讲' [Xi Jinping's keynote speech at the 2013 Boao Forum for Asia], 7 April 2013, www.gov.cn/ldhd/2013-04/07/content_2371801.htm; '习近平出席"一带一路"高峰论坛开幕式并发表主旨演讲' [Chairman Xi's keynote speech at the opening ceremony of the Belt and Road Summit Forum], 15 May 2017, www.gov.cn/xinwen/2017-05/14/content_5193658.htm.

developing countries, China will stick to the correct idea of righteousness and benefit'.[42]

The reference to the 'correct idea of righteousness and benefit', an expression often employed by Xi Jinping to stake China's claim to moral superiority, as discussed in Chapter 6, is revealing of the way the provision of benefits to surrounding states is framed. Namely, in another callback to tradition, it is depicted as another manifestation of China's benevolence towards smaller neighbours. As Qin Yaqing (2014) puts it, even as China uses engagement with the world to boost its own development, it is also demonstrating a determination, based on its virtuous Confucian tradition, to fulfil its 'unshirkable responsibility' to benefit the common good of mankind. Yet there is no doubt that China expects deference in exchange for the economic favours it grants. One official's response to a question about possible Russian objections to China's expanding activities in Central Asia was to evoke the two countries' burgeoning trade relations, implying that any undue criticism might put them in jeopardy.[43] Mongolia itself learned the hard way the economic consequences of displeasing China during the dispute around the Dalai Lama's visit, only two years after Xi Jinping's speech quoted earlier.

The Chinese government has also acknowledged the diplomatic usefulness of foreign aid, which has grown leaps and bounds since 2010.[44] A 2011 White Paper celebrated how 'through foreign aid, China has consolidated friendly relations and economic and trade cooperation with other developing countries'.[45] One Chinese scholar emphasized that the Chinese discourse of 'mutual benefits and mutual help' (*huhui huzhu*) in foreign aid giving also implies receiving political benefits in exchange for the money distributed, such as diplomatic support in international organizations, a greater acceptance of China's rise and of its status as a great power, and more influence and voice on the international stage (Luo Jianbo, 2016: 106).

---

[42] 'Xi Jinping delivers an important speech at the State Great Hural of Mongolia', 22 August 2014, www.fmprc.gov.cn/mfa_eng/wjdt_665385/zyjh_665391/201408/t20140826_678205.html.

[43] An anonymous Chinese official, quoted in 'How Vladimir Putin's embrace of China weakens Russia', *The Economist*, 25 July 2019.

[44] For recent estimations of the amount of aid given by China and its growth over time, see Kitano (2018). One impressive data point is that the amount of aid disbursed between 2010 and 2012 alone was equal to a third of the total sum given between 1950 and 2009 (Watanabe Shino, 2017: 13–4).

[45] Information Office of the State Council of the People's Republic of China, 'China's foreign aid', http://english.www.gov.cn/archive/white_paper/2014/09/09/content_281474986284620.htm.

Overall, the distribution of economic benefits to neighbours in different forms is meant to bind them close to China and use the lure of profits to obtain deference. When discussing shared development in Asia at the aforementioned 2013 Peripheral Diplomacy Work Conference, Xi Jinping spoke of 'weaving a more inseparable network of common interests' and of 'bringing the fusion of both sides' interests to a higher level'. This would bind neighbouring countries' economies to the policies adopted by Beijing and thus strengthen the incentive to avoid disrupting relations with it. Combined with the threat of physical and/or economic retaliations to any offence, this is another way to ensure that neighbours accept their place in the hierarchical order China seeks to create.

Conclusion

The purpose of this book was to deepen our understanding of China's vision for international order in Asia, by focusing on the concept of hierarchy at the centre of this vision and by highlighting the lines of continuity between the country's pre-modern past and its present foreign policy. It has argued that ancient ideas about the creation of an enduring Sinocentric political order have survived into the modern era and continue to guide Chinese foreign policy today. It was traditionally considered the ultimate mission of the Chinese emperor to bring order to 'all-under-heaven' in the form of a stable hierarchy centred on himself, where the subordinate position of all surrounding polities would be made clear and manifest through ritual diplomacy. The hierarchical structure of order was justified by the Son of Heaven's all-encompassing virtue and supported by the empire's wealth, military might, and control over names. An enduring attachment to these principles did not prevent Chinese statesmen from displaying a great degree of flexibility and adaptability in applying them to changing and sometimes adverse circumstances. Successive emperors displayed very variable degrees of attachment to the Confucian model of virtuous rulership, while making 'barbarians' adhere to proper ritual forms was a constant challenge and required negotiations and compromises. Nowhere was this more evident than in the empire's relations with its nomadic neighbours in Inner Asia, with their often superior military might and tendency to push into the Chinese heartland and establish 'conquest dynasties' of their own. Attachment to the imperial ideal of hierarchical order nevertheless remained consistent throughout this tumultuous history.

It took the trauma of the 'Western shock' to bring about a fundamental rethink in the late 19th and early 20th centuries. This rethink did not result in the complete abandonment of this ideal but in its transformation and adaptation to China's modern conditions. Achieving order was still a sacred mission, but one that implied radical change and evolution out of the parlous conditions Chinese statesmen thought international society to be in. China pursued equality with Western great powers, but other Asian nations were still considered natural subordinates and followers. Moral excellence remained the basis for this claim to leadership of Asia, but Confucian standards were replaced by pledges to offer a 'better alternative' to the exploitativeness of the imperial powers. China embraced Western-style diplomacy but still sought to demonstrate its superior status within this new framework.

The reconfiguration that accompanied China's first steps in the modern society of sovereign nation states laid the groundwork for many aspects of the PRC's foreign policy, as outlined in the last three chapters of this book. During the Maoist period, a poor country prone to bouts of revolutionary fever, alienated from a large part of international society and pressed on both its north-western and south-eastern flanks by two superpowers with potentially hostile intentions, had only limited space to pursue the vision of hierarchical order. In the rare cases where it was still solidly in a position to demonstrate its superiority, namely, in its relations with close neighbours in Indochina and on the Korean peninsula, it did seek to replicate traditional modes of hierarchical relations in a modern guise. It also vied with the Soviet Union for leadership of the broader 'anti-imperialist struggle' in the Third World but mostly lacked the power to support its ambitions. The aspiration to lead world revolution that characterized Maoist times was later abandoned, but the claim to moral superiority based on the Five Principles of Peaceful Coexistence spelled out in the 1950s proved much more enduring.

In the reform and opening period, when China's main focus was building up its wealth and power and when much of its foreign policy was oriented towards the achievement of that goal, the pursuit of a hierarchical order was again not necessarily at the centre of its preoccupations. China's quest for status in those years aimed first and foremost to secure its place as a member in good standing of international society. Its leaders understood the precariousness of their country's international position relative to a more powerful West and were keenly aware of the risk of finding themselves isolated, especially after the reputational blow of the Tiananmen crisis and of the collapse of the Soviet Union. They also recognized the undisputed dominance of the US in international society and China's role as nothing more than one potential pole in the multipolar world that they hoped would emerge under the shadow of American hegemony. For all those reasons, China's diplomatic strategy was prudent and its efforts to raise its status and obtain demonstrations of support from its neighbours largely non-confrontational.

Even as it strived to climb the international pyramid of 'comprehensive national power', China thus accommodated itself to existing international structures and emphasized how peaceful and cooperative the new type of international relations it advocated based on an evolution of the Five Principles would be. In Asia, it sought to portray itself as a regional leader through positive engagement and diplomatic activism that would raise its profile without worrying its neighbours. It also made increasing use of partnerships as a means to organize and guide the development of its foreign relations but was fairly circumspect in the use of the other tools of statecraft discussed in this book.

This changed under Xi Jinping, who is determined to achieve the 'great rejuvenation of the Chinese nation' and leads a much stronger country. China is now actively seeking to establish a Sinocentric order in Asia and to take over from the US as the overseer of the region, assuming responsibility for regional stability and prosperity in exchange for the deference of its neighbours. It has doubled down on the argument, first articulated by Sun Yat-Sen in the early 20th century, that it is uniquely qualified to take that role due to its moral superiority grounded in traditional values. To give reality to its vision of order, it has sought to become the centre of regional diplomatic life, convening countless forums where grateful neighbours gather to regularly and demonstratively reaffirm their support for its leadership. It has also set strict red lines around behaviour it considers unacceptable because they threaten its 'core interests' and disrupt the cooperative atmosphere that China says it seeks to maintain in the region. These red lines are enforced with the threat to 'punish' transgressors with China's superior might – which it hopes will by itself be enough to deter any misbehaviour – or with economic sanctions. The promise of benefits that can result from linking oneself to the Chinese economy and receiving aid and investments acts as positive reinforcement, along with participation in China's now well-developed partnership diplomacy that is meant to keep neighbouring states on the track to ever-closer cooperation.

This is China's contemporary vision for a hierarchical order in Asia, then, one where its position at the centre of regional life is recognized and where all states embrace their moral obligations towards each other. For China, this means showing benevolence by not interfering in smaller states' domestic affairs and by sharing the fruits of its economic growth. For those smaller states, this means showing deference and loyalty to China by participating in a Sinocentric pattern of diplomacy and by refraining from any 'provocative' action that would disrupt it. China's superior power is used to keep everyone in line.

There is nothing radically new about this order in its basic features. Xi Jinping's 'new type of international relations' and 'community with a shared future for mankind' remain well within the bounds of the basic Westphalian norms that underpin the contemporary international society, even if they reject the idea of international convergence around liberal ideas of human rights and democracy.[1] The Asia that China envisions is still a

---

[1] Chinese leaders have in fact argued that they are protecting the oldest and most central principles of international order against the liberal ideas that threaten to undermine them (Breslin, 2021: 200). Several observers have noted the 'back to Westphalian basics' nature of the order favoured by China as well as other East Asian states (Alagappa, 2003: 86–90;

'commonwealth of sovereign states' (Watson, 1992: 186) striving to coexist peacefully despite their different domestic socio-political systems and to solve problems of common concern through bilateral and multilateral diplomacy. The way order is maintained and China's own superior position secured is different, however.

First, China is not very keen on order preservation through binding international legal norms with judicial means of recourse to solve disputes – outside of economic treaties and contracts, that is – and has made its distaste of formal alliances in particular abundantly clear. It prefers vague pledges of friendship and mutual goodwill sustained by moral precepts. Moral cultivation and attachment to values like sincerity, trust, loyalty, and benevolence is what is supposed to push states to support international order. With strenuous adherence to those values, even the most difficult of issues in dispute will eventually become easy to resolve through friendly negotiation, it argues. China claims a superior position by being the ultimate arbiter of whether states have respected their moral obligation and by arrogating itself the right to punish those who have 'sinned'.

More concretely, though, order is maintained through participation in the Sinocentric pattern of diplomatic interactions described in Chapter 6. As we have explained in our discussion of ritual, order is in the traditional Chinese conception not only a set of abstract principles, but also something that is actively sustained, on a day-to-day basis, through the performance of one's role in accordance with the rules of propriety. Through the regular exchange of state visits and participation in frequent forums convened by Beijing, each time accompanied by pledges of mutual friendship and cooperation, states are reiterating their attachment to international order and their determination to maintain it. It is the repetition ad libitum of such actions – and conversely restraint from 'provocative' actions that would make them more difficult – that ensures order is sustained. Since ever more of Asia's diplomatic activity is centred on China and since it claims the right to define what constitutes a provocative action, its superior position is also regularly reaffirmed.

Ultimately then, even if it is underpinned by moral precepts, what China is seeking to impose on its neighbours to ensure they participate in its vision of hierarchical order is first and foremost a 'standard of behaviour'. This 'standard of behaviour' is different from the 'standard of civilization' imposed by the West on the rest of the world in the 19th and early 20th

---

Ginsburg, 2010; Lo Chang-fa, 2010). It should be noted here that references to the Westphalian origins of the current international order are a gross oversimplification of a complex history where the Westphalian settlement of 1648 did not even play a central role (Osiander, 2001). Westphalia nevertheless remains the shorthand for a pluralist vision of order, no matter how problematic that is (Hurrell 2007: 54–5).

centuries (Chapter 4). There is no talk here of dictating how other states should organize their domestic structures, which laws they should adopt and which customs they should uphold, although China does expect a firm commitment of all partner governments to protect Chinese interests on their territory. The 'standard of behaviour' is more narrowly focused on their attitude on the international stage, which should be respectful and supportive. Attendance at Chinese-led forums, endorsement of its diplomatic initiatives like the Belt and Road and of ideas like the 'community with a shared future for mankind', participation in the Chinese network of partnerships, and frequent praises and declarations of friendship are in accordance with the standard. Any action that threatens China's 'core interests', as well as public criticism of its internal affairs and foreign policy is not. The hope is that steady adherence to the standard will eventually lead it to become internalized by other Asian states so that compliance need not be enforced through the threat of punishment anymore, but comes naturally to them. The durability of the Sinocentric hierarchical order would then be fully secured. To conclude this book, we will further explore certain aspects of this order by examining how a series of opposite ideas can be reconciled within it.

Universality and Chineseness

First of all, how specifically Chinese is this vision of a hierarchical international order? After all, all empires of pre-modern times thought of themselves as the centre of the world and sought the allegiance of polities beyond their immediate realm. Often on the basis of religious beliefs, their ruler also typically argued that they were chosen by a superior being to be his representative on earth due to their possessing unique moral qualities and an ability to guide people towards enlightenment. Court rituals were also a topic of concern everywhere, the offering of tribute and the exchange of gifts in particular being common tools of diplomacy throughout history and around the world. Besides, when the Chinese imperial court sought to negotiate a modus vivendi with powerful neighbouring polities, it was certainly not the only one seeking to impose its superiority over the other side. China does stand out, though, for the way the various elements of the ideal of hierarchical order were fitted together in the manners examined in Chapter 2 to form a coherent vision of a stable social structure to cover the whole known world. Simply put, the role played by hierarchy, morality, ritual, and state power in the maintenance of social order was a topic of particular concern in Chinese political thought and the subject of remarkably sophisticated arguments and rationales, which partly explains the durability of the imperial model of government.

A similar point can be made about the specificity of China's vision of order today. As we noted in the introduction, matters of hierarchy and status may not be front and centre in the Western discourse about international relations, but that does not mean they are absent – far from it. The drive of powerful states to impose their will on their neighbourhood is a universal phenomenon. Regardless, other major states also see themselves as morally 'good' actors with a positive influence on the world. The US poses as a beacon of democracy and freedom, while Russia stands for traditional Christian values that it accuses America and Western European states of having lost, and is as keen as China to decry 'Western imperialism'. All states, furthermore, care about the way they are treated on the international stage and like to use the occasion of summits they may host to put themselves forward. As was noted, many states employ partnerships as an important tool of their foreign policy, while using military force to boost one's prestige and imposing economic sanctions on states whose conduct is considered reprehensible are common and widely used tactics. So is the use of foreign aid for political purposes.

China's particularity comes again from the way all those various elements combine together into one coherent vision of order whereby the stable hierarchy between states is what maintains international stability, China's moral leadership concerns not how states govern themselves but how they interact with each other, inter-state diplomacy serves not only to solve problems and advance cooperation but also to sustain the hierarchical international order through frequent and concrete reaffirmation, and China uses the tools mentioned previously to guide other states towards adopting a supportive attitude and punish the recalcitrant. In short, China stands out not for caring about hierarchy, morality, and status per se, but for how central those elements are to its foreign policy and for their shared role in supporting the overall objective of achieving an order China can look approvingly upon.

System and society

China's ability to obtain compliance with its vision of hierarchical order has always been highly dependent on the degree of power asymmetry between it and various neighbours, discussed in Chapter 1. The equality or even superiority in power terms of Inner Asian nomads during much of the imperial era forced China to compromise and settle for a 'patriarchal clan' system of fictive kinship instead of the tribute and investiture it preferred. Meanwhile, the empire's south-western frontier was a challenging and inhospitable environment, and Korea and Vietnam fiercely resisted any attempt at re-conquest after their initial separation. As Ogura Yoshihito argues, then, reliance on ritual was a way to proactively extend China's rule over those recalcitrant areas – to say nothing of the world beyond – even if only through the symbolic expression of the status difference between superiors and inferiors (1966: 30). In this way, the systemic realities of the prevailing balance of power and of the limits to the expansion of the Chinese empire pushed it towards reliance on ritual, thus shaping the social norms of interactions between it and various polities. In the modern era, China's weakness for most of the 20th century was, of course, a big impediment to the realization of its vision of order. The Chinese discourse about its place in the world and the way other states should interact with it could then become quite detached from reality, as it was during the Mao era when all the talk of becoming the centre of world revolution remained mostly just talk. It was only in relations with North Korea, Vietnam, Laos, and Cambodia, which remained asymmetrical despite China's relative weakness, that communist leaders could strive with some success to re-establish hierarchical relations. Conversely, China's growing strength today underpins its plans to establish itself firmly at the centre of Asia and is a necessary condition for its ability to make reality match its discourse.

As compared with the imperial era, one systemic constraint on China's pursuit of order has today virtually disappeared while another important one has replaced it. Namely, the interaction capacity of Asia has grown exponentially and geographical barriers to the deployment of Chinese power abroad have largely been overcome. However, the core principles of legitimacy of the contemporary society of sovereign states make any physical expansion through conquest on land beyond the borders China claims for itself (which include some disputed territory with India and Bhutan) or any imposition of direct Chinese administration on another state unthinkable. This means again that China must rely on modern ritual means to assert its superiority over its neighbours. In this context, the norm of equality of sovereign states in diplomatic relations serves as a constraint China has to work with and around, while the growth in the interaction capacity of Asia has reversely allowed the country to occupy the diplomatic stage almost constantly with a packed calendar of bilateral and multilateral events that continuously reaffirm China's status as the centre of regional life.

In one area, though, namely, the seas to China's east and south, few systemic constraints exist on China's ability to assert a more direct and naked form of dominance. The international norms that govern the maritime space are indeed far from attaining hegemonic status and universal acceptance, having been codified only fairly recently in the United Nations Convention on the Law of the Sea (UNCLOS), which came into effect in 1994 and remains the object of differences of interpretation. China is particularly litigious. In some cases, such as its restrictive understanding of the right of passage of military vessels in a country's Exclusive Economic Zone, it is in a minority but not alone, as several other Asian states like India, Bangladesh, Myanmar, Thailand, or Malaysia share its position (Pedrozo, 2014: 521). In other cases, such as the extent of its 'historical rights' in the South China Sea, China takes some unique positions that are largely rejected by other states in the region and by international courts, though it still claims that its interpretation is fully in accordance with the spirit of UNCLOS.[2] On this basis, it takes maximalist positions regarding its maritime claims.

In the face of this basic disagreement about rules of the road, China has followed a straightforward power-based logic. Namely, as its power has grown, it has expanded its presence in Japanese-controlled space in the East China Sea but remained constrained by the balancing effect of Japanese firmness backed by its alliance with the US. No such counterbalance exists in the South China Sea, where the clear asymmetry of power between China and its neighbours has allowed it to assert an increasing measure of administrative control over disputed areas. In this context, the hierarchical norms that it seeks to impose – laying out a standard of behaviour whereby no other state can challenge China's claims through concrete actions on the waters without opening itself to punishment, while an accommodative attitude may be rewarded with a 'permission' to access natural resources in disputed territories[3] – are a direct reflection of the systemic reality of China's superior power. This is but one of the ways in which realist considerations of power underpin the Chinese ideal of hierarchical order.

Realism and idealism

Some scholars have used studies of China's imperial history to argue that, regardless of its rhetoric, China was guided by cold strategic calculations rather than by Confucian ideals (Johnston, 1995; Wang Yuan-kang, 2011). The premise of such arguments is that the 'Chinese way of statecraft' can be neatly divided between a 'Confucian' pacifist outlook and a 'realpolitik' willingness to use force in whatever way available to achieve the empire's strategic objectives. As the analysis conducted in this book shows, however, these two aspects were in fact in a symbiotic relationship. Confucian beliefs

---

[2] For a good summary of China's arguments, see the official 'position paper' published in 2014 after the Philippines seized an international arbitration court regarding rival territorial claims over the Spratly Islands, as well as the response by a scholar at the Central Party School to the court ruling issued in 2016. 'Position paper of the government of the People's Republic of China on the matter of jurisdiction in the South China Sea arbitration initiated by the Republic of the Philippines', 7 December 2014, www.fmprc.gov.cn/mfa_eng/wjdt_665385/2649_665393/201412/t20141207_679387.html; Wang Junmin, '中国不接受南海仲裁案裁决具有法理正当性' [China doesn't accept the legitimacy of the jurisprudence of the South China Sea arbitration case ruling], *PLA Daily*, 18 July 2016.

[3] China's policy towards the Philippines in the aftermath of the aforementioned arbitral court ruling and of the election of an accommodative president, Rodrigo Duterte, soon afterwards is a good illustration of its approach. See Martin Petty, 'At strategic shoal, China asserts power through control, and concessions', *Reuters*, 10 April 2017.

do not preclude the use of force, and Chinese statesmen could exhibit both great strategic flexibility and sincere beliefs in the value of moral leadership and forbearance.

To start with, Confucianism was only one part of the mainstream of traditional Chinese political thought studied in Chapter 2. Legalism was just as important and rejected out of hand the idea of rule through virtue alone. Most Confucian thinkers themselves fully recognized the right of the virtuous ruler to use force to protect his realm against 'barbarians' who did not respond to other means of control and to punish offenders against the prevailing order. The Chinese tradition was thus to view military power as a necessary pillar to support imperial rule, to be used when necessary in cases where rule through virtue proved ineffective. To put it differently, Chinese rulers were meant to strive to follow the 'way of the king' (*wangdao*) but reserved their right to use the 'way of the hegemon' (*badao*) when circumstances required it. The moral condemnation that came with the determination that a neighbour was not fulfilling his obligation to maintain order ensured that the imperial court felt justified to take whatever punitive measure it considered appropriate. The use of force against smaller neighbours was, in short, fully a part of the ideal of a harmonious hierarchical order.

This is still the reasoning adopted by today's China when it comes to contentious issues such as the South China Sea. Having convinced itself that the islands and rocks there are part of its traditional territory – and access to fishing grounds throughout the sea its 'historical right' – to be recovered as part of the 'great rejuvenation of the Chinese nation', and facing the resistance of other claimants unwilling to accept this 'correct' view of things, China considers that it has no choice but to employ force to settle the matter despite its desire to behave benevolently by setting aside disputes and sharing resources. Establishing control over the South China Sea through the use of its military and law enforcement power is thus part and parcel of the pursuit of the ideal of a hierarchical order where China's superiority is no longer challenged and other states accept their assigned place. Once this order is secured (and free from the interference of meddling outsiders like the US), China argues, it would again be free to be gracious to its neighbours. We leave it to the reader to decide for him- or herself how plausible this narrative is – other claimants that have been the target of China's assertive tactics in the South China Sea will certainly find it difficult to accept at face value its promises of future benevolence – but this illustrates how idealism and realism merge in China's pursuit of a hierarchical order. Despite its incessant condemnations of Western-style power politics, then, China is just as ready to employ the tactics it decries when it deems that the situation requires it – even if it always claims to do so as a last resort and for purely defensive motives.

If there is an opposition between the two poles of realism and idealism in Chinese foreign policy, it is rather to be found in the concessions that China has had to make to unfavourable circumstances in the pursuit of an ideal order. In the imperial era, this was very often the case in China's relations with Inner Asian polities, where it had to accommodate itself to equal or close to equal relations due to the prevailing balance of power, and in contacts with powerful empires such as the Timurid during the Ming and Russia during the Qing.[4] Closer to today, the Maoist era stands out for its mix of idealism in the pursuit of a hierarchical revolutionary order despite China's weakness – especially during the Cultural Revolution – and realism in trying to find a pragmatic balance between various potential threats to a relatively weak PRC (Khan, 2018: Ch. 2). The same pragmatism was very much in evidence later on during the reform and opening period (and in the 1990s in particular), when China's cool-headed assessment of the precariousness of its position led it to adopt a non-confrontational attitude in raising its international status. Even today as a China more confident in its strength has become more assertive, it remains conscious of the need to preserve a stable international environment for the continued development of the Chinese economy and has thus been careful to maintain confrontations with its neighbours in the East and South China Seas at a relatively low level that does not risk disrupting international commerce or drawing too strong a reaction from the US (Martinson, 2015).

Form and interests

Another way to formulate the opposition between an idealist and a realist side to Chinese foreign policy is to distinguish between the pursuit of form and the pursuit of interests. This is the framework proposed by Amako Satoshi, who points out that the distinction made in China between diplomacy based on 'abstract principles' (*xu*) and that based on 'reality' (*shi*) amounts to a debate between the prioritization of 'form' (*xing*) and that of 'benefits' or 'interests' (*li*) respectively (2014: 4–5). This book has mostly discussed the diplomacy of form, which understands China's relations with its neighbours through the prism of hierarchy and emphasizes demonstrations of superiority in the way foreign policy is formulated and implemented. This was the main purpose of ritual interactions in imperial times and continues to inspire Chinese efforts to establish a Sinocentric pattern of diplomacy among Asian states, through which its position of regional leader is clearly expressed. The framing of China's use of force or of economic sanctions as

---

[4] On China's attunement to the ever-shifting balance of power in Inner Asia in particular, see Kwan (2016) in addition to the relevant parts of Chapters 2 and 4.

a 'punishment' of wayward neighbours and the pledges to 'share the fruits of China's development' with supportive states similarly puts the emphasis on the superior-to-inferior relation between the two sides.

The diplomacy of interests, on the other hand, privileges China's material needs and the reinforcement of its economic and military power. Examples of it in imperial times include, for instance, the opening of border markets on the empire's Inner Asian frontiers, where little fuss was made about ritual matters, in order to maintain stability in the borderlands and to acquire horses to bolster the Chinese army (Yü Ying-shi, 1967: 99–111; Rossabi, 1970; Millward, 1992; Iwami, 1997: 68–71). More recently, the main focus of Chinese diplomacy after the beginning of reform and opening was to facilitate the country's economic development, which is why Amako calls this period 'benefit-heavy' (2014: 9). This was also the period when what Deng Yong calls the 'worship of national interest' developed in the Chinese discourse about foreign affairs, which privileged bolstering national security and growing the economy above any other objective (1999: 49–50). The pursuit of national interests is still a priority today, but has under Xi Jinping been merged with the diplomacy of form. Indeed, we have discussed in Chapter 6 how China now insists on respect for its 'core interests' as a test of its neighbours' acknowledgement of its superior position, with failure leading to 'punishment'.

This is but one way in which creating the aforementioned Sinocentric pattern of regional diplomacy helps safeguard China's interests. The countless international meetings it convenes and the secondary cooperation mechanisms that proliferate around the main forums between China and different groups of states are so many opportunities to raise issues of concern and to obtain the agreement of partners to protect Chinese interests abroad. The fact that Beijing has a large degree of control over the agenda and format of discussions makes its task easier. More broadly, establishing China's superior position and reminding others of its 'standard of behaviour' serves to make them think twice before adopting any policy that might endanger its interests.[5] To evaluate how successful this strategy is would require us to examine how China's neighbours respond to it, which is unfortunately beyond the scope of this book.

Asia and the world

Our analysis has focused not only on the Chinese side of things, but also geographically on Asia. There are good reasons for this choice: Chinese

---

[5] On China's enhancement of its prestige as a means to defend its interests, see also Heath (2018).

leaders consider the continent of particular strategic importance and their efforts to establish a modern hierarchical order – an integral part of the 'great rejuvenation of the Chinese nation' – are focused first and foremost on the country's 'periphery' where, as they see it, it used to enjoy the deference and respect of other polities. Although the 'new type of international relations' and the 'community with a shared future for mankind' are meant to encompass the whole world, Xi Jinping has stressed the need to put them into practice in China's neighbourhood first. Asia has also received the biggest share of China's attention (and money) in implementing the Belt and Road, another major initiative with a wider scope (Aoyama, 2016: 5–7). In short, China may increasingly present a vision of order with a global scale, but this vision is more precise and developed closer to its shores and attempts at implementation occur regionally first. Asia is also where the range and intensity of interactions between China and other states is greatest, and is most likely to include conflicts and disputes. It is finally where the full weight of China's power can most directly be brought to bear on other states.

This makes Asia the best area to study China's designs for international order, but the implications of such a study are increasingly relevant for the rest of the world. China's international footprint continues to expand, and it is now a crucial actor all around the globe. As noted earlier, many major policies and initiatives, from the promotion of a 'community with a shared future for mankind' and of the BRI to its forum diplomacy and partnership network cover every region of the world. China has made particular efforts to strengthen its relations with developing countries in and beyond its immediate 'periphery', since it sees them as a natural constituency and allies in the struggle against US 'hegemonism' (Eisenman and Heginbotham, 2019; Rolland, 2020). Yet it increasingly seems that it seeks to establish hierarchical relations with every state outside the US itself. Other Western states certainly are potential targets for 'punishment' if they cross China's red lines, as happened to Norway in 2010 after the Nobel Committee attributed the Peace Prize to famous political dissident Liu Xiaobo (Harrell, Rosenberg, and Saravalle, 2018: 42–3), and ten years later to Australia for various 'offences', and to Lithuania for demonstratively raising the level and intensity of its relations with Taiwan.[6] China's expanding ambitions are therefore being felt all around the globe, which makes it all the more important to understand its designs for international order close to home, where they have been fleshed out the most. We hope this book was of some help in that endeavour.

---

[6] On the two latter cases, see respectively Stephen Dziedzic, 'Chinese official declares Beijing has targeted Australian goods as economic punishment', *ABC News*, 7 July 2021, and 'China reduces ties with Lithuania in Taiwan spat', *Associated Press*, 21 November 2021.

References

Ai, J. (2015) *The Political Use of Tradition in Contemporary China*, Singapore: World Scientific.

Alagappa, M. (2003) 'Constructing security order in Asia: conceptions and issues', in M. Alagappa (ed), *Asian Security Order: Instrumental and Normative Features*, Stanford: Stanford University Press, pp 70–105.

Amako, S. (2014) 'China's diplomatic philosophy and view of the international order in the 21st century', *Journal of Contemporary East Asia Studies*, 3(2): 3–33.

Ames, R.T. (1994) *The Art of Rulership: A Study of Ancient Chinese Political Thought*, Albany: State University of New York Press.

Ames, R.T. (2002) 'Observing ritual "propriety (*li*禮)" as focusing the "familiar" in the affairs of the day', *Dao: A Journal of Comparative Philosophy*, 1(2): 143–56.

Aoyama, R. (2013) *China's Asia Diplomacy* (青山瑠妙：中国のアジア外交), Tokyo: University of Tokyo Press.

Aoyama, R. (2014) 'Defensive, assertive and then aggressive public diplomacy: three elements in China' (青山瑠妙：防御的、積極的、そして攻撃的パブリック・ディプロマシー—中国における3つの要素—), *International Affairs*, 635: 15–25.

Aoyama, R. (2016) '"One belt, one road": China's new global strategy', *Journal of Contemporary East Asia Studies*, 5(2): 3–22.

Aoyama, R. and Amako, S. (2015) *The Future of China as a Superpower 2: Diplomacy and International Order* (青山瑠妙・天児慧：超大国・中国のゆくえ2—外交と国際秩序—), Tokyo: University of Tokyo Press.

Arakawa, M. (2010) *Communication and Trade in Eurasia and the Tang Empire* (荒川正晴：ユーラシアの交通・交易と唐帝国), Nagoya: The University of Nagoya Press.

Avila, A.P.C. and Goldman, J. (2015) 'Philippine–US relations: the relevance of an evolving alliance', *Bandung: Journal of the Global South*, 2(6): 1–18.

Ba, A. (2006) 'Who's socializing whom? Complex engagement in Sino–ASEAN relations', *The Pacific Review*, 19(2): 157–79.

Balzacq, T. (2020) 'Rituals and diplomacy', in T. Balzacq, F. Charillon, and F. Ramel (eds) *Global Diplomacy: An Introduction to Theory and Practice*, translated by W. Snow, New York: Palgrave Macmillan, pp 111–22.

Barfield, T.J. (1992) *The Perilous Frontier: Nomadic Empires and China, 221 BC to AD 1757*, Cambridge, MA: Blackwell.

Barmé, G.R. (2008) *The Forbidden City*, London: Profile Books.

Beckwith, C.I. (2009) *Empires of the Silk Road: A History of Central Eurasia from the Bronze Age to the Present*, Princeton: Princeton University Press.

Beeson, M. (2004) 'U.S. hegemony and Southeast Asia', *Critical Asian Studies*, 36(3): 445–62.

Beeson, M. and Berger, M.T. (2003) 'The paradoxes of paramountcy: regional rivalries and the dynamics of American hegemony in East Asia', *Global Change*, 15(1): 27–42.

Bell, C. (2009) *Ritual Theory, Ritual Practice*, Oxford: Oxford University Press.

Bello, D.A. (2015) 'To go where no Han could go for long: malaria and the Qing construction of ethnic administrative space in frontier Yunnan', *Modern China*, 31(3): 283–317.

Bielenstein, H. (2005) *Diplomacy and Trade in the Chinese World 589–1276*, Leiden: Brill.

Bodde, D. (1968) 'Harmony and conflict in Chinese philosophy', in A.F. Wright (ed), *Studies in Chinese Thought*, Chicago: University of Chicago Press, pp 19–80.

Bol, P.K. (1992) *'The Culture of Ours': Intellectual Transitions in T'ang and Sung China*, Stanford: Stanford University Press.

Bradley, D. (2014) 'A "new situation": China's evolving assessment of its security environment', *China Brief*, 14(15): 6–8.

Brazinsky, G.A. (2017) *Winning the Third World: Sino–American Rivalry during the Cold War*, Chapel Hill: The University of North Carolina Press.

Breslin, S. (2021) *China Risen? Studying Chinese Global Power*, Bristol: Bristol University Press.

Brook, T., van Walt van Praag, M., and Boltjes, M. (eds) (2018) *Sacred Mandates: Asian International Relations since Chinggis Khan*, Chicago and London: Chicago University Press.

Bull, H. (2002) *The Anarchic Society: A Study of Order in World Politics*, 3rd edition, New York: Palgrave.

Busbarat, P. (2016) '"Bamboo swirling in the wind": Thailand's foreign policy imbalance between China and the United States', *Contemporary Southeast Asia: A Journal of International and Strategic Affairs*, 38(2): 233–57.

Buzan, B. (2010) 'China in international society: is "peaceful rise" possible?', *The Chinese Journal of International Politics*, 3(1): 5–36.

Buzan, B. (2018) 'China's rise in English School perspective', *International Relations of the Asia-Pacific*, 18(3): 449–76.

Buzan, B. and Little, R. (2000) *International Systems in World History: Remaking the Study of International Relations*, Oxford: Oxford University Press.

Cai, P. (2017) 'Understanding China's Belt and Road Initiative', Lowy Institute Analysis, March.

Callahan, W.A. (2004) *Contingent States: Greater China and Transnational Relations*, Minneapolis: University of Minnesota Press.

Callahan, W.A. (2008) 'Chinese visions of world order: post-hegemonic or a new hegemony?' *International Studies Review*, 10: 749–61.

Callahan, W.A. (2010) *China: The Pessoptimist Nation*, Oxford: Oxford University Press.

Callahan, W.A. (2011) 'Introduction: tradition, modernity, and foreign policy in China', in W.A. Callahan and E. Barbantseva (eds), *China Orders the World: Normative Soft Power and Foreign Policy*, Washington, DC: Woodrow Wilson Center Press, pp 1–17.

Callahan, W.A. (2012) 'Sino-speak: Chinese exceptionalism and the politics of history', *The Journal of Asian Studies*, 71(1): 33–55.

Callahan, W.A. (2015) 'History, tradition and the China Dream: socialist modernization in the world of great harmony', *Journal of Contemporary China*, 24(96): 983–1001.

Callahan, W.A. (2016) 'China's "Asia Dream": the Belt Road Initiative and the new regional order', *Asian Journal of Comparative Politics*, 1(3): 226–43.

Cannadine, D. (1987) 'Introduction: divine rites of kings', in D. Cannadine and S. Price (eds), *Rituals of Royalty: Power and Ceremonial in Traditional Societies*, Cambridge: Cambridge University Press, pp 1–19.

Carr, E.H. (2016) *The Twenty Years Crisis, 1919–1939: An Introduction to the Study of International Politics*, reissue, London: Palgrave Macmillan.

Ceulemans, E. (2021) 'Ceremonial or convivial gifts: two forms of gift-giving in contemporary Chinese diplomacy', *The Hague Journal of Diplomacy*, 16(1): 133–44.

Chan, G. (1999) *Chinese Perspectives on International Relations: A Framework for Analysis*, London: Macmillan.

Chang Chun-shu (2007) *The Rise of the Chinese Empire, Volume One: Nation, State, and Imperialism in Early China, ca. 1600 BC-A.D. 8*, Ann Arbor: University of Chicago Press.

Charap, S., Drennan J., and Noël P. (2017) 'Russia and China: a new model of great-power relations', *Survival*, 59(1): 25–42.

Ch'en, K.K.S. (1973) *The Chinese Transformation of Buddhism*, Princeton: Princeton University Press.

Chen Dongxiao (2014) 'China's "host diplomacy": opportunities, challenges and tasks' (陈东晓：中国的"主场外交"—机遇，挑战和任务), *China International Studies*, 5: 4–16.

Chen Jian (2001) *Mao's China and the Cold War*, Chapel Hill: The University of North Carolina Press.

Chen Kanling (2015) 'A tentative discussion of the rule through ritual of traditional East Asian order: an analytical framework' (陈康令：试论传统东亚秩序的礼治——一种分析框架), *Journal of Contemporary Asia-Pacific Studies*, 3: 29–59.

Chen Kanling (2017) *Ritual and All-Under-Heaven: The Long Stability of the Traditional East Asian Order* (陈康令：礼和天下——传统东亚秩序的长稳定), Shanghai: Fudan University Press.

Chen Xiaochen (2016) 'An inventory of China's foreign "partnerships"' (陈晓晨：中国对外"伙伴关系"大盘点), Hexun Online, 21 April.

Chen Zhigang (2010) 'A few theoretical issues in the study of the tributary system' (陈志刚：关于封贡体系研究的几个理论问题), *Journal of Tsinghua University (Philosophy and Social Sciences)*, 6: 59–69.

Chen Zhimin (2009) 'International responsibility and China's foreign policy', Iida, M. (ed), *China's Shift: Global Strategy of the Rising Power*, Tokyo: The National Institute for Defense Studies, pp 7–28.

Cheng, J.Y.S. (2018) *Multilateral Approach in China's Foreign Policy*, Singapore: World Scientific Publishing.

Cheng, J.Y.S. and Zhang Wankun (2002) 'Patterns and dynamics of China's international strategic behaviour', *Journal of Contemporary China*, 11(31): 235–60.

Chia Ning (1993) 'The Lifanyuan and the Inner Asian rituals in the early Qing (1644–1795)', *Late Imperial China*, 14(1): 60–92.

Chiang Kai-shek (1947) *China's Destiny*, translated and edited by P. Jaffe, New York: Roy Publishers.

Ch'ü T'ung-tsu (1965) *Law and Society in Traditional China*, Paris: Mouton & Co.

Chun, A.J. (1989) 'The Ching tribute system as guest ritual: a preliminary description', in *Proceedings on the Second International Conference on Sinology*, Taipei, Taiwan: Academia, pp 169–208.

Chung, J.H. (2001) 'South Korea between eagle and dragon: perceptual ambivalence and strategic dilemma', *Asia Survey*, 41(5): 777–96.

Chuwattananurak, W. (2016) 'China's comprehensive national power and its implications for the rise of China: reassessment and challenges', paper presented to the CEEISA-ISA 2016 Joint International Conference, Ljubljana, 23–25 June.

Clark, I. (1989) *The Hierarchy of States: Reform and Resistance in the International Order*, Cambridge: Cambridge University Press.

Clark, I. (2005) *Legitimacy in International Society*, Oxford: Oxford University Press.

Clark, I. (2009) 'Towards an English School theory of hegemony', *European Journal of International Relations*, 15(2): 203–28.

Clark, I. (2011a) 'China and the United States: a succession of hegemonies?', *International Affairs*, 87(1): 13–28.

Clark, I. (2011b) *Hegemony in International Society*, Oxford: Oxford University Press.

Clark, I. (2014) 'International society and China: the power of norms and the norms of power', *The Chinese Journal of International Politics*, 3(1): 315–40.

Cohen, P. (1967) 'Wang T'ao's perspective on a changing world', in A. Feuerwerker, R. Murphey, and M.C. Wight (eds), *Approaches to Modern Chinese History*, Berkeley: University of California Press, pp 133–62.

Danjō, H. (2013) *The System of Maritime Exclusion=Tribute Bringing and the Hua Yi Order in the Ming Dynasty* (壇上寛：明代海禁＝朝貢システムと華夷秩序), Kyoto: Kyoto University Press.

Danjō, H. (2016) *Chinese History as All-Under-Heaven and Imperial Court* (壇上寛：天下と天朝の中国史), Tokyo: Iwanami Shinsho.

Dardess, J.W. (1984) *Confucianism and Autocracy: Professional Elites in the Founding of the Ming Dynasty*, Berkeley: University of California Press.

de Bary, W.T. (1988) *East Asian Civilizations: A Dialogue in Five Stages*, Cambridge, MA: Harvard University Press.

d'Encausse, H.C. and Schram, S.R. (1969) *Marxism and Asia: An Introduction with Readings*, London: Allen Lane, Penguin Press.

Deng Xiaoping (1994) *Selected Works of Deng Xiaoping (1982–1992)*, Beijing: Foreign Languages Press.

Deng Yong (1999) 'Conception of national interests: realpolitik, liberal dilemma, and the possibility of change', in Deng Yong and Wang Feiling (eds), *In the Eyes of the Dragon: China Views the World*, Lanham, MA: Rowman & Littlefield Publishers, Inc, pp 47–72.

Deng Yong (2008) *China's Struggle for Status: The Realignment of International Relations*, Cambridge: Cambridge University Press.

Deng Yong (2011) 'The power and politics of recognition: status in China's foreign relations', in T.J. Volgy, R. Corbetta, K.A. Grant, and R.G. Baird (eds), *Major Powers and the Quest for Status in International Politics Global and Regional Perspectives*, New York: Palgrave Macmillan, pp 77–95.

Deng Yong (2014) 'China: the post-responsible power', *The Washington Quarterly*, 37(4): 117–32.

Di Cosmo, N. (1998) 'Qing colonial administration in Inner Asia', *The International History Review*, 20(2): 287–309.

Di Cosmo, N. (2002) *Ancient China and Its Enemies: The Rise of Nomadic Power in East Asian History*, Cambridge: Cambridge University Press.

Donnelly, J. (2009) 'Rethinking political structures: from "ordering principles" to "vertical differentiation" – and beyond', *International Theory*, 1(1): 49–86.

Doshi, R. (2021) *The Long Game: China's Grand Strategy to Displace American Order*, Oxford: Oxford University Press.

Dreyer, E.L. (2007) *Zheng He: China and the Oceans in the Early Ming Dynasty, 1405–1433*, New York: Pearson Longman.

Dubs, H.H. (1928) *The Works of Hsüntze*, London: Arthur Probsthain.

Dunne, T. (2003) 'Society and hierarchy in international relations', *International Relations*, 17(3): 303–20.

Dunne, T. and Little, R. (2014) 'The international system – international society distinction', in C. Navari and D. Green (eds), *Guide to the English School in International Studies*, Oxford: Wiley-Blackwell, pp 91–107.

Ebihara, T. (2000) 'Chinese diplomacy as seen in the construction of "partnerships": focusing on relations with the "great powers" around the 15th Party Congress of the Chinese Communist Party' (海老原毅：「パートナーシップ」構築に見られる中国外交—中国共産党十五全大会前後の『大国』との関係を中心として—), *East Asian Area Studies*, 7: 17–34.

Economy, E.C. (2018) *The Third Revolution: Xi Jinping and the New Chinese State*, Oxford: Oxford University Press.

Edwards, R.R. (1973) 'Imperial China's border control law', *Columbia Journal of Asian Law*, 1(1): 33–62.

Eisenman, J. and Heginbotham, E. (2019) 'Building a more "democratic" and "multipolar" world: China's strategic engagement with developing countries', *China Review*, 19(4): 55–83.

Elliott, M.C. (2009) *Emperor Qianlong: Son of Heaven, Man of the World*, New York: Pearson Longman.

Elliott, M.C. and Chia Ning (2004) 'The Qing hunt at Mulan', in J.A. Millward, R.W. Dunnell, M.C. Elliott, and P. Forêt (eds), *New Qing Imperial History: The Making of the Inner Asian Empire at Qing Chende*, London: RoutledgeCurzon, pp 66–83.

Fairbank, J.K. (1968) 'A preliminary framework', in J.K. Fairbank (ed), *The Chinese World Order*, Cambridge, MA: Harvard University Press, pp 1–19.

Fairbank, J.K. (1969) 'China's foreign policy in historical perspective', *Foreign Affairs*, 47(3): 449–63.

Fairbank, J.K. (1978) 'Introduction: the old order', in J.K. Fairbank (ed), *The Cambridge History of China, Volume 10: Late Ch'ing, 1800–1911, Part 1*, Cambridge: Cambridge University Press, pp 1–34.

Fairbank, J.K. and Goldman, M. (2006) *China: A New History*, 2nd edition, Cambridge, MA: Belknap Press of Harvard University Press.

Fairbank, J.K. and Teng Ssu-yu (1941) 'On the Ch'ing tributary system', *Harvard Journal of Asiatic Studies*, 6(2): 135–246.

Farmer, E.L. (1995) *Zhu Yuanzhang and Early Ming Legislation: The Reordering of Chinese Society Following the Era of Mongol Rule*, Leiden, New York, and Köln: E.J. Brill.

Fehl, N.E. (1971) *Li: Rites and Propriety in Literature and Life: A Perspective for a Cultural History of Ancient China*, Hong Kong: The Chinese University of Hong Kong.

Fei Xiaotong (1992) *From the Soil: The Foundations of Chinese Society*, translated by G.G. Hamilton and Wang Zheng, Berkeley: University of California Press.

Feng Huiyun (2007) *Chinese Strategic Culture and Foreign Policy Decision-Making: Confucianism, Leadership and War*, New York: Routledge.

Feng Zhongping and Huang Jing (2014) 'China's strategic partnership diplomacy: engaging with a changing world', ESPO Working Papers No 8, June.

Finnane, A. (2010) 'Zhou Enlai in Bandung: film as history in the People's Republic of China', in D. McDougall and A. Finnane (eds), *Bandung 1955: Little Histories*, Caulfield: Monash University Press, pp 109–30.

Fitzgerald, C.P. (1964) *The Chinese View of their Place in the World*, Oxford: Oxford University Press.

Fitzgerald, C.P. (1972) *The Southern Expansion of the Chinese People: 'Southern Fields and Southern Ocean'*, London: Barrie & Jenkins.

Fletcher, J.F. (1968) 'China and Central Asia, 1368–1884', in J.K. Fairbank (ed), *The Chinese World Order*, Cambridge, MA: Harvard University Press, pp 206–24.

Foot, R. (1998) 'China in the ASEAN Regional Forum: organizational processes and domestic modes of thought', *Asian Survey*, 38(5): 425–40.

Foot, R. (2005) 'China's regional activism: leadership, leverage, and protection', *Global Change, Peace & Security*, 17(2): 141–53.

Foot, R. (2009) 'China and the United States: between cold and warm peace', *Survival*, 51(6): 123–46.

Foot, R. (2017) 'China and the international human protection regime: beliefs, power and status in a changing normative order', Kokusai Mondai (International Affairs) No 661, May.

Foot, R. (2020) *China, the UN, and Human Protection: Beliefs, Power, Image*, Oxford: Oxford University Press.

Ford, C.A. (2010) *The Mind of Empire: China's History and Modern Foreign Relations*, Lexington: The University Press of Kentucky.

Ford, C.A. (2015) 'The party and the sage: communist China's use of quasi-Confucian rationalizations for one-party dictatorship and imperial ambition', *Journal of Contemporary China*, 24(96): 1032–47.

Franke, H. (1983) 'Sung embassies: some general observations', in M. Rossabi (ed), *China Among Equals: The Middle Kingdom and its Neighbors, 10th-14th Centuries*, Berkeley: University of California Press, pp 116–48.

Fravel, M.T. (2008) *Strong Borders, Secure Nation: Cooperation and Escalation in China's Territorial Disputes*, Princeton: Princeton University Press.

French, H.W. (2017) *Everything Under the Heavens: How the Past Helps Shape China's Push for Global Power*, London: Scribe.

Friedman, J. (2015) *Shadow Cold War: The Sino-Soviet Competition for the Third World*, Chapel Hill: The University of North Carolina Press.

Fu Ying and Wu Shicun (2016) 'South China Sea: how we got to this stage', The National Interest, 9 May.

Fuma, S. (2007a) '"Propriety" and "chastisement" in Ming-Qing China's diplomacy towards Korea' (夫馬進：明清中国の対朝鮮外交における「礼」と「問罪」), in S. Fuma (ed), *Studies on the History of Chinese Diplomacy and Exchanges in East Asia* (夫馬進編：中国東アジア外交交流史の研究), Kyoto: Kyoto Universty Press, pp 311–53.

Fuma, S. (2007b) 'Ming-Qing China's policy towards Vietnam as a mirror of its policy towards Korea: with a focus on the question of investiture and "punitive expeditions"', *Memoirs of the Research Department of the Toyo Bunko*, 65: 1–33.

Galvany, A. (2013) 'Beyond the rule of rules: the foundations of sovereign power in the *Han Feizi*', in P.R. Goldin (ed), *Dao Companion to the Philosophy of Han Fei*, Dordrecht: Springer, pp 87–106.

Galyamova, V. (2010) 'Central Asian countries and China: managing the transition', in Zhang Yunling (ed), *China-Central Asian Countries: Making New Partnership*, Beijing: Social Sciences Academy Press, pp 285–323.

Garver, J.W. (2006) 'China's decision for war with India in 1962', in A.I. Johnston and R.S. Ross (eds), *New Directions in the Study of China's Foreign Policy*, Stanford: Stanford University Press, pp 86–130.

Garver, J.W. (2016) *China's Quest: The History of the Foreign Relations of the People's Republic of China*, Oxford: Oxford University Press.

Ge Zhaoguang (2014) *Rethinking China: Its Territory, People and Culture* (葛兆光：中国再考ーその領域・民族・文化ー), translated by S. Nagata, Tokyo: Iwanami Shoten.

Gilpin, R. (1981) *War and Change in World Politics*, Cambridge: Cambridge University Press.

Ginsburg, T. (2010) 'Eastphalia as the perfection of Westphalia', *Indiana Journal of Global Legal Studies*, 17(1): 27–45.

Goh, E. (2005) 'The US–China relationship and Asia-Pacific security: negotiating change', *Asian Security*, 1(3): 216–44.

Goh, E. (2013a) 'Conceptualizing the relationship between bilateral and multilateral security approaches in East Asia: a great power regional order framework', in W.T. Tow and B. Taylor (eds), *Bilateralism, Multilateralism and Asia-Pacific Security: Contending Cooperation*, New York: Routledge, pp 169–82.

Goh, E. (2013b) *The Struggle for Order: Hegemony, Hierarchy, and Transition in Post-Cold War East Asia*, Oxford: Oxford University Press.

Golding, P.R. (2011) 'Persistent misconceptions about Chinese "Legalism"', *Journal of Chinese Philosophy*, 38(1): 88–104.

Goldstein, A. (2001) 'The diplomatic face of China's grand strategy: a rising power's emerging choice', *The China Quarterly*, 168: 835–64.

Goldstein, A. (2005) *Rising to the Challenge: China's Grand Strategy and International Security*, Stanford: Stanford University Press.

Gong, G.W. (1984) *The Standard of 'Civilization' in International Society*, Oxford: Oxford University Press.

Graham, A.C. (1989) *Disputers of the Tao: Philosophical Argument in Ancient China*, La Salle, IL: Open Court.

Hakoda, K. (2009) 'The tradition and modernity of oversea missions: oversea missions in the ocean affairs period and their personnel' (箱田恵子：在外公館の伝統と近代—洋務時期の在外公館とその人材—), in T. Okamoto and S. Kawashima (eds), *Emerging Diplomacy in Late Imperial China* (岡本隆司・川島真編：中国近代外交の胎動), Tokyo: University of Tokyo Press, pp 117–38.

Hamashita, T. (1990) *International Forces of Change in Modern China: The Tribute Trade System and Modern Asia* (浜下武志：近代中国の国際的契機—朝貢貿易システムと近代アジア—), Tokyo: University of Tokyo Press.

Hamashita, T. (1997) *The Tribute System and Modern Day Asia* (浜下武志：朝貢システムと近代アジア), Tokyo: Iwanami Shoten.

Hamashita, T. (2003) 'Tribute and treaties: maritime Asia and treaty port networks in the era of negotiation, 1800–1900', in G. Arrighi, T. Hamashita, and M. Selden (eds), *The Resurgence of East Asia: 500, 150 and 50 Year Perspectives*, New York: RoutledgeCurzon, pp 17–50.

Han Feizi (2003) *Basic Writings*, translated by B. Watson, New York: Columbia University Press.

Han Yu-shan (1955) *Elements of Chinese Historiography*, Hollywood, CA: W.M. Hawley.

Haneda, M. (ed) (2013) *East Asian History Viewed from the Sea* (羽田正編：海から見た歴史), Tokyo: University of Tokyo Press.

Hao Cheng (1980) 'Intellectual change and the reform movement, 1890–8', in D. Twitchett and J.K. Fairbank (eds), *The Cambridge History of China, Volume 11: Late Ch'ing, 1800–1911, Part 2*, Cambridge: Cambridge University Press, pp 274–338.

Hao Yen-p'ing and Wang Erh-min (1980) 'Changing Chinese views of Western relations, 1840–95', in D. Twitchett and J.K. Fairbank (eds), *The Cambridge History of China, Volume 11: Late Ch'ing, 1800–1911, Part 2*, Cambridge: Cambridge University Press, pp 142–201.

Harle, V. (1998) *Ideas of Social Order in the Ancient World*, London: Greenwood Press.

Harrell, P., Rosenberg, E., and Saravalle, E. (2018) *China's Use of Coercive Economic Measures*, Washington, DC: Center for a New American Security.

Harris, S. (2014) *China's Foreign Policy*, Cambridge: Polity.

Harrison, H. (2000) *The Making of the Republican Citizen: Political Ceremonies and Symbols in China 1911–1929*, Oxford: Oxford University Press.

Hayden, S. (2016) 'What China's big nation complex means for the future of Asia', War on the Rocks, 13 June.

Hayton, B. (2018) 'The modern origins of China's South China Sea claims: maps, misunderstandings, and the maritime geobody', *Modern China*, 45(2): 127–70.

Hayton, B. (2020) *The Invention of China*, New Haven: Yale University Press.

Heath, T.R. (2014) *China's New Governing Party Paradigm: Political Renewal and the Pursuit of National Rejuvenation*, Surrey: Ashgate.

Heath, T.R. (2018) 'China's endgame: the path towards global leadership', Lawfare, 5 January.

Herman, J.E. (2006) The cant of conquest: Tusi offices and China's political incorporation of the southwest frontier', in P.K. Crossley, H.F. Siu, and D.S. Sutton (eds), *Empire at the Margins: Culture, Ethnicity, and Frontier in Early Modern China*, Berkeley: University of California Press, pp 135–68.

Herman, J.E. (2007) *Amid the Cloud and Mist: China's Colonization of Guizhou, 1200–1700*, Cambridge, MA: Harvard University Press.

Hevia, J.L. (1989) 'A multitude of lords: Qing court ritual and the Macartney embassy of 1793', *Late Imperial China*, 10(2): 72–105.

Hevia, J.L. (1995) *Cherishing Men from Afar: Qing Guest Ritual and the Macartney Embassy of 1793*, Durham, NC: Duke Universty Press.

Hirano, S. (2007) *The Empire of the Great Qing and the Turmoil of the Chinese World* (平野聡：大清帝国と中華の混迷), Tokyo: Kodansha.

Hobson, J.M. and Sharman, J.C. (2005) 'The enduring place of hierarchy in world politics: tracing the social logics of hierarchy and political change', *European Journal of International Relations*, 11(1): 63–98.

Holcombe, C. (1997) 'Ritsuryō Confucianism', *Harvard Journal of Asiatic Studies*, 57(2): 543–73.

Holcombe, C. (2001) *The Genesis of East Asia, 221 B.C.–A.D. 907*, Honolulu: University of Hawaii Press.

Hollis, M. and Smith, S. (1990) *Explaining and Understanding International Relations*, Oxford: Clarendon Press.

Hori, T. (1993) *China and the Ancient East Asian World: The Chinese World and Various People* (堀敏一：中国と古代東アジア世界—中華的世界と諸民族—), Tokyo: Iwanami Shoten.

Hori, T. (2006) *The Shape of the East Asian World: China and the Surrounding States* (堀敏一：東アジア世界の形成―中国と周辺国家—), Tokyo: Kyuko Shoin.

Horton, C. (2020) 'China's engagement with Cambodia: developing a strategic foothold in Southeast Asia', in N. Rolland (ed), *An Emerging China-Centric Order: China's Vision for a New World Order in Practice*, NBR Special Report No 87, August, pp 1–17.

Hsiao Kung-chuan (1979) *A History of Chinese Political Thought, Volume One: From the Beginnings to the Sixth Century A.D.*, translated by F.W. Mote, Princeton: Princeton University Press.

Hsiung, J.C. (1972) *Law and Policy in China's Foreign Relations: A Study of Attitudes and Practice*, New York: Columbia University Press.

Hsiung, J.C. (2012) *China into its Second Rise: Myths, Puzzles, Paradoxes, and Challenges to Theory*, Singapore: World Scientific.

Hsü, I.C.Y. (1960) *China's Entrance into the Family of Nations: The Diplomatic Phase, 1858–1880*, Cambridge, MA: Harvard University Press.

Hsü, L.S. (1932) *The Political Philosophy of Confucianism: An Interpretation of the Social and Political Ideas of Confucius, his Forerunners, and his Early Disciples*, London: George Routledge.

Hu Jintao (2016) *Selected Works of Hu Jintao, Volume 2* (胡锦涛：胡锦涛文选，第二卷), Beijing: Renmin Chubanshe.

Huang Chun-chieh (2004) 'Salient features of Chinese historical thinking', *Medieval History Journal*, 7(2): 243–54.

Huang Donglan (2005) 'Expression of space in late Qing and republican period geography textbooks: territory, boundaries and national humiliation' (黄東蘭：清末・民国期地理教科書の空間表象—領土・疆域・国恥—), *Chinese Studies Monthly*, 59(3): 24–39.

Huang Shuofeng (1992) *On Comprehensive National Power* (黄硕风：综合国力论), Beijing: China Social Sciences Press.

Huang Zhilian (1992) *The East Asian Chinese Order: A Discussion of the Pattern of Relations between China and East Asian States* (黄枝连：亚洲的华夏秩序—中国与亚洲国家关系形态论), Beijing: Renmin University Press.

Huang Zhilian (1994) *The East Asian Ritual and Righteousness World: A Discussion of the Pattern of Relations between the Chinese Feudal Dynasties and the Korean Peninsula* (黄枝连：东亚的礼义世界—中国封建王朝与朝鲜半岛关系形态论), Beijing: Renmin University Press.

Hunt, M.H. (1984) 'Chinese foreign relations in historical perspective', in H. Harding (ed), *China's Foreign Relations in the 1980s*, New Haven: Yale University Press, pp 1–42.

Hurrell, A. (2007) *On Global Order: Power, Values, and the Constitution of International Society*, Oxford: Oxford University Press.

Hwang Kwang-Kuo (2011) *Foundations of Chinese Psychology: Confucian Social Relations*, New York: Springer.

Iida, M. (2015) 'China's maritime advance' (飯田将史：中国の海洋進出), in S. Kawashima (ed), *China Risk* (川島真編：チャイナ・リスク), Tokyo: Iwanami Shoten, pp 175–99.

Ikenberry, G.J. (2004) 'American hegemony and East Asian order', *Australian Journal of International Affairs*, 58(3): 353–67.

Ikenberry, G.J., Wang Jisi, and Zhu Feng (eds) (2015) *America, China, and the Struggle for World Order: Ideas, Traditions, Historical Legacies, and Global Visions*, New York: Palgrave Macmillan.

Ing, M.D.K. (2012) *The Dysfunction of Ritual in Early Confucianism*, Oxford: Oxford University Press.

Inoguchi, T. and Bacon, P. (2005) 'Empire, hierarchy, and hegemony: American grand strategy and the construction of order in the Asia-Pacific', *International Relations of the Asia-Pacific*, 5(2): 117–32.

Institute of Linguistics, CASS (ed) (2012) *Xinhua Dictionary* (中国社会科学院语言研究所：新华字典), 11th edition, Beijing: Commercial Press.

Ishikawa, H. (2003) *A Study on the Thought of Li and Fa in Ancient China* (石川英昭：中国古代礼法思想の研究), Tokyo: Sobunsha.

Iwai, S. (2005) 'The system of hegemony through ritual of Ming era China and the order of East Asia' (岩井茂樹：明代中国の礼制覇権主義と東アジアの秩序), *Oriental Culture*, 85: 121–60.

Iwai, S. (2006) 'International trade and the mutual trade system in 16–18 century East Asia' (岩井茂樹：16–18世紀の東アジアにおける国際商業と互市体制), *East Asian Studies*, 46: 3–24.

Iwai, S. (2007) 'The mutual trade markets of the Qing Dynasty and its "quiet diplomacy"' (岩井茂樹：清代の互市と"沈黙外交"), in S. Fuma (ed), *Studies on the History of Chinese Diplomacy and Exchanges in East Asia* (夫馬進編：中国東アジア外交交流史の研究), Kyoto: Kyoto Universty Press, pp 354–90.

Iwai, S. (2009) 'Empire and mutual trade: friendly relations in 16–18 century East Asia' (岩井茂樹：帝国と互市—十六‐十八世紀東アジアの通交—), in N. Kagotani and K. Wakimura (eds), *Empire and Asian Networks: The Long 19th Century* (籠谷直人・脇村孝平編：帝国とアジア・ネットワーク—長期の19世紀—), Kyoto: Sekai Shisosha, pp 30–59.

Iwami, K. (1997) 'A few questions surrounding Tang foreign trade and foreign residents' (石見清裕：唐代外国貿易・在留外国人をめぐる諸問題), in M. Tanigawa, T. Hori, O. Ikeda, H. Kikuchi, and Y. Satake (eds), *Basic Questions Regarding Wei, Jin, Northern and Southern Dynasties, Sui and Tang Times* (谷川道雄・堀敏一・池田温・菊池英夫・佐竹靖彦 編：魏晋南北朝隋唐時代史の基本問題), Tokyo: Kyoko Shoin, pp 61–91.

Jacques, M. (2009) *When China Rules the World: The End of the Western World and the Birth of a New Global Order*, New York: Penguin.

Jakóbowski, J. (2018) 'Chinese-led regional multilateralism in Central and Eastern Europe, Africa and Latin America: 16+1, FOCAC, and CCF', *Journal of Contemporary China*, 27(113): 659–73.

James, A. (1993) 'System or Society?', *Review of International Studies*, 19: 269–88.

Jia Qingguo (2005) 'Learning to live with the hegemon: evolution of China's policy toward the US since the end of the Cold War', *Journal of Contemporary China*, 14(44): 395–407.

Jia Wenshan (2017) 'Host diplomacy for a new world order', China Daily, 8 August.

Jiang Junbo (2015) 'From "nation-state system" to "tianxia system": a possible international order?' (简军波：从"民族国家体系"到"天下体系":可能的国际秩序?), *International Relations Research*, 1: 37–40.

Jiang Zemin (2006) *Selected Works of Jiang Zemin*, Volume 2 (江泽民：江泽民文选, 第二卷), Beijing: Renmin Chubanshe.

Jin Canrong (2014) *What is Great Power Responsibility: The Path to China's Peaceful Development* (金燦栄：大国の責任とは—中国平和発展への道のり—), translated by T. Honda, Tokyo: Duan Press.

Jin Canrong (2017a) 'Two kinds of strategic thinking must learn to accommodate each other' (金燦栄：两种战略維須学会相互包容), Global Times, 21 June.

Jin Canrong (2017b) 'When the American first master meets the Chinese sweeping monk' (金灿荣：当美国第一高手 遇到中国扫地僧), US-China Perception Monitor, 29 June.

Jin Fenglin (2018) 'On the transformation and upgrading of the politics of the Way of the King and the community of destiny for mankind' (靳凤林：王道政治的转型升级与人类命运共同体), *Morality and Civilization*, 3: 89–93.

Johnson, C.K. (2016) 'President Xi Jinping's "Belt and Road" Initiative: a practical assessment of the Chinese Communist Party's roadmap for China's global resurgence', CSIS Report, March.

Johnston, A.I. (1995) *Cultural Realism: Strategic Culture and Grand Strategy in Chinese History*, Princeton: Princeton University Press.

Johnston, A.I. (1996) 'Cultural realism and strategy in Maoist China', in P.J. Katzenstein (ed), *The Culture of National Security: Norms and Identity in World Politics*, New York: Columbia University Press, pp 216–68.

Johnston, A.I. (2008) *Social States: China in International Institutions, 1980–2000*, Princeton: Princeton University Press.

Johnston, A.I. (2019) 'China in a world of orders: rethinking compliance and challenge in Beijing's international relations, *International Security*, 44(2): 9–60.

Jones, C. (2018) *China's Challenge to Liberal Norms: The Durability of International Order*, London: Palgrave Macmillan.

Kaneko, S. (1974) 'Regarding the form of Tang international letters' (金子修一：唐代の国際文書形式について), *Journal of Historical Studies*, 83(10): 29–51.

Kaneko, S. (2001) *The International Order of the Sui and Tang and East Asia* (金子修一：隋唐の国際秩序と東アジア), Tokyo: Meicho Kankokai.

Kang, D.C. (2003) 'Hierarchy and stability in Asian international relations', in G.J. Ikenberry and M. Mastanduno (eds), *International Relations Theory and the Asia-Pacific*, New York: Columbia University Press, pp 163–90.

Kang, D.C. (2007) *China Rising: Peace, Power, and Order in East Asia*, New York: Columbia University Press.

Kang, D.C. (2010) *East Asia before the West: Five Centuries of Trade and Tribute*, New York: Columbia University Press.

Kardon, I. (2015) 'China's maritime rights and interests: organizing to become a maritime power', paper presented at the China as a Maritime Power Conference, Washington, DC, 28–29 July.

Kataoka, K. (1998) 'The Qing Dynasty's relations with outer vassals and tributary states as seen in the regulations for the New Year ceremony' (片岡一忠：朝賀規定からみた清朝と外藩・朝貢国の関係), *The Journal of the Historical Association of Komazawa University*, 52: 240–63.

Kaufman, A.A. (2014) 'In pursuit of equality and respect: China's diplomacy and the League of Nations', *Modern China*, 40(6): 605–38.

Kausikan, B. (2016) 'Pavlovian conditioning and "correct thinking" on the South China Sea', The Straits Times, 1 April.

Kavalski, E. (2013) 'The struggle for recognition of normative powers: normative power Europe and normative power China in context', *Cooperation and Conflict*, 48(2): 247–67.

Kawashima, S. (2004) *The Formation of Modern Chinese Diplomacy* (川島真：中国近代外交の形成), Nagoya: The University of Nagoya Press.

Kawashima, S. (2006) 'International status as a symbol in Chinese diplomacy: the Hague Peace Conference, the League of Nations and the path to the United Nations' (川島真：中国外交における象徴としての国際的地位——ハーグ平和会議、国際連盟、そして国際連合へ—), *International Politics*, 145: 17–35.

Kawashima, S. (2007) 'The history of Chinese diplomacy' (川島真：中国外交の歴史), in S. Kawashima (ed), *The Diplomacy of China: Self-Consciousness and Challenges* (川島真編：中国の外交—自己認識と課題—), Tokyo: Yamakawa Shuppansha, pp 9–34.

Kawashima, S. (2009) 'China's reinterpretation of the Chinese world order, 1900–40s', in A. Reid and Zheng Yangwen (eds), *Negotiating Asymmetry: China's Place in Asia*, Singapore: NUS Press, pp 139–58.

Kawashima, S. (2012) 'China', in B. Fassbender and A. Peters (eds), *The Oxford Handbook of The History of International Law*, Oxford: Oxford University Press, pp 451–74.

Kawashima, S. and Hattori, R. (2007) *History of the International Politics of East Asia* (川島真・服部龍二：東アジア国際政治史), Nagoya: The University of Nagoya Press.

Keene, E. (2009) 'International society as an ideal type', in C. Navari (ed), *Theorising International Society: English School Methods*, London: Palgrave Macmillan, pp 104–24.

Kertzer, D.I. (1988) *Rituals, Politics, and Power*, New Haven: Yale University Press.

Kim, J.C. (2010) 'Politics of regionalism in East Asia: the case of the East Asia summit', *Asian Perspectives*, 34(3): 113–36.

Kim, J.Y. (2015) 'The rule of ritual: crimes and justice in Qing–Vietnamese relations during the Qianlong period (1736–1796)', in J.A. Anderson and J.K. Whitmore (eds), *China's Encounters on the South and Southwest: Reforging the Fiery Frontier Over Two Millennia*, Leiden: Brill, pp 288–321.

Kim, S.S. (1979) *China, the United Nations, and World Order*, Princeton: Princeton University Press.

Kinoshita, I. (2009) *The International History of Embassies: Understanding World Affairs from the Distribution of Foreign Diplomatic Missions* (木下郁夫：大使館国際関係史—在外公館の分布で読み解く世界情勢—), Tokyo: Shakai Hyōronsha.

Kitano, N. (2018) 'Estimating China's foreign aid using new data', *IDS Bulletin*, 49(3): 49–72.

Khan, S.W. (2018) *Haunted by Chaos: China's Grand Strategy from Mao Zedong to Xi Jinping*, Cambridge, MA: Harvard University Press.

Knoblock, J. (1988) *Xunzi: A Translation of the Complete Works*, Volume I Books 1–6, Stanford: Stanford University Press.

Knoblock, J. (1990) *Xunzi: A Translation of the Complete Works*, Volume II Books 7–16, Stanford: Stanford University Press.

Knoblock, J. (1994) *Xunzi: A Translation of the Complete Works*, Volume III Books 17–32, Stanford: Stanford University Press.

Kominami, I. (2001) 'Introduction' (小南一郎：序論), in I. Kominami (ed), *The Ritual System and the Study of Ritual in China* (小南一郎編：中國の禮制と禮學), Kyoto: Hoyu Books, pp 1–9.

Kotani, S. (2013) 'Regarding China's maritime advance in the South China Sea and its "maritime rights and interests" preservation activities' (小谷俊介：南シナ海における中国の海洋進出および「海洋権益」維持活動について), *Reference*, 754: 27–41.

Ku, S.C.Y. (2006) 'China's changing political economy with Southeast Asia: starting a new page of accord', *Asian Perspective*, 30(4): 113–40.

Kuhn, F. (2019) 'International status relations: a study of China and Japan from the 15th ct. to the Treaty of Versailles', PhD dissertation, National University of Singapore.

Kurihara, T. (1969) *Studies in Qin and Han History* (栗原朋信：秦漢史の研究), Tokyo: Yoshikawa Kobunkan.

Kwan, A.C.C.K. (2016) 'Hierarchy, status and international society: China and the steppe nomads', *European Journal of International Relations*, 22(2): 362–83.
Lai, C. (2018) 'Acting one way and talking another: China's coercive economic diplomacy in East Asia and beyond', *The Pacific Review*, 31(2): 169–87.
Laidlaw, J. (1999) 'On theatre and theory: reflections on ritual in imperial Chinese politics', in J.P. McDermott (ed), *State and Court Ritual in China*, Cambridge: Cambridge University Press, pp 399–416.
Lake, D.A. (2009) *Hierarchy in International Relations*, Ithaca: Cornell University Press.
Langlois, J.D. (1981) 'Political thought in Chin-hua under Mongol rule', in J.D. Langlois (ed), *China under Mongol Rule*, Princeton: Princeton University Press, pp 137–85.
Lantegne, M. (2005) *China and International Institutions: Alternate Paths to Global Power*, London: Routledge.
Leach, E. (1965) 'The cult of informality', *New Society*, 6(145): 9–12.
Lee, J.Y. (2013) 'Diplomatic ritual as a power resource: the politics of asymmetry in early modern Chinese-Korean relations', *Journal of East Asian Studies*, 13(2): 309–36.
Lee, L.T. (1967) 'Treaty relations of the People's Republic of China: a study in compliance', *University of Pennsylvania Law Review*, 116: 244–314.
Lee, S. (2000) *The Making of the East Asian Cultural Sphere* (李成市：東アジア文化圏の形成), Tokyo: Yamakawa Shuppansha.
Leifer, M. (1974) *The Foreign Relations of the New States*, Melbourne: Longman.
Levanthes, L. (1994) *When China Ruled the Seas: The Treasure Fleet of the Dragon Throne 1405–1433*, New York: Simon & Schuster.
Levenson, J.R. (1958) *Confucian China and Its Modern Fate, Volume 1: The Problem of Intellectual Continuity*, Berkeley: University of California Press.
Levine, S.I. (1984) 'China in Asia: the PRC as a regional power', in H. Harding (ed), *China's Foreign Relations in the 1980s*, New Haven: Yale University Press, pp 107–45.
Lewis, M.E. (1999) *Writing and Authority in Early China*, Albany: State University Press of New York.
Lewis, M.E. (2005) *The Construction of Space in Early China*, Albany: State University of New York Press.
Lewis, M.E. (2009a) *China between Empires: The Northern and Southern Dynasties*, Cambridge, MA: Belknap Press of Harvard University Press.
Lewis, M.E. (2009b) *China's Cosmopolitan Empire: The Tang Dynasty*, Cambridge, MA: Belknap Press of Harvard University Press.
Leys, S. (1999) *Essais sur la Chine*, Paris: Robert Laffont.
Li Baojun and Liu Bo (2011) 'An analysis of the "tribute-titles" order' (李宝俊,刘波："朝贡-册封"秩序论析), *Foreign Affairs Review*, 2: 109–21.

Li Cheng and Lucy Xu (2014) 'Chinese enthusiasm and American cynicism: the "new type of great power relations"', China–US Focus, 4 December.

Li Danhui and Xia Yafeng (2008) 'Competing for leadership: split or détente in the Sino-Soviet bloc, 1959–1961', *The International History Review*, 30(3): 545–74.

Li Jie (2007) 'The transition of the international system: from the perspective of the theory of responsibility', *China International Studies*, 4: 138–58.

Li Kangying (2010) *The Ming Maritime Trade Policy in Transition, 1368 to 1567*, Wiesbaden: Harrassowitz Verlag.

Li Mingjiang (2012) 'Chinese debates of South China Sea policy: implications for future developments', RSIS Working Paper No 239, May.

Li Xiao and Li Junjiu (2015) '"One Belt, One Road" and the reshaping of China's geopolitical and geoeconomic strategy' (李晓·李俊："一带一路"与中国地缘政治经济战略的重构), *World Economics and Politics*, 10: 30–59.

Li Yunquan (2004) *A History of the Tribute System: Research on China's Pre-Modern Foreign Relations System* (李云泉：朝贡制度史论—中国古代对外关系体制研究), Beijing: Xinhua Publishing House.

Li Yunquan (2006) 'The theoretic origins of the tributary system and its character in different historical periods' (李云泉：朝贡制度的理论渊源与时代特征), *China's Borderland History and Geography Studies*, 16(3): 37–42.

Li Yunquan (2011) 'Re-discussing the Qing tribute system' (李云泉：再论清代朝贡体制), *Journal of Shandong Normal University (Humanities and Social Sciences)*, 5: 93–100.

Lin Ming-te (1991) 'Li Hung-chang's suzerain policy toward Korea, 1882–1894', *Chinese Studies in History*, 24(4): 69–96.

Lin Xuezhong (2009) *From the Law of Nations to Legal Diplomacy: The Introduction, Interpretation and Application of International Law in the Late Qing* (林学忠：从万国公法到公法外交—晚清国际法的传入, 诠释与应用), Shanghai: Shanghai Ancient Works Publishing House.

Lind, J. (2018) 'Life in China's Asia: what regional hegemony would look like', *Foreign Affairs*, 97(2): 71–82.

Ling Shengli (2017) '"Host diplomacy" helps promote China's strategic capabilities' (凌胜利："主场外交"助力中国战略能力提升), *Contemporary World*, 9: 24–27.

Link, P. (2013) *An Anatomy of Chinese: Rhythm, Metaphor, Politics*, Cambridge, MA: Harvard University Press.

Liu Bowei and Fang Changping (2016) 'China's peripheral network of partnerships and its peripheral security environment' (刘博文·方长平：周边伙伴关系网络与中国周边安全环境), *Journal of Contemporary Asia-Pacific Studies*, 3: 68–100.

Liu Feitao (2004) 'Power, responsibility and great power consciousness: also discussing the proper attitude in China's response to responsibility in international society' (刘飞涛：权力、责任与大国认同—兼论中国应对国际社会责任的应有态度), *Pacific Bulletin*, 12: 25–32.

Liu Tiewa (2014) 'Chinese strategic culture and the use of force: moral and political perspectives', *Journal of Contemporary China*, 23(87): 556–74.

Liu Tuyao and Cheng Ruishan (2007) 'Regarding Zhou Enlai's diplomatic thought of seeking common ground while reserving differences' (刘土尧·程瑞山：试论周恩来的求同存异外交思想), People's Daily Online, 9 January.

Liu Xinru (1988) *Ancient India and Ancient China: Trade and Religious Exchanges, AD 1–600*, Dehli: Oxford University Press.

Lo Chang-fa (2010) 'Values to be added to an "Eastphalia order" by the emerging China', *Indiana Journal of Global Legal Studies*, 17(1): 13–25.

Lo Chi-Kin (1989) *China's Policy toward Territorial Disputes: The Case of the South China Sea Islands*, New York: Routledge.

Lo Jung-pang (2012) China as a *Sea Power 1127–1368: A Preliminary Survey of the Maritime Expansion and Naval Exploits of the Chinese People During the Southern Song and Yuan Periods*, edited by B.A. Elleman, Singapore: NUS Press.

Loewe, M.A.N. (1974) 'The campaigns of Han Wu-ti', in F. Kierman and J.K. Fairbank (eds), *Chinese Ways in Warfare*, Cambridge, MA: Harvard University Press, pp 67–122.

Loewe, M.A.N. (1986) 'The former Han Dynasty', in D. Twichett and J.K. Fairbank (eds), *The Cambridge History of China, Volume 1: The Ch'in and Han Empires, 221 B.C.-A.D. 220*, Cambridge: Cambridge University Press, pp 103–222.

Luard, E. (1976) *Types of International Society*, New York: The Free Press.

Luo Jianbo (2016) 'Nine big characteristics of Chinese foreign aid' (罗建波：中国对外援助的九大特色), *International Development Cooperation*, 4: 102–6.

Lüthi, L.M. (2008) *The Sino–Soviet Split: Cold War in the Communist World*, Princeton: Princeton University Press.

Lynch, D. (2009) 'Chinese thinking on the future of international relations: realism as the Ti, rationalism as the Yong?', *The China Quarterly*, 197: 87–107.

Mcconaughey, M., Musgrave, P., and Nexon, D.H. (2018) 'Beyond anarchy: logics of political organization, hierarchy, and international structure', *International Theory*, 10(2): 181–218.

Maeda, H. (2012) 'The national interest controversy and core interests in China' (前田宏子：中国における国益論争と核心的利益), *PHP Policy Review*, 6(48): 1–10.

Mancall, M. (1963) 'The persistence of tradition in Chinese foreign policy', *The Annals of the American Academy of Political and Social Science*, 349(1): 14–26.

Mancall, M. (1968) 'The Ch'ing tribute system: an interpretative essay', in J.K. Fairbank (ed), *The Chinese World Order*, Cambridge, MA: Harvard University Press, pp 63–89.

Mancall, M. (1971) *Russia and China: Their Diplomatic Relations to 1728*, Cambridge, MA: Harvard University Press.

Martinson, R. (2015) 'China's great balancing act unfolds: enforcing maritime rights vs. stability', The National Interest, 11 September.

Martinson, R. and Yamamoto, K. (2017) 'Three PLAN officers may have just revealed what China wants in the South China Sea', The National Interest, 9 July.

Marukawa, T. (2015) *Chinese Nationalism: Reading Another Modern Times* (丸川哲史：中国ナショナリズム—もう一つの近代をよむ—), Kyoto: Hōritsu Bunka Sha.

Mastanduno, M. (2003) 'Incomplete hegemony: the United States and security order in Asia', in M. Alagappa (ed), *Asian Security Order: Instrumental and Normative Features*, Stanford: Stanford University Press, pp 141–70.

Masuda, M. (2000) 'China's great power diplomacy: regarding "strategic partnerships"'(増田雅之：中国の大国外交—「戦略パートナーシップ」をめぐって—), *East Asia*, 402: 85–104.

Matsuda, H. (1986) *History of the Nomads* (松田壽男：遊牧民の歴史), Tokyo: Rokko Shuppan.

Mattern, J.B. and Zarakol, A. (2016) 'Hierarchies in world politics', *International Organization*, 70(3): 623–45.

Mayer, M. (2018) 'China's historical statecraft and the return of history', *International Affairs*, 94(6): 1217–35.

Mearsheimer, J.J. (2010) 'The gathering storm: China's challenge to US power in Asia', *The Chinese Journal of International Politics*, 3(4): 381–96.

Medeiros, E.S. (2009) *China's International Behavior: Activism, Opportunism, and Diversification*, Santa Monica, CA: Rand Corporation.

Meisner, M. (1967) *Li Ta-chao and the Origins of Chinese Marxism*, Cambridge, MA: Harvard University Press.

Men Honghua (2001) 'International regimes and China's strategic choice' (门洪华：国际机制与中国的战略选择), *Chinese Social Science*, 2: 178–87.

Men Honghua and Liu Xiaoyang (2015) 'Evaluation and prospects of China's partnerships strategy' (门洪华·刘笑阳：中国伙伴关系战略评估与展望), *World Economics and Politics*, 2: 65–95.

Miller, A.L. (2009) 'Some things we used to know about China's past and present (but now, not so much)', *The Journal of American–East Asian Relations*, 16(1/2): 41–68.

Miller, T. (2017) *China's Asian Dream: Empire Building along the New Silk Road*, London: Zed Books.

Millward, J.A. (1992) 'Qing silk–horse trade with the Qazaqs in Yili and Tarbaghatai, 1758–1853', *Central and Inner Asian Studies*, 7: 1–42.

Millward, J.A. (1998) *Beyond the Pass: Economy, Ethnicity, and Empire in Qing Central Asia, 1759–1864*, Stanford: Stanford University Press.

Minzner, C. (2018) *End of an Era: How China's Authoritarian Revival is Undermining its Rise*, Oxford: Oxford University Press.

Mitter, R. (2003), 'An uneasy engagement: Chinese ideas of global order and justice in historical perspective', in R. Foot, J. Gaddis, and A. Hurrell (eds), *Order and Justice in International Relations*, Oxford: Oxford University Press, pp 120–51.

Mitter, R. (2004) *A Bitter Revolution: China's Struggle with the Modern World*, Oxford: Oxford University Press.

Mitter, R. (2020) *China's Good War: How World War II Is Shaping a New Nationalism*, Cambridge, MA: The Belknap Press of Harvard University Press.

Miyazaki, M. (1997) *Zheng He's Great Voyages to the South Sea: The Yongle Emperor's Reorganization of World Order* (宮崎正勝：鄭和の南海大遠征永— 楽帝の世界秩序再編—), Tokyo: Chuokoron-sha.

Mizoguchi, Y., Ikeda, T., and Kojima, T. (2007) *History of Chinese Thought* (溝口雄三・池田知久・小島毅：中国思想史), Tokyo: University of Tokyo Press.

Morgenthau, H. (1948) *Politics among Nations: The Struggle for Power and Peace*, New York: Alfred A. Knopf.

Mote, F.W. (1999) *Imperial China 900–1800*, Cambridge, MA: Harvard University Press.

Motegi, T. (1997) *The Changing International Order of Modern East Asia* (茂木敏夫：変容する近代東アジアの国際秩序), Tokyo: Yamakawa Shuppansha.

Motegi, T. (2009) 'Change and restructuring of the Chinese image of the world' (茂木敏夫：中国的世界像の変容と再編), in W. Iijima, T. Kubo, and Y. Murata (eds), *History of 20th Century China I: The Chinese World and Modern Times* (飯島渉・久保亨・村田雄二郎編：20世紀中国史1—中華世界と近代—), Tokyo: University of Tokyo Press, pp 37–58.

Mount, F. (1972) *The Theatre of Politics*, London: Weidenfeld and Nicolson.

Murakami, K. (2016) 'The changing degree of Asia's economic dependence on the United States and China' (村上和也：変化するアジア経済の対米・対中依存度), Mitsui Mitomo Banking Trust Report, September.

Nahlik, S.E. (1984) 'À l'aube de la codification du droit international', in J. Makarczyk (ed), *Essays in International Law in Honour of Judge Manfred Lachs*, The Hague: Martinus Nijhoff Publishers, pp 201–16.

Nakajima, G. (2018) 'The structure and transformation of the Ming tribute trade system', in M.P. Garcia and L. De Sousa (eds), *Global History and New Polycentric Approaches: Europe, Asia and the Americas in a World Network System*, Singapore: Palgrave Macmillan, pp 137–62.

Nakamura, H. (1964) *Ways of Thinking of Eastern Peoples: India-China- Tibet-Japan*, Honolulu: East-West Center Press.

Nakanishi, T. (2013) *China as an Empire: The Logic and Reality of Hegemony* (中西輝政：帝国としての中国—覇権の論理と現実—), new edition, Tokyo: Toyo Keizai Shinposha.

Nathan, A.J. and Scobell, A. (2012) *China's Search for Security*, New York: Columbia University Press.

Navari, C. (2009) 'What the classical English School was trying to explain, and why its members were not interested in causal explanation', in C. Navari (ed), *Theorising International Society: English School Methods*, London: Palgrave Macmillan, pp 39–57.

Newby, L.J. (2005) *The Empire and the Khanate: A Political History of Qing Relations with Khoqand C. 1760–1860*, Leiden: Brill.

Ni Chen (2011) 'The evolving Chinese government spokesperson system', in Wang Jian (ed), *Soft Power in China: Public Diplomacy through Communication*, New York: Palgrave Macmillan, pp 57–71.

Ni Lexiong (2008) 'The implications of ancient Chinese military culture for world peace', in D.A. Bell (ed) *Confucian Political Ethics*, Princeton: Princeton University Press, pp 201–25.

NIDS (2000) *East Asian Strategic Review 2000*, Toyko: Japan Times.

Ning Sao (2000) 'Choosing the partnership strategy and building partnerships: China's diplomacy entering the 21st century' (宁骚：选择伙伴战略 营造伙伴关系—跨入21世纪的中国外交), *Expanding Horizons*, 2: 4–7.

Nishi, S. and Koito, N. (1941) *The Meaning and Structure of Ritual* (西晋一郎・小糸夏次郎：禮の意義と構造), Tokyo: National Spiritual Culture Research Center.

Nishijima S. (1983) *The Ancient Chinese State and the East Asian World* (西嶋定生：中国古代国家と東アジア世界), Tokyo: Tokyo University Press.

Nordin, A.H.M. (2016) *China's International Relations and Harmonious World: Time, Space and Multiplicity in World Politics*, New York: Routledge.

Ogura, Y. (1966) 'The formation of the Sino-barbarian thought' (小倉芳彦：華夷思想の形成), *Thought*, 503: 23–32.

Okamoto, T. (2009) 'The independence of Korea and Qing diplomacy: between independence and autonomy' (岡本隆司：韓国の独立と清朝の外交—独立と自主の間—), in T. Okamoto and S. Kawashima (eds), *Emerging Diplomacy in Late Imperial China* (岡本隆司・川島真編：中国近代外交の胎動), Tokyo: University of Tokyo Press, pp 161–80.

Onodera, S. (2017) *Chinese Nationalism: The Modern History of Nation and Patriotism* (小野寺史郎：中国ナショナリズム—民族と愛国の近現代史—), Tokyo: Chuokoron-Shinsha.

Osiander, A. (2001) 'Sovereignty, international relations, and the Westphalian myth', *International Organization*, 55(2): 251–87.

Oxman, B.H. (2006) 'The territorial temptation: a siren song at sea', *The American Journal of International Law*, 100(4): 830–51.

Paine, S.C.M. (2003) *The Sino-Japanese War of 1894–1895: Perceptions, Power, and Primacy*, Cambridge: Cambridge Universty Press.

Pan Yihong (1997) *Son of Heaven and Heavenly Qaghan: Sui-Tang China and its Neighbors*, Bellingham, WA: Center for East Asian Studies, Western Washington University.

Pang Zhongying (2001) 'China's Asia strategy: flexible multilateralism' (庞中英：中国的亚洲战略—灵活的多边主义), *World Economics and Politics*, 10: 30–5.

Pantsov, A.V. and Levine, S.I. (2012) *Mao: The Real Story*, New York: Simon & Schuster.

Paul, T.V., Larson, D.W., and Wohlforth, W.C. (eds) (2014) *Status in World Politics*, Cambridge: Cambridge University Press.

Pedrozo, R. (2014) 'Military activities in the Exclusive Economic Zone: East Asia focus', *International Law Studies*, 90(1): 514–43.

Perdue, P.C. (2005) *China Marches West: The Qing Conquest of Central Eurasia*, Cambridge, MA: The Belknap Press of Harvard University Press.

Perdue, P.C. (2010) 'Boundaries and trade in the early modern world: negotiations at Nerchinsk and Beijing', *Eighteenth-Century Studies*, 43(3): 341–56.

Pillsbury, M. (2000) *China Debates the Future Security Environment*, Washington, DC: National Defense University Press.

Pines, Y. (2000) 'Disputers of the "Li": breakthroughs in the concept of ritual in preimperial China', *Asia Major*, 13(1): 1–41.

Pines, Y. (2002) *Foundations of Confucian Thought: Intellectual Life in the Chunqiu Period, 722–453 B.C.E.*, Honolulu: University of Hawaii Press.

Pines, Y. (2005) 'Beasts or humans: pre-imperial origins of the "Sino-barbarian" dichotomy', in R. Amitai and M. Biran (eds), *Mongols, Turks, and Others: Eurasian Nomads and the Sedentary World*, Leiden: Brill, pp 59–102.

Pines, Y. (2012) *The Everlasting Empire: The Political Culture of Ancient China and Its Imperial Legacy*, Princeton: Princeton University Press.

Pines, Y. (2013) 'Submerged by absolute power: the ruler's predicament in the Han Feizi', in P.R. Goldin (ed), *Dao Companion to the Philosophy of Han Fei*, Dordrecht: Springer, pp 67–86.

Pocock, J.G.A. (1973) *Politics, Language, and Time: Essays on Political Thought and History*, New York: Atheneum.

Pouliot, V. (2016) *International Pecking Orders: The Politics and Practice of Multilateral Diplomacy*, Cambridge: Cambridge University Press.

Prasirtsuk, K. (2013) 'The implications of U.S. strategic rebalancing: a perspective from Thailand', *Asia Policy*, 15: 31–7.

Puett, M. (2006) 'Innovation as ritualization: the fractured cosmology of early China', *Cardozo Law Review*, 28(1): 23–36.

Pye, L.W. (1968) *The Spirit of Chinese Politics: A Psychocultural Study of the Authority Crisis in Political Development*, Cambridge, MA: The M.I.T. Press.

Pye, L.W. (1988) *The Mandarin and the Cadre: China's Political Cultures*, Ann Arbor, MI: Center for Chinese Studies, the University of Michigan.

Pye, L.W. (1990) 'China: erratic state, frustrated society', *Foreign Affairs*, 69(4): 56–74.

Qin Yaqing (2011) 'Rule, rules, and relations: towards a synthetic approach to governance', *The Chinese Journal of International Politics*, 4(2): 117–45.

Qin Yaqing (2014) 'The correct view of righteousness and interest: the conceptual innovation and practical principle of Chinese diplomacy in the new era' (秦亚青：正确义利观—新时期中国外交的理念创新和实践原则), Seeking Truth, 6 June.

Qin Yaqing (2016) 'A relational theory of world politics', *International Studies Review*, 18(1): 33–47.

Queen, S.A. (2013) 'Han Feizi and the old master: a comparative analysis and translation of Han Feizi Chapter 20, "Jie Lao," and Chapter 21, "Yu Lao"', in P.R. Golding (ed), *Dao Companion to the Philosophy of Han Fei*, Dordrecht: Springer, pp 197–256.

Rajah, R. (2019) 'East Asia's decoupling', Lowy Institute Working Paper, 1, January.

Rawski, E.S. (2015) *Early Modern China and Northeast Asia: Cross-Border Perspectives*, Cambridge: Cambridge University Press.

Reilly, J. (2012) 'China's unilateral sanctions', *The Washington Quarterly*, 35(4): 121–33.

Renshon, J. (2017) *Fighting for Status: Hierarchy and Conflict in World Politics*, Princeton: Princeton University Press.

Ringmar, E. (2012) 'Performing international systems: two East-Asian alternatives to the Westphalian order', *International Organization*, 66(1): 1–25.

Robinson, T. (1991) 'China confronts the Soviet Union: warfare and diplomacy on China's Inner Asian frontiers', in R. MacFarquhar and J.K. Fairbank (eds), *The Cambridge History of China, Volume 15: The People's Republic, Part 2 – Revolutions with the Chinese Revolution, 1966–1982*, Cambridge: Cambridge University Press, pp 218–301.

Rolland, N. (2017) *China's Eurasian Century? Political and Strategic Implications of the Belt and Road Initiative*, Seattle: National Bureau of Asian Research.

Rolland, N. (2020) 'China's vision for a new world order', NBR Special Report No 83, January.

Rossabi, M. (1970) 'The tea and horse trade with Inner Asia during the Ming', *Journal of Asian History*, 4(2): 136–68.

Rossabi, M. (1976) 'Two Ming envoys to Inner Asia', *T'oung Pao*, 62(1/3): 1–34.

Rozman, G. (2012) 'East Asian regionalism and Sinocentrism', *Japanese Journal of Political Science*, 13(1): 143–53.

San Pablo-Baviera, A. (2002) 'Perceptions of a China threat: a Philippine perspective', in H. Yee and I. Storey (eds), *The China Threat: Perceptions, Myths and Reality*, New York: RoutledgeCurzon, pp 253–69.

San Pablo-Baviera, A. (2003) 'The China factor in US alliances in East Asia and the Asia Pacific', *Australian Journal of International Affairs*, 57(2): 339–52.

Sato, M. (2003) *The Confucian Quest for Order: The Origin and Formation of the Political Thought of Xun Zi*, Leiden: Brill.

Sato, M. (2014) 'Li as a way to order: the intellectual characteristics and historical role of Xun Zi's theory of Li', *Social Sciences in China*, 35(1): 136–45.

Satō, S. (1992) 'Kang Youwei: the discourse on peace at the end of the Qing and the "Book of Datong"' (佐藤慎一：康有為—清末の平和論と『大同書』—), *Political Science Yearbook*, 43: 79–93.

Satō, S. (1996) *Intellectuals and Civilization in Modern China* (佐藤慎一：近代中国の知識人と文明), Tokyo: University of Tokyo Press.

Sawyer, R.D. (1993) *The Seven Military Classics of Ancient China*, New York: Basic Books.

Schell, O. and Delury, J. (2013) *Wealth and Power: China's Long March to the Twenty-First Century*, New York: Random House.

Schram, S.R. (1969) *The Political Thought of Mao Tse-tung*, revised and enlarged edition, New York: Praeger.

Schram, S.R. (ed) (2005) *Mao's Road to Power: Revolutionary Writings 1912–1949, Volume 7: New Democracy (1939–1941)*, Armonk, NY: M.E. Sharpe.

Schuman, M. (2020) *Superpower Interrupted: The Chinese History of the World*, New York: Public Affairs.

Schwartz, B.I. (1964) *In Search of Wealth and Power: Yen Fu and the West*, Cambridge, MA: Belknap Press of Harvard University Press.

Schwartz, B.I. (1968) 'The Chinese perception of world order: past and present', in J.K. Fairbank (ed), *The Chinese World Order*, Cambridge, MA: Harvard University Press, pp 276–88.

Schwartz, B.I. (1985) *The World of Thought in Ancient China*, Cambridge, MA: Belknap Press of Harvard University Press.

Schwartz, B.I. (1996) *China and Other Matters*, Cambridge, MA: Harvard University Press.

Scobell, A. (2002) *China and Strategic Culture*, Carlisle: Strategic Studies Institute, US Army War College.

Scobell, A. (2003) *China's Use of Military Force: Beyond the Great Wall and the Long March*, Cambridge: Cambridge University Press.

Scott, D. (2010) 'China and the "responsibilities" of a "responsible" power: the uncertainties of appropriate power rise language', *Asia-Pacific Review*, 17(1): 72–96.

Seligman, A.B., Weller. R.P., Puett, M.J., and Simon, B. (2008) *Ritual and Its Consequences: An Essay on the Limits of Sincerity*, Oxford: Oxford University Press.

Sen, T. (2003) *Buddhism, Diplomacy and Trade: The Realignment of Sino–Indian Relations, 600–1400*, Honolulu: University of Hawaii Press.

Serruys, H. (1967) *Sino–Mongol Relations during the Ming, II: The Tribute System and Diplomatic Missions (1400–1600)*, Brussels: Institut Belge des Hautes Etudes Chinoises.

Shambaugh, D. (2004/05) 'China engages Asia: reshaping the regional order', *International Security*, 29(3): 64–99.

Shen Zhihua (2016) *The Last 'Imperial Court': China and North Korea in the time of Mao Zedong and Kim Il Sung, Volume 2* (沈志華：最後の「天朝」—毛沢東・金日成時代の中国と北朝鮮—下), translated by Zhu Jianrong, Tokyo: Iwanami Shoten.

Shi Hua (1979) 'Deng Xiaoping on Sino-Vietnam war', *China Report*, 15(3): 53–7.

Shi Yinhong (2015) 'China's traditional experience and contemporary practice: strategic adjustment, strategic overdraft and the question of the great rejuvenation' (时殷弘：传统中国经验与当今中国实践: 战略调整、战略透支和伟大复兴问题), *Foreign Affairs Review*, 6: 57–68.

Shi Zhe and Chen Jian (1993) 'With Mao and Stalin: the reminiscences of Mao's interpreter part II: Liu Shaoqi in Moscow', *Chinese Historians*, 6(1): 67–90.

Shih Chih-yu (1990) *The Spirit of Chinese Foreign Policy: A Psychocultural View*, New York: Palgrave Macmillan.

Shih Chih-yu (1993) *China's Just World: The Morality of Chinese Foreign Policy*, Boulder, CO: Lynne Rienner Publishers.

Shirk, S.L. (2007) *China: Fragile Superpower*, Oxford: Oxford University Press.

Simpson, G. (2004) *Great Powers and Outlaw States: Unequal Sovereigns in the International Legal Order*, Cambridge: Cambridge University Press.

Skaff, J.K. (2012) *Sui-Tang China and its Turko-Mongol Neighbors: Culture, Power, and Connections, 580–800*, Oxford: Oxford University Press.

Smith, R.J. (2012) *Mapping China and Managing the World: Culture, Cartography and Cosmology in Late Imperial Times*, New York: Routledge.

Song Guoyou (2015) 'The strategic conception of the "Belt and Road" and the new development of China's economic diplomacy' (宋国友："一带一路"战略构想与中国经济外交新发展), *International Review*, 4: 22–34.

Sorace, C.P. (2017) *Shaken Authority: China's Communist Party and the 2008 Sichuan Earthquake*, Ithaca: Cornell University Press.

Stevenson, A. (ed) (2010) *Oxford Dictionary of English*, 3rd Edition, Oxford: Oxford University Press.

Storey, I. (2015) 'Thailand's post-coup relations with China and America: more Beijing, less Washington', Trends in Southeast Asia No 20.

Strüver, G. (2017) 'China's partnership diplomacy: international alignment based on interests or ideology', *The Chinese Journal of International Politics*, 10(1): 31–65.

Su Hao (2000) 'The "partnerships" framework of Chinese diplomacy' (苏浩：中国外交的"伙伴关系"框架), *World Affairs*, 5: 11–12.

Su Hao (2009) 'Harmonious world: the conceived international order in framework of China's foreign affairs, in M. Iida (ed), *China's Shift: Global Strategy of the Rising Power*, Tokyo: The National Institute for Defense Studies, pp 29–55.

Sun Baoshan (1999) 'A tentative discussion of partnerships in post-Cold War international relations' (孙宝珊：试论冷战后国际关系中的伙伴关系), *Pacific Journal*, 2: 84–90.

Sun Jingxin and Lin Janwei (2015) 'Partnerships contribute to great power diplomacy with Chinese characteristics' (孙敬鑫·林剑贞：伙伴关系助力中国特色大国外交), *Contemporary World*, 10: 34–7.

Sun Shiqiang and Luan Chunyu (2013) 'Hu Jintao's "harmonious world" outlook' (孙士强·栾淳钰：论胡锦涛的"和谐世界"观), *Journal of Yanbian Party School*, 29(1): 24–7.

Suzuki, C. (1981) 'Qing–Burma relations: war and peace, 1766–1790' (鈴木中正：清・ビルマ関係―戦争と和平1766～1790―), *Southeast Asia: History and Culture*, 10: 3–16.

Suzuki, S. (2008) 'Seeking 'legitimate' great power status in post-Cold War international society: China's and Japan's participation in UNPKO', *International Relations*, 22(1): 45–63.

Suzuki, S. (2009) *Civilization and Empire: China and Japan's Encounter with European International Society*, New York: Routledge.

Suzuki, S. (2017) '"Delinquent dangs" in the international system hierarchy', in A. Zarakol (ed), *Hierarchies in World Politics*, Cambridge: Cambridge University Press, pp 219–40.

Svarverud, R. (2007) *International Law as World Order in Late Imperial China: Translation, Reception and Discourse, 1847–1911*, Leiden: Brill.

Swaine, M.D. (2010) 'China's assertive behavior, part one: on "core interests"', China Leadership Monitor No 34, November.

Swaine, M.D. (2017) 'Chinese views on South Korea's deployment of THAAD', China Leadership Monitor No 52, February.

Swaine, M.D. and Tellis, A.J. (2000) *Interpreting China's Grand Strategy: Past, Present, and Future*, Santa Monica, CA: Rand.

Swanström, N. (2005) 'China and Central Asia: a new great game or traditional vassal relations?', *Journal of Contemporary China*, 14(45): 569–84.

Swisher, E. (1958) 'Chinese intellectuals and the western impact, 1838–1900', *Comparative Studies in Society and History*, 1(1): 26–37.

Takagi, S. (2003) 'China's "new security concept"' (高木誠一郎：中国の「新安全保障観」)', *National Institute for Defense Studies Bulletin*, 5(2): 68–89.

Takagi, S. (2011) 'A new aspect of Chinese diplomacy: the pursuit of international "discourse power"' (高木誠一郎：中国外交の新局面—国際「話語権」の追求—), *Aoyama Journal of International Politics, Economics and Business*, 85: 3–19.

Takahara, A. (2004) 'China's multilateral diplomacy: the advocacy of the new security concept and the mew development of peripheral diplomacy' (高原明生：中国の多角外交ー新安全保障観の唱道と周辺外交の新展開ー)', *International Issues*, 527: 17–30.

Tang Xuejun and Chen Xiaoxia (2015) 'China's thinking and strategic position for the post-American age: shaping a "China following the Way of the King" from the Chinese character' (唐学军·陈晓霞：后美国时代的中国思维与战略定位—以华夏性格塑造王道中国), *Journal of Shanxi Normal University (Social Sciences)*, 45: 142–4.

Tanigawa, M. (1979) 'The historical construction of the formative period of the East Asian world: centering on the investiture system' (谷川道雄：東アジア世界形成期の史的構造—冊封体制を中心として—), in Research Society on Tang History (ed), *The Sui and Tang Empire and the East Asian World* (唐代史研究会編：隋唐帝国と東アジア世界), Tokyo: Kyuko Shoin, pp 87–111.

Tao Jing-shen (2009) 'The move to the South and the reign of Kao-tsung (1127–1162)', in D. Twichett and P.J. Smith (eds), *The Cambridge History of China, Volume 5: Part One: The Sung Dynasty and Its Precursors, 907–1279*, Cambridge: Cambridge University Press, pp 644–709.

Terada, T. (2017) *Zheng He, Pioneer in World History of Maritime Voyage* (寺田隆信：世界航海史上の先駆者鄭和), Tokyo: Shimizu Shoin.

Tobin, D. (2020) 'How Xi Jinping's "new era" should have ended U.S. debate on Beijing's ambitions', *CSIS Research Report*, May.

Tomiya, I. (2016) *The Dilemma of the Chinese Empire: Ritual Thought and Legal Order* (富谷至：中華帝国のジレンマ：礼的思想と法的秩序), Tokyo: Chikuma Shobo.

Twichett, D. (1979) 'Hsuan-tsung (reign 712-56)', in D. Twichett (ed) *The Cambridge History of China, Volume 3: Sui and T'ang China, 589-906, Part 1*, Cambridge: Cambridge University Press, pp 333–463.

Ueda, M. (2005) *Sea and Empire: The Qing Dynasty Era* (上田信：海と帝国—明清時代—), Tokyo: Kodansha.

Van Ness, P. (1970) *Revolution and Chinese Foreign Policy: Peking's Support for Wars of National Liberation*, Berkeley: University of California Press.

Volgy, T.J., Corbetta, R., Grant, K.A., and Baird, R.G. (eds) (2011) *Major Powers and the Quest for Status in International Politics Global and Regional Perspectives*, New York: Palgrave Macmillan.

Von Glahn, R. (2016) *The Economic History of China: From Antiquity to the Nineteenth Century*, Cambridge: Cambridge University Press.

Wade, G. (2000) 'The Southern Chinese borders in history', in G. Evans, C. Hutton, and K.K. Eng (eds), *Where China Meets Southeast Asia: Social and Cultural Change in the Border Regions*, Singapore: Institute of Southeast Asian Studies, pp 28–50.

Wade, G. (2005) 'The Zheng He voyages: a reassessment', *Journal of the Malaysian Branch of the Royal Asiatic Society*, 78(1): 37–58.

Waldron, A. (1990) *The Great Wall of China: From Myth to History*, Cambridge: Cambridge University Press.

Waley-Cohen, J. (2006) *The Culture of War in China: Empire and the Military under the Qing Dynasty*, London: I.B. Tauris.

Wang Fei-ling (1999) 'Self-image and strategic intentions: national confidence and political insecurity', in Deng Yong and Wang Fei-ling (eds), *In the Eyes of the Dragon: China Views the World*, Lanham, MA: Rowman & Littlefield Publishers, Inc, pp 21–46.

Wang Fei-ling (2015) 'From Tianxia to Westphalia: the evolving Chinese conception of sovereignty and world order', in G.J. Ikenberry, Wang Jisi, and Zhu Feng (eds), *America, China, and the Struggle for World Order: Ideas, Traditions, Historical Legacies, and Global Visions*, New York: Palgrave Macmillan, pp 43–68.

Wang Fei-ling (2017) *The China Order: Centralia, World Empire, and the Nature of Chinese Power*, Albany: State University of New York Press.

Wang Gungwu (1958) 'The Nanhai trade: a study of the early history of Chinese trade in the South China Sea', *Journal of the Malayan Branch of the Royal Asiatic Society*, 31(2): 1–135.

Wang Gungwu (1983) 'The rhetoric of a lesser empire: early Sung relations with its neighbors', in M. Rossabi (ed), *China Among Equals: The Middle Kingdom and its Neighbors, 10th-14th Centuries*, Berkeley: University of California Press, pp 47–65.

Wang Gungwu (1984) 'The Chinese urge to civilize: reflections on change', *Journal of Asian History*, 18(1): 1–34.

Wang Gungwu (1998) 'Ming foreign relations: Southeast Asia', in D. Twitchett and F.W. Mote (eds), *The Cambridge History of China, Volume 8: The Ming Dynasty, 1368–1644, Part 2*, Cambridge: Cambridge University Press, pp 301–32.

Wang Hongying (2003) 'National image building and Chinese foreign policy', *China: An International Journal*, 1(1): 46–72.

Wang Hui (2004) *China from Empire to Nation State*, translated by M.G. Hill, Cambridge, MA: Harvard University Press.

Wang Hung-jen (2015) 'Contextualising China's call for discourse power in international politics', *China: An International Journal*, 13(3): 172–89.

Wang Shengcai (2006) 'A modern interpretation of the Confucian ideas of justice and benefits and their influence on China's foreign policy making' (王生才：儒家义利观的现代解读及其对中国外交决策的影响), *Journal of the Second Northwest University for Nationalities*, 2: 24–7.

Wang Yizhou (1999) 'Chinese diplomacy oriented toward the 21st century: pursuing and balancing three needs' (王逸舟：面向21世纪的中国外交—三种需求的寻求及其平衡), *Strategy and Management*, 99(6): 18–27.

Wang Yizhou (2007) *New Thinking on Chinese Diplomacy* (王逸舟：中国外交の新思考), translated by S. Amako and R. Aoyama, Tokyo: University of Tokyo Press.

Wang Yuan-kang (2011) *Harmony and War: Confucian Culture and Chinese Power Politics*, New York: Columbia University Press.

Wang Zheng (2012) *Never Forget National Humiliation: Historical Memory in Chinese Politics and Foreign Relations*, New York: Columbia University Press.

Wang Zheng (2013) 'The Chinese dream: concept and context', *Journal of Chinese Political Science*, 19: 1–13.

Wang Zhenping (2013) *Tang China in Multi-Polar Asia: A History of Diplomacy and War*, Honolulu: University of Hawaii Press.

Watanabe Shinichirō (1996) *The Heavenly Throne: Government by the Imperial Court and Rituals of the Chinese Ancient Empire* (渡辺信一郎：天空の玉座—中国古代帝国の朝政と儀礼—), Tokyo: Kashiwahobo.

Watanabe Shino (2017) 'The expansion of China's foreign aid and the limitations of international development assistance' (渡辺紫乃：中国の対外援助の拡大と国際開発援助の限界), *Oriental Culture*, 97: 11–30.

Watson, A. (1987) 'Hedley Bull, states systems and international societies', *Review of International Studies*, 13(2): 147–53.

Watson, A. (1992) *The Evolution of International Society: A Comparative Historical Analysis*, New York: Routledge.

Watson, A. (2007) *Hegemony & History*, New York: Routledge.

Weber, M. (1949) *The Methodology of the Social Sciences*, translated by E.A. Shils and H.A. Finch, New York: Free Press.

Weber, M. (1968) *Economy and Society: An Outline of Interpretive Sociology*, translated by E. Fischoff, H. Gerth, A.M. Henderson, F. Kolegar, C.W. Mills, T. Parsons, M. Rheinstein, G. Roth, E. Shils, and C. Wittish, Berkeley: University of California Press.

Wen Jian (2016) 'Seizing international discourse power, effectively spreading China's voice: analyzing Xi Jinping's thinking and ideas on foreign propaganda work' (文建：把握国际话语权 有效传播中国声音—习近平外宣工作思路理念探析), *Chinese Journalist*, 4: 35–7.

Westad, O.A., Chen, J., Tønnesson, S., Nguyen V.T., and Hershberg, J.G. (eds) (1998) '77 conversations between Chinese and foreign leaders on the wars in Indochina, 1964–1977', Woodrow Wilson International Center for Scholars Working Paper No 22, May.

Wight, M. (1978) *Power Politics*, Leicester: Leicester University Press.

Wight, M. (1991) *International Relations: The Three Traditions*, Leicester: Leicester University Press.

Wilentz, S. (ed) (1985) *Rites of Power: Symbolism, Ritual, and Politics since the Middle Ages*, Philadelphia: University of Pennsylvania Press.

Wills, J.E., Jr (1984) *Embassies and Illusions: Dutch and Portuguese Envoys to K'ang-his, 1666–1687*, Cambridge, MA: Council on East Asian Studies, Harvard University.

Wills, J.E., Jr (2009) 'How many asymmetries? Continuities, transformations, and puzzles in the study of Chinese foreign relations', *The Journal of American-East Asian Relations*, 16(1/2): 23–39.

Wills, J.E., Jr (2012) 'Functional, not fossilized: Qing tribute relations with Đại Việt (Vietnam) and Siam (Thailand), 1700–1820', *T'oung Pao*, 98(4–5): 439–78.

Wilson, J.L. (2021) 'Russia and China in Central Asia: deepening tensions in the relationship', *Acta Via Serica*, 6(1): 55–90.

Womack, B. (2006) *China and Vietnam: The Politics of Asymmetry*, Cambridge: Cambridge University Press.

Womack, B. (2009) 'Recognition, deference, and respect: generalizing the lessons of an asymmetric Asian order', *The Journal of American-East Asian Relations*, 16(1/2): 105–18.

Wood, J.R. and Serres, J. (1970) *Diplomatic Ceremonial and Protocol: Principles, Procedures and Practices*, London: Palgrave Macmillan.

Worden, A. (2020) 'China at the UN Human Rights Council: conjuring a "community of shared future for humankind"?', in N. Rolland (ed), *An Emerging China-Centric Order: China's Vision for a New World Order in Practice*, NBR Special Report No 87, August, pp 33–48.

Wright, D.C. (1996) 'Parity, pedigree, and peace: routine Sung diplomatic missives to the Liao', *Journal of Song-Yuan Studies*, 26: 55–85.

Wright, D.C. (2005) *From War to Diplomatic Parity in Eleventh Century China*, Leiden: Brill.

Wright, M.C. (1958) 'The adaptability of Ch'ing diplomacy: the case of Korea', *Journal of Asian Studies*, 17(3): 363–81.

Wu Qiang (2014) 'China's maritime surveillance conducts regular law-enforcement patrols in all waters' (吴琼：中国海监定巡执法全海域), *China Ocean News*, 22 July.

Xiao Huanrong (2003) 'China's responsibility as a great power and its strategy of regionalism' (肖欢容：中国的大国责任与地区主义战略), *World Economics and International Politics*, 1: 46–51.

Xiao Xi and Niu Yong (2010) 'The influence of the idea of "harmony" in traditional Chinese culture on China's diplomacy' (肖晞·牛勇：中国传统文化中的'和'对中国外交的影响), *Wuhan University Journal (Philosophy & Social Sciences)*, 2: 187–94.

Xu Jilin (2012) 'Social Darwinism in modern China', *Journal of Modern Chinese History*, 6(2): 182–97.

Yamagoshi, T. (2004) 'The propagation of Wilsonianism and the May Fourth Movement in China' (山腰敏寛：中国におけるウィルソン主義の宣伝と五四運動), *Modern and Contemporary China Studies*, 14/15: 79–87.

Yamaguchi, S. (2016) 'The continuity and changes in China's perception of the international order', *NIDS Journal of Defense and Security*, 17: 63–81.

Yamamuro, S. (2001) *Asia as a Subject of Thought: Standards, Connections, Projects* (山室信一：思想課題としてのアジア—基軸・連鎖・投企—), Tokyo: Iwanami Shoten.

Yan Xuetong (2001) 'The rise of China in Chinese eyes', *Journal of Contemporary China*, 10(26): 33–9.

Yan Xuetong (2006) 'The rise of China and its power status', *The Chinese Journal of International Politics*, 1(1): 5–33.

Yan Xuetong (2008) 'Xun Zi's thoughts on international politics and their implications', *Chinese Journal of International Politics*, 2(1): 135–65.

Yan Xuetong (2011a) *Ancient Chinese Thought, Modern Chinese Power*, Princeton: Princeton University Press.

Yan Xuetong (2011b) 'From a unipolar to a bipolar superpower system: the future of the global power dynamic', Global Times, 30 December.

Yan Xuetong (2014) 'From keeping a low profile to striving for achievement', *The Chinese Journal of Chinese Politics*, 7(2): 153–84.

Yan Xuetong (2015a) 'In Chinese diplomacy, the "periphery" is more important than the United States' (阎学通：中国外交,"周边"比美国更重要), International Online, 14 January.

Yan Xuetong (2015b) 'Why a bipolar world is more likely than a unipolar or multipolar one', *New Perspectives Quarterly*, 32(3): 52–6.

Yan Ziyou (1999) 'The Qing Dynasty's outer vassal feudal nobility system' (晏子有：清朝外藩封爵制度), *Social Science Front*, 9: 162–5.

Yang Bing (2009) *Between Winds and Clouds: The Making of Yunnan (Second Century BCE to Twentieth Century CE)*, New York: Columbia University Press.

Yang Bing (2010) 'The Zhang on Chinese southern frontiers: disease constructions, environmental changes, and imperial colonization', *Bulletin of the History of Medicine*, 84(2): 163–92.

Yang Lien-sheng (1968) 'Historical notes on the Chinese world order', J.K. Fairbank (ed), *The Chinese World Order*, Cambridge, MA: Harvard University Press, pp 20–33.

Ye Sang and Barmé, G.R. (2009) 'Thirteen national days, a retrospective', *China Heritage Quarterly* No 17, March.

Ye Zicheng (2007) 'The ideas of justice and benefits in traditional Chinese culture and China's diplomacy' (叶自成：中国传统文化中的义利观与中国外交), *International Politics Quarterly*, 3: 24–9.

Yoo, H.J. (2012) 'The Korea-US alliance as a source of creeping tension: a Korean perspective', *Asian Perspectives*, 36(2): 331–51.

Yoshida, K. (1984) *Russia's Eastward Advance and the Treaty of Nerchinsk* (吉田金一：ロシアの東方進出とネルチンスク条約), Tokyo: Modern China Study Center.

You Ji (2013) 'Deciphering Beijing's maritime security policy and strategy in managing sovereignty disputes in the China Seas', S. Rajaratnam School of International Studies Policy Brief, October.

Yu Shicun (2012) 'How do we read history today?' (余世存：今天怎样读历史?), *Divine Land*, 19: 23–8.

Yü Ying-shi (1967) *Trade and Expansion in Han China: A Study in the Structure of Sino-Barbarian Economic Relations*, Berkeley: University of California Press.

Yü Ying-shi (1986) 'Han foreign relations', in D. Twichett and J.K. Fairbank (eds), *The Cambridge History of China, Volume 1: The Ch'in and Han Empires, 221 B.C.–A.D. 220*, Cambridge: Cambridge University Press, pp 377–462.

Zarakol, A. (ed) (2017) *Hierarchies in World Politics*, Cambridge: Cambridge University Press.

Zarrow, P. (2001) 'Political ritual in the early Republic of China', in K. Chow, K.M. Doak, and P. Fu (eds), *Constructing Nationhood in Modern East Asia*, Ann Arbor: The University of Michigan Press, pp 149–88.

Zeng Jinghan (2017) 'Does Europe matter? The role of Europe in Chinese narratives of "One Belt One Road" and "new type of great power relations"', *Journal of Common Market Studies*, 55(5): 1162–76.

Zeng Jinghan and Breslin, S. (2016) 'China's "new type of great power relations": a G2 with Chinese characteristics?', *International Affairs*, 92(4): 773–94.

Zhang Feng (2014) 'International societies in pre-modern East Asia: a preliminary framework', in B. Buzan and Zhang Yongjin (eds), *Contesting International Society in East Asia*, Cambridge: Cambridge University Press, pp 29–50.

Zhang Guozuo (2009) 'A few thoughts regarding discourse power' (张国祚：关于"话语权"的几点思考), *Qiushi*, 9: 43–6.

Zhang Jinfan (2014) *The Tradition and Modern Transition of Chinese Law*, Berlin: Springer.

Zhang Rongming (2015) 'Way of the Hegemon, Way of the King and the new Way of the King: reflecting on China's development strategy' (张荣明：霸道、王道与新王道—中国发展战略思考), *Journal of Tianjin Normal University (Social Sciences)*, 238: 6–10.

Zhang Shu Guang (1999) 'China's traditional and revolutionary heritage', in K. Booth and R. Trood (eds), *Strategic Culture in the Asia-Pacific Region*, Basingstoke: Macmillan, pp 29–50.

Zhang Shu Guang (2007) 'Constructing "peaceful coexistence": China's diplomacy toward the Geneva and Bandung Conferences, 1954–55', *Cold War History*, 7(4): 509–28.

Zhang Tiejun (2002) 'Chinese strategic culture: traditional and present features', *Comparative Strategy*, 21(2): 73–90.

Zhang Xiaoming (2011) 'A rising China and the normative changes in international society', *East Asia*, 28(3): 235–46.

Zhang Xiaoming (2015) *Deng Xiaoping's Long War: The Military Conflict between China and Vietnam, 1979–1991*, Chapel Hill: The University of North Carolina Press.

Zhang Ying (2018) 'China's diplomacy toward Africa: concepts and practice' (张颖：中国对非洲外交一理念与实践), *International Studies*, 1: 27–40.

Zhang Yongjiang (2017) 'The Libu and Qing perception, classification and administration of non-Han people', in D. Schorkowitz and Chia Ning (eds), *Managing Frontiers in Qing China: The Lifanyuan and Libu Revisited*, Leiden: Brill, pp 116–43.

Zhang Yongjin (1991a) *China in the International System, 1918–20: The Middle Kingdom at the Periphery*, London: Palgrave Macmillan.

Zhang Yongjin (1991b) 'China's entry into international society: beyond the standard of "civilisation"', *Review of International Studies*, 17(1): 3–16.

Zhang Yongjin (1998) *China in International Society since 1949: Alienation and Beyond*, New York: Palgrave.

Zhang Yongjin (2014) 'The idea of order in ancient Chinese political thought: a Wightian exploration', *International Affairs*, 90(1): 167–83.

Zhang Yongjin (2015) 'China and the struggle for legitimacy of a rising power', *The Chinese Journal of International Politics*, 8(3): 301–22.

Zhang Yongjin (2016) 'China and liberal hierarchies in global international society: power and negotiation for normative change', *International Affairs*, 92(4): 795–816.

Zhang Yongjin and Buzan, B. (2020) 'China and the global reach of human rights', *The China Quarterly*, 241: 169–90.

Zhang Yunling and Tang Shiping (2005) 'China's regional strategy', in D. Shambaugh (ed), *Power Shift: Chain and Asia's New Dynamics*, Berkeley: University of California Press, pp 48–78.

Zhao Dingxin (2015) *The Confucian–Legalist State: A New Theory of Chinese History*, Oxford: Oxford University Press.

Zhao Kejin (2016) 'China's rise and its discursive power strategy', *Chinese Political Science Review*, 1(3): 539–64.

Zhao Suisheng (2015a) 'A new model of big power relations? China–US strategic rivalry and balance of power in the Asia-Pacific', *Journal of Contemporary China*, 24(93): 377–97.

Zhao Suisheng (2015b) 'Rethinking the Chinese world order: the imperial cycle and the rise of China', *Journal of Contemporary China*, 24(96): 961–82.

Zhao Suisheng (2018) 'For what purpose does China reshapes world order?' (赵穗生：中国凭什么重塑世界秩序?), US–China Perception Monitor, 25 August.

Zhao Tinyang (2006) 'Rethinking empire from a Chinese concept "All-under-Heaven" (Tian-xia,天下)', *Social Identities*, 12(1): 29–41.

Zheng Yongnian (1999) *Discovering Chinese Nationalism in China: Modernization, Identity, and International Relations*, Cambridge: Cambridge University Press.

Zhou Fangyin (2017) 'Chinese scholars' understanding of and debates about the international structure' (周方银：中国学者对国际格局的认识及争鸣), *Quarterly Journal of International Politics*, 2(2): 1–32.

Zhu Liqun (2010) 'China's foreign policy debates', Chaillot Papers No 121, September.

Index

References to footnotes show both the page number and the note number (154n17).

A

adaptability, Chinese foreign policy 63–4, 121, 167
Afghanistan 151, 152, 153, 154n17
agriculturalists 23
Amako Satoshi 5, 176, 177
Ames, Roger 49
Amity and Cooperation, Treaty of (1967) 110, 131
The Analects (Confucius) 49, 52, 55
anti-imperialism 90, 105, 168
ASEAN (Association of Southeast Asian Nations) 110, 152
  China's 10+1 formula 135
ASEAN-centred forums 131
ASEAN Regional Forum (ARF) 131
ASEAN+3 mechanism 110, 132
Asia 4–5
  as an asymmetrical system *see* asymmetry
  China as rightful leader of 80, 89, 92–3, 98, 104, 115–18, 129–30
  as an international system 20–41
  Western emissaries 83
Asia-Pacific Economic Cooperation (APEC) summit 135
Asian financial crisis (1997) 110, 131
Asian Infrastructure Investment Bank (AIIB) 2, 114, 133
asymmetry 21–33
  archetypal asymmetry 26
  in international relations 21
  reverse asymmetry 24
  theory 21
Australia 178
awesomeness (*wei*) 51
  as a defensive response 161
  demonstrating 157–9
  deterrence 161
  establishing 53–6
  military parades 158–9
  military power 75–7
  in the near seas 159–62

punishments 162
regular rights protection patrols 160

B

Bandung conference (1955) 123
Bangladesh 151, 152, 153, 154, 154n17, 173
barbarians (*yidi*) 11, 72, 78, 83, 84, 91, 167, 175
  Chinese superiority over 60–1, 62
  force against 76
  reliance on 74
  titles awarded to 73
BARF (Belt and Road Forum) 133, 135, 136, 137, 138, 164
Belt and Road Initiative (BRI) *see* BRI (Belt and Road Initiative)
benevolence (*ren*) 141, 165, 169, 170, 175, 130
  in Chinese political thought 47–8, 49, 62–3
  pledges of 170
  of the Son of Heaven 78
Boao Forum (2013) 164
Book of Change 54
Book of Odes (*Shijing*) 76
Book of Rites 56–7
Brazil 147
BRICS 114, 115, 136
BRI (Belt and Road Initiative) 2, 133, 164
  21st Maritime Silk Road 155
  aim of 133
  ambition of 133
  benefits of host diplomacy 137
  control by Chinese bureaucrats 137
  Memorandums of Understanding (MoUs) 138
  recognition of enlightened leadership 138–9
  related events hosted in China 135
  shaping of partnerships 137
  Silk Road Economic Belt 155

symbolic value of 133, 134
Xi's pledge 133
BRICS 114, 115, 136
Brunei 152
Buddhism 15–16, 28, 35
Bull, Hedley 11
Burma 26, 87
  see also Myanmar (Burma)
Buzan, Barry 33–4

C
Callahan, William 141
Cambodia 30, 152, 173
Canrong, Jin 116–17
Carr, E.H. 54
CCP (Chinese Communist Party) 1, 89
  alternative centre of communist movement 105
  international discourse strategy 146
  new situation (*xin xingshi*) 1–2, 112, 158
  objective 6
  propaganda apparatus 145
  readings of history 6
  regional custodial role 117
  revised history of WWII 107
  road to rejuvenation 102
  Soviet Union and
    challenge to central position of 122
    criticism of leadership 122
    support for worldwide revolutionary movements 145–6
    vanguard of national liberation 122
Central Asia 27–8, 32
century of humiliation 40, 116, 120, 140
  see also national humiliation
Chanyu 67
chaos (*luan*) 44
Chen Jian 123–4
Cheng, Joseph 148
Chiang Kai-shek 92–3
Chiang Mai initiative 110
Chih-Yu Shih 120
China 135
  adaptability to changing circumstances 121
  Asia
    central position, establishing 132–9
    centre central position, perception 89
    charm offensive with 110
    BRICS 114, 115, 136
  colonial domination 87
  communication with other states see interaction capacity
  conflicts 141
  deference to see deference
  delimitation of territory 39–40
  as a discursive state 145
  economic and diplomatic initiatives 2
  economic growth 1, 108, 112
  external propaganda 147

foreign policy see foreign policy (China)
foreign relations see foreign relations (China)
as friendly neighbour 129–30
great powers
  equality with 88, 115
  favourable comparison with 80–1
  language of great power management 8–9
  self-perception as 8
great rejuvenation of 116–17, 140, 169
increasing assertiveness of 2–3
international order see international order: China
international society see international society: China
international stage, first steps 121–4
  exchanges with North Korea and Vietnam 123–4
  expectations of deference 124
international status see international status (China)
international structure 108–9
intolerance of challenge or criticism 142–3
linking imperial past and present 5–7
nationalism 89
'new era' 2
and its 'periphery' 4–5, 101, 178
policy towards Korea
  equal treaty (1899) 87
  evolving 87
  property and taxation rights 87–8
power of 21
punitive expeditions 55, 158
relations with smaller states 9–10, 21–2
United Nations
  admission to (1971) 106
  supportive attitude towards 114–15
visions
  of an Asian society 12
  of order 3–4, 5
  of a Sinocentric order 134–6
wars
  defeat against Japan (1894–5) 87
  with India (1962) 157
  with Vietnam (1979) 157–8
world order
  maintaining 61–2
  perception of 60
China-ASEAN free trade agreement 110
China's Destiny (Chiang Kai-shek) 92
Chinese communism 16
Chinese Communist Party (CCP) see CCP (Chinese Communist Party)
Chinese culture 14–15
Chinese National Tourist Administration 163
Chinese traditional culture 6, 42, 127, 128
Clark, Ian 38
coercion 53–6

INDEX

Cold War 110, 122, 131
Commentary of Zuo to the Spring and Autumn Annals (*Chunqiu Zuo zhuan*) 53, 75
community with a shared future for mankind 125–6, 140, 169, 178
comprehensive national power 1, 18, 109, 168
Conference on Interaction and Confidence-Building Measures in Asia (CICA) 133, 135, 136
Confucian-Legalist synthesis 17, 43, 44, 51
Confucianism 10, 15n16, 16, 35, 174–5
  harmonious society 43, 55
  rejection of 80, 92
  use of force 175
Confucians
  approval of benefits 56
  awesomeness 53
  education 53
  poor view of self-interest 56
  punishments 55–6
  rulers and ruling 51
Confucius 47, 49, 52, 128, 145
  The Analects 49, 52, 55
  correct punishments 55
  rectification of names 52
Congress of Vienna (1815) 96
conquest dynasties 15
core interests 139–40, 142, 160, 164, 169, 171
correct behaviour 18, 139, 141
correct view of righteousness and interests 127–8
Court for the Administration of the Outer Regions 68
Covenant of Chanyuan 67, 70
covenants (*meng*) 67–8, 70
Cultural Revolution 103n3, 104, 106, 122

D

Dalai Lama 163, 166
Dali kingdom 25
Danjō Hiroshi 61, 62, 66
de see virtue
deference
  in exchange for economic favours 165, 166
  of North Korea, lack of 123
  of smaller neighbours 26, 36, 60, 117, 140, 141–2, 169
  of Vietnam 25, 124
Delury, John 80–1
democracy 114, 114n24
Deng Xiaoping 2, 102, 106, 107–8, 140–1, 158
  economic development 107
  'seeking truth from fact' 108
  speech at UN General Assembly (1974) 106, 124
Deng Yong 109, 177

diplomacy 12
  ASEAN Regional Forum (ARF) 131
  Asian financial crisis (1997) 131
  bilateral treaties 80
  bilateral visits 131–2
  Chinese character and style 8
  diplomatic protocol 38, 87, 95
  equality and 86, 96
  of form 176–7
  hierarchy and 96
  host diplomacy 134–5, 136–7
  initiatives 2
  interactions with other states 36, 37, 38, 39, 73
  of interests 177
  League of Nations strategy 98–9
  limitations on 36
  moralism and 118
  multilateralism 131, 132, 134–5
  regional 110–11, 130–2
  ritual rules 95–6
  Six Party Talks (2003) 132
  Western customs and norms 36, 93, 95–6, 97–8
  see also partnerships
diplomatic envoys 95–6
  Chinese 96, 97, 98
    Hague peace conferences (1899, 1907) 96–8
    treated as lower ranks 96, 98
    visiting Europe 96
  equal footing 71
  ethics and respect 96
  reception of 68, 69, 70
  Western 96
discourse power 146–7
Dong Zhongshu 77
Double Ten (10 October) anniversary 95
Dubs, Homer 48
duties
  of China 114
  of great powers 7
  hosting duties 137
  of international society 37
  moral 42, 47
  of sovereign leaders 45, 53
Dzungars 63

E

East Asia 8, 29–31, 132
  alliances and relations with the US 29–30
  asymmetrical system 29–31
  economic realm
    decline of the US 31
    rise of China 31
  exposure to Chinese military power 30–1
East Asia Summit (EAS) 132
East Asian world 34–5

215

East China Sea 26, 159, 160, 174
East Timor 152
economic benefits *see* profits (benefits)
economic sanctions *see* sanctions
English School 3–4, 11
equality 38, 39, 88, 115
  Chinese definition of 38, 85, 86
  diplomacy and 86, 96
  disorder and 45
  international law and 85
  kingly way and 91
  of nation states 38, 39, 84
  power and 85
  see also sovereign equality
era of negotiation 80, 86, 93
evolution 82, 83
Exclusive Economic Zone 159, 173
expos 137

F
Fairbank, John 5, 62
Fei Xiaotong 47
Five Principles of Peaceful Coexistence
    103–4, 121–2, 123, 125, 168
foreign aid 164, 165, 172
foreign policy (China) 2
  adaptability 63–4, 121, 167
  anti-imperialism 90, 105, 168
  diplomacy 122–3
  form and interests 176–7
  hierarchical understanding of the
      world 10, 12
  moral leadership 121–2
  posture 2
  realism and idealism 174–6
  reinforcing domestic stability 22
foreign relations (China) 10, 13–14
  Central Asia and 27–8, 32
  cultural exchanges 26–7
  entente with the US 29
  under foreign cultural influence 28
  historical patterns of 14
  with India 32
  with Inner Asia 22–4
  with Korea and the South 24–6, 76, 87
  maritime world 26–7, 32, 173–4
  modern transition 28–9
  'new China' 28
  partnerships 150
  preoccupation
    with territorial security 29
    with the US 29
  with Russia 32, 113n21, 151, 152, 156
  with South Asia 27–8, 32–3
  trade 26
form, diplomacy of 176–7
formal alliances 170
forum diplomacy 135

G
G20 1, 115
G77 108
Galvany, Albert 57–8
Gaozong 63
Gaozu 63
Gilpin, Robert 54
Global Development Initiative (GDI) 133–4
Global Security Initiative (GSI) 133–4
Goh, Evelyn 3
Gong, Gerrit 83
good neighbourhood 129
governance (*zhi*) 44
  see also rulership
great powers 88
  China and 8–9, 80–1, 88, 115
  division with small states 89
  hegemonic behaviour of 85
  on Korean territory 88
  management of international affairs 7
  responsible great power 8, 111, 114, 119
  superior might of 86
  see also Western great powers
Guanzi 48–9, 54

H
Hague peace conferences (1899, 1907) 96–8
Hamashita Takeshi 80
Han dynasty 15, 23, 23–4, 61
  indoctrination campaign 75
  seals 69
  titles 73–4
Han Fei 46, 50–1, 52, 55
  see also rulership
Han Feizi 51
Han Wudi 24
harmonious world 111, 125
  Confucian society 43, 55
harmony (*he*) 44, 127
hegemon
  definition 9
  way of 9–10
hegemony 7–8
  of the great powers 85
  of international society 37–8
  negative connotation of 9
  of the US 8, 9
  see also way of the hegemon
heqin policy 67, 75, 77
Hevia, James 71
hierarchical order
  Chineseness of 171–2
  contemporary vision 167–9
  ideal type 42–57
    moral superiority 46–8, 90–3
    order 43–4
    ritual 48–50
    social inequality 44–6
    Weberian 12–17

INDEX

hierarchy 7–11
  China's imperial past 10
  Chinese conception of 10–11
  definition 7
  diplomacy and 12
  of international order 12
  moral qualities of leaders 16–17
  order and 13, 60–2, 81–9
  of power in modern international society 7–8
Hong Kong 159
Hongwu 76–7
host diplomacy 134–5, 136–7
  grand venues 137
Hu Jintao 2–3, 109, 111, 117, 127, 158, 164
  harmonious world 111, 125
  win-win cooperation 125
human relationships (*renlun*) 45
human rights 114, 114n24
humaneness *see* benevolence (*ren*)
Hundred Days' Reform movement 87

I

ideal type 13–15
  as an abstraction 13
  construction of 14
  definition 13
  formation of 13
  as a heuristic tool 13
  of hierarchical order 16, 42–57
    moral superiority 46–8, 90–3
    order 43–4
    ritual 48–50
    social inequality 44–6
  moral duties 42
idealism, realism and 174–6
Imperial Confucianism 15
Imperial Hunt 68
imperialism 80, 90, 106, 107, 120, 172
  alternative to 91–2
  Chiang Kai-shek's fight against 92
  nationalism in response to 89
  Sun's condemnation of 91
improper behaviour 139–43
incentives 56–7
India 123, 152, 154, 173
  BRICS 114, 115, 136
  China and
    partnership 151
    relations with 32
    war with (1962) 157
Indonesia 30, 152, 155
Inner Asia 22–4
Inner Asian sea 27
interaction capacity 33–7
  of Asia 34–5, 36
  communication 33–4, 35, 36, 37
  definition 33–4
  diplomatic interactions 36–7

geography and 34
Great Firewall 37
limitations 36
southern ecological barrier 35–6
interests, diplomacy of 177
international justice
  Chinese advocacy for 107, 115, 120, 125–6, 127
  definition 120
international law 38, 40, 84–5
  central role of 85
  duality of 85
international legitimacy 86
international order
  China's vision of 3–4, 10, 11, 69
    ambition of 111–12
    commitment to 107
    confidence in advancing 111
    equality with the US 115
    as guardian and defender 102
    hierarchical 12
    protector 114
    specificity of 4, 80–1, 171–2
    superiority of 93, 115
    support of neighbours 117
  definition 3
  reform of 3
  Western-led 90
  see also international society
international personality 39
international relations 7, 12, 21, 38, 40–7, 85, 89, 102
  better model of 120, 121, 122, 124
  new type of 125, 139, 141, 150, 169, 178
  social and systemic aspects 11
  theory 3–4
international society 2–3
  China and
    acceptance of redefined role in 87–8
    acceptance of Western diplomatic norms 93–4
    aspirations of leadership 106
    centre stage 2–3
    Chinese intellectuals' assessment of 83, 84
    creation of subgroup 106
    diminished status in 80–1
    entrance into 38, 40, 80–100
    equal relationship with the US 113–14
    guarantor of peace 90, 91, 92
    Hague peace conferences (1899, 1907) 97–8
    international moral leadership 92
    kingly way *see* way of the king 91
    League Council 98–9
    oceanic affairs 93–4
    pessimistic assessment of 86
    power dynamics 113
    principle of legal equality 88
    as a proletariat nation 90–1, 92

217

rejection of imperial powers'
  intentions 86
rightful place 112–18, 120
superiority over neighbours 88, 89, 93
traditional ritual order, idealized
  vision 91–2
unequal treaties 84, 88, 96, 98
utopian vision for 90–1
virtuous kingship 93
world status 99
competition and power struggle 86
definition 3n4
era of negotiation 80, 86, 93
hegemonic beliefs 37–8
legitimate members of 38
liberal values 90
modern 7, 38, 40
nation states 38
norms of 38, 86
post-Cold War East Asia 8
power competition 103, 104
rights and obligations of sovereign states 86
sovereign equality 39, 83, 84–5, 86, 93, 173
undisputed dominance of the US 168
see also international order
international status (China) 81, 85, 102
  assessment of 111
  importance of 109–10
  in international society 99
  obsession with 10, 100, 109
  raising of 110
  recovering 98
  report on 110
  solidifying 97–8
international structures 2, 3, 4, 108–9, 113, 168
investiture 65–6
Ishikawa Hideaki 48–9
Iwai Shigeki 70

J
Japan 26, 31, 87, 110, 159, 163
  alliance with the US 29–30, 31
  great power, lack of recognition 88
  special status 98
  war with China (1894–5) 87
Jia Qingguo 9
Jia Yi 77
Jiang Zemin 108, 109, 125, 127, 131, 158
Jin dynasty 66n7, 67–8

K
Kang, David 5
Kang Youwei 82–3
Kausikan, Bilahari 141
Kawashima Shin 88, 96
Kazakhstan 152, 153
keep a low profile 2, 108
Kerry, John 116

Kertzer, David 94
Khrushchev, Nikita 105
Khubilai Khan 63
Kim Jaymin 72
Kim, Samuel 104
kinship (*heqin*) 66–7, 75, 77
Korea 25–6, 76, 87
  equal treaty with China (1899) 87
  independence 87
  Japanese annexation of 87
  non-reciprocal rights of the great powers 88
  see also North Korea; South Korea
Kuhn, Felix 38
Kyrgyzstan 152, 154

L
Laidlaw, J. 64–5
language 52–3, 73–5
Laos 30, 152, 173
Lattimore, Owen 22–3
Leach, Edmund 94
League Council 98–9
League of Nations 98
Legalism 15n16, 16, 175
  strong and authoritarian state 43
  see also Confucian-Legalist synthesis
Legalists
  awesomeness 53, 54
  education 53
  punishments 54–5, 55–6
  rulers and ruling 46, 51
legitimacy 37–40, 46–8
  principles of 38–40
Leifer, Michael 103
Lenin, Vladimir Ilyich 90
Levine, Steven 105
Lewis, Mark 43
li 48–50, 51
  criticisms of 50
  see also ritual (*li*)
Li Dazhao 90, 92, 93
Li Peng 129
Liang Qichao 84, 85
Liao dynasty 66n7, 67–8, 71
Lifanyuan 68, 82
Link, Perry 145
Lithuania 178
Little, Richard 33–4
Liu Shaoqi 122
Liu Xiaobo 178
Liu Zhenmin 118
long imperial era 59–79
Lotte 162, 163

M
Macartney, George 71
majesty *see* awesomeness (*wei*)
Malaysia 30, 152, 173
Maldives 152
Mancall, Mark 5

Manchuria 24
Mao Zedong 93, 102, 103–7, 119, 123
  ambitions of 104–5
  as a benevolent suzerain 123
  condescending view of Asian countries 105
  Cultural Revolution 106
  international order 103
    Chinese leadership 106–7
    power and exploitation 106
  leaders of Asia 103, 104–5
  Moscow speech (1957) 157
  rectification of names 145
  revolutionary zeal 103, 106
  support for national liberation movements 120
  'three worlds theory' 106
  underdog perspective 104
  understanding with Stalin 105
Maoist era 112
  dissatisfaction with Soviet leadership 106
  Five Principles of Peaceful Coexistence 103–4, 168
  hierarchical order, limited scope for 168
  idealism and realism 176
  leaders of opposition to superpowers 106, 168
  revolutionary diplomacy 103
  revolutionary fervour 103, 168
  rivalry with the US 103–4
  Soviet Union and 105–6, 168
  utopian vision of socialism 119
maritime 26–7, 32, 159–62, 173–4
market capitalism 37
Marxism-Leninism 80, 119
  Chinese interpretation 90, 124, 145
May Fourth Movement 90, 92n8
Mekong region 134, 151, 154, 156
Mencius 44, 45
miasma (*zhang*) 35
Middle Kingdom 4, 5, 15, 27
military force/power 21, 30–1, 75–7
  maritime 159–62
  parades 158–9
  see also awesomeness (*wei*)
Ming dynasty 24, 26, 27
  military expeditions 74, 76–7
  reception of envoys 69
  tributary trade system 66n6, 78
  Yongle emperor 24, 64, 77
Mischief Reef 30, 159
Mongolia 86, 152, 163, 164, 166
Mongols 24, 26
moral hierarchy 120, 121
moral leadership 62–3, 120, 121–2
moral precepts 170
moral superiority 46–8, 62–4, 90–3
  community with a shared future for mankind 125–6, 140, 169, 178

Five Principles of Peaceful Coexistence 103–4, 121–2, 123
  new security concept 125
  peripheral diplomacy 129–30
  status 122–3
  superior-to-inferior relationship 123–4
  traditional virtues 126–8
moral virtues 118
moralism, international justice 120
Morgenthau, Hans 122–3
Mote, Frederick 22–3, 71
Motegi Toshio 91
Mount, Ferdinand 94
Mozi 54
multilateral diplomacy 131, 132, 134–5
Myanmar (Burma) 30, 123, 152, 153, 173

N
names
  correct names 145
  proper names 145
  rectification of 44, 52–3, 73–5, 145
Nanzhao kingdom 25
Nathan, Andrew 112
nation states 38
  equality, right to 38, 39, 84
national humiliation 88, 89, 99, 100
national liberation movements 92, 104, 120, 122
national self-determination 90
nationalism 80, 89
near seas 159–62
Nepal 138, 152, 154, 156
Ness, Peter Van 103
new China 5, 28, 80, 157
New Development Bank 114
new security concept 125
new situation 1–2, 112, 158
new type of international relations 125, 139, 141, 150, 169, 178
Nishijima Sadao 18
nomads 15, 23, 24, 39
North Korea 30, 38, 156, 173
  nuclear programme 132
  relations with China 123
Northern and Southern dynasties 66, 71
Norway 178

O
obedience, incentivizing 56–7
Okamoto Takashi 87
Opium Wars 28, 84, 93
order
  Chinese intellectual crisis 82
  hierarchy and 13, 60–2, 81–9
  as highest value 43–4
  Kang Youwei's 'three ages' discourse 82–3
  Li Dazhao's vision 90
  traditional understanding of 81–2

Western ideas 82
see also international order
Oriental civilization 91
Outer Mongolia 94

P
pacts *see* covenants
Pakistan 149, 151, 152, 156
Pan Guangdan 45
Pan Yihong 76
Paracel islands 159
partnership diplomacy 147
partnerships 147–57, 168–9
  with African countries 151
  agreements 148
  ambiguities in 152, 153–4, 155
  appeal of 148
  in Asia 152
  contingent nature of 154
  criteria of attribution 149, 151, 155
  foreign relations 150
  friendships and intimacy 155–6
  hierarchy of 148–9, 156
  joint declarations 150
  as a network of 148, 149–50, 154
  origins of 147–8
  perfecting stage 150
  qualifiers of 149, 154
  ranking of 151, 152, 155, 156
  Sinocentric pattern of diplomacy 150–1
  strategic importance 155
  strategic objectives 148
  structure of 151–2
  types of 151, 152–3
  upgrade of 150, 151, 153, 154, 156
patriarchal clan order 66, 70, 172
peace (*ping*) 44
People's Liberation Army (PLA) 157–9, 158
People's Liberation Army Daily 160
People's Republic of China (PRC) *see* China
peripheral diplomacy 5, 116, 117, 129–30
Peripheral Diplomacy Work Conference (2013) 164, 166
peripheral geostrategic support 111
Philippines 30, 152, 159, 161–2, 163
Pilgrimage to the Emperor 68
Pines, Yuri 73
policy of prestige 123
power 84
  asymmetry of *see* asymmetry
  definition 21
  elements of 21
  equality and 85
  of modern states 21
  see also awesomeness; military force/power
PRC (People's Republic of China) *see* China
prestige 54
  see also awesomeness

profits (benefits)
  bestowing and withdrawing 162–6
  deference 165, 166
  as diplomatic tools 164–6
  economic costs imposed 163
  foreign aid 164, 165
  sanctions 162–3, 163–4
  support from Asian states 164–5
  trade restrictions 163
  taming of barbarians with 77–8
  in traditional Chinese political thought 56–7
progress 82, 83
propaganda 6, 18, 145, 147
proper behaviour 50
public diplomacy 146
punishment (*xing*) 54–5, 55–6, 162
  favour and 56
  purpose of 76
Pye, Lucian 5, 47

Q
Qian Qichen 125
Qin dynasty 15, 23–4
Qin Yaqing 165
Qing dynasty 24, 26
  barbarians and 62
  Chinese sovereignty in Inner Asia territories 86–7
  Court for the Administration of the Outer Regions 68
  defeat against Japan (1895) 84
  era of negotiation 86
  historical records 61
  Imperial Hunt 68
  national humiliation 88, 89
  Pilgrimage to the Emperor 68
  policy towards Korea 87
  private trade 78
  ranking system 74
  respecting traditional order 82
  rituals 68
  Russian empire 28
  tributaries 88
  war with France 86
  Yan Fu 84
Qing Qianlong 63, 72
punitive expedition 77
quad 115

R
ranks and titles system 18–19, 50, 67, 69, 70, 73–4
reactive assertiveness 162
realism, idealism and 174–6
rectification (*zheng*) 44, 52, 73–5, 145
rectifying words 52–3
regional diplomacy 130–2
Regulation on the Precedence of Diplomatic Agents 96
ren see benevolence (*ren*)

responsible great power 8, 111, 114, 119
revolutionary diplomacy 103
rewards 77–8
rich neighbourhood 129
righteousness (*yi*) 47–8, 48–9, 63, 127–8
ritual (*li*) 51, 57, 64–72, 93–9, 173
  as a common language 65
  compromise by Chinese statesman 71–2
  concrete practical performance 71
  covenants 67–8, 70
  diplomacy and 95–6
  flexibility of 72
  maintaining social hierarchy 48–50
  mode of interaction 64–5
  national days 95
  pacts 66, 67, 70
  patriarchal clan order 66, 70
  peace through kinship 66–7
  precedents 71
  reception of envoys and court ceremonies 68–9
  relationships with seafaring merchants 71–2
  repurposing of 94
  stable framework 70–1
  state ceremonies 65–6, 69, 70
  status and 64, 67–8, 69, 70, 71
  traditional concepts 94
  tribute and investiture 65–6, 70, 72
  twin purposes of 70–2
  in the West 94–5
  Western *li* 96
ritual order (rule through ritual)
  awesomeness 75–7, 79
  ending of 80, 93, 94
  foreigners' inclusion in 73
  idealized vision of 91–2
  lure through profits 77–8
  maintaining order 65–9
  mutual trade (*hushi*) 72, 72n17
  standard of behaviour 97
Rolland, Nadège 4
Rozman, Gilbert 115
Ruan Zongze 164
rulership 50–1
  coercion 53–6
  incentives 56–7
  punishments 54–5
  rectification 52–3
  titles and ranks system 73–4
  tools of 72–8
    awesomeness 75–7, 157–9, 159–62
    language 73–5, 145
    profits 56–7, 77–8, 162–6
Rumi, Aoyama 5
Russia 28, 61, 110, 113, 137, 152
  BRICS 114, 115, 136
  relations with China 32, 113n21, 151, 152, 156
  SCO 110, 132, 154

see also Soviet Union
Ryukyu Islands 27, 35, 88
Ryukyu Kingdom 74, 86

S
safe neighbourhood 129
sanctions 142–3, 162–3, 163–4
Sawyer, R.D. 75
Scarborough shoal 161–2, 163
Schell, Orville 80–1
Schwartz, Benjamin 55, 60
Scobell, Andrew 112
seafaring transportation 34
seeking common ground while reserving differences 140, 141
Shandong peninsula 86
Shang Yang 44, 50, 51, 54
  on punishment 55
Shanghai Cooperation Organization (SCO) 110, 132, 154
Shen Zhihua 123
Shi Yinhong 164
Shun 45
Siam *see* Thailand
Singapore 30, 152, 155
Sino-Indian War (1962) 32, 157
Six Party Talks 110, 132
Smith, R.J. 43, 60
social Darwinism 84, 89
social hierarchy 48–50
social inequality 44–6
social order 42–3, 44–5
social rules 42–3
society 172–4
  see also international society
society of states *see* international society
soft power 146, 146n2
Son of Heaven 10, 27, 46
  interaction with foreign rulers 65–6
  top of the hierarchy 62, 64, 67, 69, 70
  virtuous leadership 78–9
Song dynasty 15, 25, 27, 61, 64, 66, 71
  Covenant of Chanyuan 67, 70
  covenants 67–8
  reception of envoys 69
  ritual relationship with seafaring merchants 71–2
Song Guoyou 164
Sorace, Christian 145
South Africa, BRICS 114, 115, 136
South Asia 27–8, 32–3
South China 26, 35
South China Sea 26, 30, 88, 141–2, 159, 160, 162, 173
  artificial islands 160
  China's sovereignty claims and rights 142
  declaration 110
  military force 175
South-East Asia 29, 30, 88, 103, 134, 151, 152, 155, 162

South Korea 30, 31, 110, 131, 132, 149, 151, 152, 153
  alliance with the US 30
  American-built missile defence system 142–3, 162–3
  China and
    assurances to 143
    sanctions 162–3
South Vietnam 159
sovereign equality 39, 83, 84–5, 86, 93, 173
Soviet Union 28, 29, 32, 104, 124, 146
  fall of 108, 168
  leader of communist movement 105–6
    China's contestation of position 122, 123, 145, 168
  see also Russia
Spratly Islands 160
Spring and Autumn period 44, 83
Sri Lanka 151, 152, 153, 154, 154n17
stability (*ding*) 44
stability in unity 45–6
Stalin, Joseph 105
standard of behaviour 97, 170–1, 174, 177
standard of civilization 83, 84, 86, 98, 170–1
state capitalism 37
state ceremonies 65–6, 69, 70
statecraft 59–79, 174
  moral superiority 62–4
  order and hierarchy 60–2
  ritual 64–72
  tools of rulership 72–8
state(s)
  power of 21
  see also nation states
status
  allocation of 73
  ritual 64, 67–8, 69, 70, 71
  titles 73
  see also international status (China)
status foundations 38–9
status treatment 38, 39
steppes 23–4
stratification 7
Su Hao 149
subjective adequacy 10
Sui dynasty 26
Sun Shuxian 161–2
Sun Yat-sen 91, 92, 92–3, 127, 169
supremacy, legitimation of 46–8
system
  definition 11
  society and 172–4
  system-society distinction 11
  systemic analysis 12
  systemic pressures 11

T

Taiwan 38, 140, 141, 150, 158, 159, 160, 161n29, 178

Taizong 24, 63
Tajikistan 152, 154
Takagi Seiichirō 146
Tang dynasty 24, 25, 35, 76
  covenants 67
  Indian subcontinent 27
  ranks system 74
  reception of envoys 69
  ritual relationship with seafaring merchants 71–2
Tang emperors 63–4
Tang Jiaxuan 129
Tang Taizong 24
Thailand 30, 152, 173
  balancing relations with the US and China 30–1
  Joint Vision Statement (2012) 30
Third World 106, 108
  China as leader
    postponement of aspiration 108
    sacred duty 107
  New International Economic Order 107
Tiananmen incident 107, 108, 168
Tibet 27, 32, 67, 87, 141
titles 52
  allocated to barbarians 73–4
  awarded by the Tang 74
  ritual connection 73
  upgrading and downgrading 74
  see also ranks and titles system
tools of rulership see rulership: tools of
traditional virtues 126–8
tranquillity (*an*) 44
Trans-Pacific Partnership 31
travelling embassies see diplomatic envoys
tribute system 65–6, 70, 72
Trotsky, Leon 90
true principle 64
Trump, Donald 114
Turkey 137, 152
Turkmenistan 152, 154

U

UN Security Council 115
unequal treaties 84, 88, 96, 98
United Nations Convention on the Law of the Sea (UNCLOS) 173, 174
United Nations Security Council 8
United States of America (USA)
  alliance with Japan 29–30, 31
  alliances and relations with East Asia 29–30
  China
    entente 29
    equal relationship 113–14
    rivalry with 103–4
  hegemony of 8, 9
  military assets 29
  undisputed dominance of 168

universality 171–2
urge to classify 74, 79, 149
Uzbekistan 152

V

vanguard of international revolutionary struggle 90, 92, 112, 122
Versailles Treaty 90
Vietnam 25, 30, 33, 77, 152, 173
  relations with China 123–4
  war with China (1979) 157–8
  see also South Vietnam
virtue (*de*) 42–3, 46–7, 63–4
  traditional 126–8
  see also moral superiority

W

Wang Hui 82
Wang Yi 118, 125–6, 128, 134–5, 136n29, 141, 142, 149–50, 163
Wang Zheng 116
Wang Zhenping 63
Warring States 44, 45–6, 83
Watson, Adam 11
way of the hegemon 9, 91, 127, 175
way of the king 9, 91, 127, 128, 175
Weber, Max 13
wei see awesomeness (*wei*)
Wen Jiabao 129
Western emissaries
  as educators and missionaries 83
  sense of superiority 83
  standard of civilization 83–4, 84–5
Western great powers
  China and
    as an alternative to 93, 100, 121, 128
    aspirations 98
    collision with 81
    equal ranking 98, 99
    partnerships with 148–9
    hegemonism and power politics 9
    historic 8
    as predatory and corrupt 17
Western international society *see* international society
Western shock 12, 28, 40, 167
Western states
  norms of legitimacy 86
  two faces of 85
Western Xia 66n7, 69
Westphalian norms 169
Wight, Martin 21, 54
Wilson, Woodrow 90
win-win cooperation 125, 130, 133, 135, 153
Womack, Brantly 21
world proletariat 90–1
Wuzi 75

X

Xi Jinping 2, 3, 4, 93, 101, 109
  address to Central Conference on Work (2014) 127–8
  China's core interests 140
  China's rightful place 112–18
  Chinese dream 116
  community with a shared future for mankind 125–6, 140, 169
  defining mission of 117
  foreign trips 136n29
  Global Development Initiative (GDI) 133–4
  Global Security Initiative (GSI) 133–4
  leadership aspirations 112, 114
  military parades 158–9
  new type of international relations 125, 139, 141, 150, 169
  partnerships 141
  peripheral diplomacy 116, 117, 129–30
  reforms to international order 102
  rejuvenation of Chinese nation 116–17, 140, 169
  self-promotion of 101
  on traditional virtues 127, 128
  understanding of international order 114
  views and comments of 115–16
  views and comments on
    Asia 9, 115–16
    correct idea of righteousness and benefit 164–5
    discourse power 147
    foreign intrusions 161
    Pacific Ocean 116
  see also BRI (Belt and Road Initiative)
Xiangshan Forum 118
Xinhai Revolution (1911) 80, 85, 95
Xinjiang 32, 76, 87, 141, 155
Xiongnu 61
  enemy state 73
  heqin policy 67, 75, 77
  nomadic federation 23–4
  status 73
Xunzi 45, 47, 50, 51, 51n22, 53–4, 55
  on self-interest 56

Y

Yamamuro Shinichi 85
Yan Xuetong 117, 128
Yang Jiechi 127, 136n29, 142n43
Yao 45
yi see righteousness (*yi*)
Yongle emperor, Ming dynasty 26, 61, 64, 77
Yü Ying-shi 76, 78
Yuan dynasty 63, 81, 82
Yunnan 25, 26

Z

Zhang Wankun 148

Zhang Wentian 145
Zhao Suisheng 115
Zhao Yi 64
Zhao Ziyang 107
Zheng He 26, 34, 77

Zhou dynasty 83
Zhou Enlai 104, 140
Zhu Yuanzhang 81–2
Zhuge Liang 25